LOVING SOMEONE GAY

Loving Someone Gay

Revised and Updated

Don Clark, Ph.D.

CELESTIALARTS

Berkeley, California

Cover design by Ken Scott
Text design by Hal Hershey
Composition by The Recorder Typesetting Network

Original edition, 1977
Revised edition, 1987

0 9 8 7 6

Library of Congress Cataloging-in-Publication Data

Clark, Donald H., 1930–
    Loving someone gay/Don Clark. —Rev. and updated.
      p.   cm.
    Includes index.
    ISBN 0-89087-505-7
    1. Homosexuality, Male—United States.   I. Title.
HQ76.2.U5C57   1991
306.76′62—dc20   90-20831
                                               CIP

For Barbara and Michael

Contents

Preface to the New Edition

Not long ago, a nurse in Australia wrote to me. Because a number of gay men had come to her hospital to be treated for diseases resulting from Acquired Immune Deficiency Syndrome (AIDS), she had decided to learn more about gay men and lesbians. One of her patients gave her his copy of *Loving Someone Gay*. She wanted to thank me for writing it not only because she believed it had helped her to understand gay people better, but because, while reading the book, her son had told her that he is gay, and she was better prepared for his disclosure. She said that she was curious to know if there were thoughts I might add if I were writing the book now.

It was twelve years ago, in 1975, that I wrote the book, hoping it would reach some of the people who needed a more positive view of gay identity than was offered in print by mental health professionals at that time. Today, the book continues to reach thousands of new readers each year. Indeed, there are thoughts to be added and some to be reconsidered. There has been much change in the human world and more change than most of us could have imagined in the world of gay men and lesbians. It is for these reasons that this new edition is presented.

The original *Loving Someone Gay* is presented as Part II of this book. Outdated references have been eliminated. In almost all other respects it is the original book. I wanted to maintain its integrity because something about it continues to be helpful to people.

There is one small but significant change that you will find in the book presented as Part I. At the time the original book was published, I insisted that the word "gay" be capitalized. It seemed very important to me that readers be reminded that we gay people are a sub-culture within larger cultures, like Blacks and Jews. With or without my insistence on that capital letter, in the intervening years we have been recognized as such a group, and the literate world has not seen the need for the capital letter to differentiate us in the English language from the connotation of people who are happy or merry. Though few of us gay people are happy or merry all of the time, I am happy that we are now recognized, and I no longer feel the need to insist on capitalizing the word that points to our shared identity.

You may notice also that in Part II, I more often speak of "gay people" while in Part I there is the more usual current usage of "lesbians and gay men." I continue to feel an affection for speaking of us as gay people, as a reminder that we are related by our affectional orientation whether we are women or men. But I am well aware of the present need to remind the world that lesbians carry a double oppression, first as women and second as gay people. Perhaps in another twelve years the cumbersome use of "lesbians and gay men" will be as unnecessary as my once insistent use of the capital "G". I hope so.

Part I of the new edition contains my altered and additional thoughts and observations, based on my continued professional and personal involvement in the experiences of gay men and lesbians in the amazing years since *Loving Someone Gay* was first written.

Don Clark
San Francisco
April 1987

PART ONE
Our Changing Lives

1
One Dozen Years

These past twelve years have been dramatic. We gay men and lesbians have been hurt and helped, battered as our lives have improved. We stand on the brink of true liberation while in the shadow of threatened attempts to harm us.

There are people who would like to use the AIDS epidemic as an excuse to seize us and our property, strip us of all civil rights, and quarantine us. There are people who hope to use genetic engineering to eliminate us from future generations.

Yet, at the same time, there are more people in the world than ever before who know us—visible at last—as their relatives, friends, neighbors, and co-workers. There are more people than ever before who care for us and want to help to right the wrongs that have been heaped on us in centuries of bigotry, prejudice, and xenophobia.

We are truly on a cutting edge. The past dozen years have placed us at a watershed in human history. It is an exciting and frightening time. If the original edition of *Loving Someone Gay* was filled with the optimistic language of the days of the human potential movement, this edition contains the language of a fast changing, dangerous, unpredictable world. One dozen years have placed lesbians and gay men center stage in the drama of a world trying to find its values.

Once Upon a Time

David telephoned me this morning. I usually have dinner with my friends David and Bill sometime each week. We see one another or talk on the telephone at times between our dinners, too. We have shared the personal aspects of our lives for years, more family than friends. Bill has had a nagging cough for the past several weeks and has noticed some weight loss. He has an appointment for a medical checkup later this week. There is worry along with the hope that this may be no more than a persistent cold.

David telephoned me because he needed to talk. He has been trying to be optimistic about Bill's health and not add to Bill's anxiety. But this morning David arrived at work and realized that he has been keeping himself exhaustingly busy with projects at his office and at home so that he would not dwell on thoughts about what will happen if Bill is diagnosed with AIDS. He had closed himself into a private office in order to telephone me. A good part of our time on the telephone was spent with his crying at last while I gladly waited and listened at my end of the line, wishing that I could hold him and that there was more that I could do to help.

"I feel as if I am living inside someone else's life," David said between sobs this morning. There have been many times in recent years when most of us gay people have felt as if we were living in someone else's life. They were the times when change was coming along so fast in our personal lives that we simply could not assimilate it. "I guess we just have to get through this somehow," David said, "or we'll never appreciate what we have."

True. We cannot grasp the gains of the past twelve years until our most personal and painful fears and losses have been admitted, felt, wept for, and accepted. Only then can each of us embrace, appreciate and enjoy the gifts that have come to us. It is our tears that cleanse our vision, and our sorrow that opens our hearts.

It is true also that one of the great gifts of human nature is our inability to foresee the future. Had I been able to foresee all that was to come in the past twelve years, I would not only have been astonished to the point of disbelief at the prospect of

4

the added richness, but surely the fear that I would have experienced in the face of all of the impending losses and pain would have immobilized me. I pick twelve years as a seemingly arbitrary time frame because twelve years ago I was completing the manuscript for the original *Loving Someone Gay*.

One week ago a stunned man sat in my office, having just lost his third close friend to an AIDS death. "It's wild," he said. "Eleven years ago I read your book in Chicago when it first came out. I was thinking about making the move to San Francisco. Sometimes it seems like the years since then have been almost too full of everything. More has happened than I thought I'd experience in my whole lifetime." He described the first half dozen years as full of adventure. "It was definitely scary sometimes, but it was fun." He described the last five years as having been full of sickness, pain, fear, death, and a search for some kind of meaning to it all. "It's not much fun now. It feels like when I was playing football in school. I keep wanting to ask for time out so I can get my bearings again, but the action just doesn't stop. Nothing and nobody can or will stop the clock."

After a pensive moment, he added, "And yet I feel real alive these days—definitely awake. My family and straight friends know who I am now and that's a lot better than back in Chicago days. But they still don't really understand. And now they're worried about my health all the time and afraid to talk about it. Why can't we all just love one another and get on with it? I've got to learn to take it the way it is."

He was speaking for many of us gay men, lesbians, and the people who care about us. A dozen years ago, enough of us had found one another to discover that we were as good and diverse a group of people as any on the planet. There was a sweet joy in the discovery and a sense of urgency. We wanted to get the word out to those who were still in hiding. We wanted them to come out where we could see them and offer them a hand. We wanted them to join us. We wanted to find the rest of our family. We had discovered that we were not bad people and we sensed that, together, we could heal our wounds and lift the sad, unnecessary yoke of shared oppression.

We came to our liberation riding the crest of the wave of surging social change that followed the Second World War. There is no documented beginning to the story of gay liberation. There have been gay men and lesbians for as long as there have been humans. Like other humans, when oppressed, we gay men and lesbians make efforts to become free of the oppression. We have been unpopular in some parts of the world during many of the past centuries because varying styles of religion and rulers have made us so. Our attempts to right the wrongs of subjugation have been poorly chronicled. But the social changes following the Second World War led directly to the Stonewall Rebellion in New York City in June of 1969. From that time forward, people around the world who had been ridiculed and punished because of natural erotic preference seriously began to question the right of other people with presumed heteroerotic orientation to place them in second class positions of social contempt.

The pace of the gay movement for equal rights has continued to accelerate since the Stonewall Rebellion. It continues to grow everywhere in the world except in those areas dominated by the most repressive and punitive rulers. Even in those parts of the world, many people have some awareness of the increased freedom experienced by gay people elsewhere. The seed is well planted.

The path of change for gay people has been, and will continue to be, unpredictable. The cost of the struggle in this century to free ourselves has been painful every step of the way. Gay people remain in prisons and mental institutions in various parts of the world for no reason other than their determination to tell the truth and insist on equal rights regardless of erotic orientation. In the most enlightened areas of the world, it was only a very short time ago that adults "caught" in mutually consenting homoerotic activity were arrested, sometimes imprisoned or placed in mental institutions, frequently had their names and addresses published in newspapers, and lost their employment as well as the respect and support of friends, neighbors, and families.

The original edition of *Loving Someone Gay* was published seven and a half years after the Stonewall Rebellion, though I had begun the search for a publisher for it two years earlier. Reputable publishers and those with no particular reputation worth protecting warned that they would not consider having the name of their publishing company on a book written by a gay psychologist who persisted in saying that being gay was not necessarily in any way pathological. One important New York book editor went to a great deal of trouble to write her own critique which she backed up with the expert opinion of an anonymous consultant, both pointing out that it was impossible to give a "responsible, balanced view of homosexuals" without discussing the sad pathology so often involved. She was able, of course, to find a psychologist who wrote a book for her on the subject with a point of view that was more comfortable for her.

So much has happened in our lives in the intervening twelve years since *Loving Someone Gay* was written that the time seems strangely elongated. It seems almost as if one might tell the story of this period using the traditional opening of fables, "Once upon a time. . . ." A striking difference, of course, is that one could not end the tale with the traditional matching ending, "and they all lived happily ever after". We gay men and lesbians know better now than to expect to live happily ever after. We know it more starkly than ever before. We have had a rapid, brief period of maturation. Though it is more comfortable for some people not to notice who we are, what is happening to us, or that we exist at all, our story is not a fairy tale. It is the story of very real men, women, and children, finding our way in difficult circumstances. It is a story the rest of the human world would do well to heed.

Finding Our Way

One of the faces of change ushered in by the twentieth century's social revolution came to be known as the human potential movement. It was a marriage of the philosophy of humanism with the rapidly expanding fields of psychology and other social sciences. The human potential movement was able to move forward only with determined permissiveness, questioning all time-honored articles of social faith and human limitation.

Such an orientation was helpful to gay liberationists. It helped us gain perspective. We, too, were determinedly permissive, trying to question any assumed reason for prohibition. If that sounds adolescent, it is worth remembering that it represented a major leap forward from the second class child-like position in which we had been held.

The human potential movement set the tone, asking some of the questions we needed to ask and others that were subtly related. Why should a man wear a suit and necktie instead of a loose embroidered shirt, sandals or bare feet, and beads? Why should a woman marry in order to have children? For that matter, why should a woman feel obliged to have children? Why should people live in small family units rather than in chosen collective communes? Why not smoke marijuana and dance in the streets rather than drink whiskey and dance in night clubs? Why should a man not choose another man as his sexual partner or spouse? Why should a woman not choose a woman? Why should a person not have respectable multiple partners for the night or for life?

We question askers and truth seekers, gay or not, wanted to be all that we could be and live life as fully as possible. It was not a new phenomenon in human history, but it was new for most of us within our lifetimes. And the technological revolution in communication permitted the questions and visions of freedom to spread around the globe like wildfire. We were as determined in our permissive exploration as any army engaged in a holy war, with one difference. An emerging ethic of the time was that while gaining more, it was important not to take away from another person. The lust for power and property so evident in warfare and the petty civil variations on its theme had been tried and found not only wanting but plainly wrong.

Lesbians and gay men, along with other people, made important gains during that period of questioning assumptions that moved us along the path of self understanding. It is likely that the world will never again be as smugly ignorant of its propensity for damaging prejudice. The right of any group of people to subjugate and limit the lives of another group is more easily and quickly called to question now as a result of that period in human history. The false gel of shame that had kept gay men and lesbians from demanding our full civil rights had begun to melt away.

Our willingness to conform to a code of strident permissiveness would have a price, of course, and many of us knew it at the time. Clearly, it would be difficult later to establish the necessary new code of personal and group morality in which not everything would be encouraged or permitted. But we had to sample widely before knowing where restrictive caution might be helpful.

The problem we humans encounter again and again is our propensity to conform to a current code even when that code prescribes nonconformity. The stunned man from Chicago, sitting in my office after the death of his third close friend, said, "There didn't seem to be time to stop and take stock when the fun was on, and there doesn't seem to be time to stop and take it now either. I was doing what all my friends were doing then and I'm doing it even now. Then I was running to the next party or political meeting. Now I'm running to the next sick friend or memorial service. What's going on right now always seems so darned urgent. I know I need to get my own perspective somehow, but how?" So saying, he spoke for most of the human world today. Perspective is in short supply.

In these past twelve years, the gay community has gone from insistent necessary free-wheeling permissiveness, questioning and exploring, to being a visible, highly diverse community with demonstrated strength and focused ability to respond to any threat to its well being. We have demonstrated a remarkable ability to rally together when confronted with crisis. We have made great gains in understanding ourselves as a group and as individuals. And while growing into this maturity, we have managed to continue relentlessly to demand our full civil rights in the communities and nations in which we happen to find ourselves.

We have startled the watching world and ourselves not only with our strength and our capacity for caring but with our capacity for violence when pushed too far. There was a hint of it contained in the Stonewall Rebellion. But it was demonstrated more clearly the following decade in the United States in San Francisco, when the city's mayor and first elected openly gay member of the Board of Supervisors were assassinated by a homophobic former member of the city's Board of Supervisors. The assassin's name was Dan White. When, at the end of his murder trial, it was announced that he had been given a prison sentence that would permit him to be on the streets again five years later, the full impact of the shameful insult was felt. Within hours a large spontaneous protest rally had turned into what was to be known as the White Night Riot as the City Hall was assaulted and police cars were overturned and burned in the frustrated, angry, anguished protest.

Later that same night we learned the difference between our potential for violence and the potential for violence in the world that surrounds us. The White Night Riot was followed by a police riot during which uniformed police charged the center of the predominantly gay section of the city, wantonly smashing property and the people they found in their angry path. The White Night Riot had registered protest by damaging the property that was the symbol of unfair rulers, laws, and enforcers. The police riot damaged not only property but purposely attacked and harmed unarmed, defenseless people. It was a painful but profitable reminder that our power resides in the strength of our truth combined with our willingness to continue moving forward in non-violent ways. It is the newer way, just finding its following in modern times, but a far more profound and potent way to effect lasting social change.

We have learned a lot in twelve years. We have learned to guard against harming one another as individual members of an oppressed group are so tempted to do in their moments of impotent frustration. We have had our share of forming circular firing squads in the early days of our social revolution, targeting comrades whose ideology did not seem exactly correct. Like other searching groups we have been guilty of being too quick to pick a truth to shout louder than people whose goals are the same as ours. We have had to learn quickly to cooperate and take care of one another. We have found one another and have learned that we can only move forward together.

Because we represent change we are viewed as a threat by some. Because we are unknown to many we seem foreign and therefore frightening or dangerous. Because some view us as dangerous we agitate the deeper fears that lie hidden in their personal insecurity. It is inevitable and necessary that the larger community get to know us as the individuals we are, rather than as the stereotype they have learned to believe us to be.

We had just begun to introduce ourselves with our disclosures to family and friends. We had begun to present ourselves in the media. Progress was steady but slow. And then we were catapulted into public awareness in a way no one could have anticipated.

Sudden Change

AIDS took us by surprise. The disease was not new. The epidemic was not new. But it was not deemed newsworthy in our part of the world until it became obvious that there was a disease epidemic infecting gay men in the United States. It was a strange disease that revealed itself in the form of a variety of other seldom seen diseases. It was concluded that it involved a disorder of the body's immune system which regularly fights off microbes that can cause a wide variety of diseases. One of the first names given to the disease was GRID, or Gay Related Immune Deficiency. Because gay men were seen stereotypically as sexually promiscuous people, it was guessed that it might be a disease that was easily transmitted sexually. Not all gay men were sexually promiscuous, but the guess that the disease could be transmitted sexually later proved to be a correct guess. It was not known in those days how else it might be transmitted from one person to another, nor was it yet understood that this is a human disease rather than a gay disease. Thus do fear and prejudice so often go hand in hand.

Gay men had been punished for generations for daring to show homosexual desire. (Lesbians were less harshly and regularly punished since they were seen as mere women and axiomatically second class.) It seemed urgent to keep male citizens in heterosexual line because they were the presumed bedrock of respectable society. In fact, *homoerotic preference* was the real issue but too subtle a distinction and too uncomfortable an issue for most people to examine. Sexual behavior was easier to observe and control. It was better understood since many people with heteroerotic preference sometimes indulge in homosexual behavior.

Though rule makers usually are too bigoted and/or prejudiced to permit themselves such thoughts, all evidence has consistently pointed to the truth that human erotic desire can *only* be viewed as a continuum. To view it in categories is to do no

11

more than invent artificial categories by breaking the continuum into pieces. But a continuum is subtle and categories are easy to remember. So we persist in placing people into the categories of heterosexuals, homosexuals, and bisexuals. These pretend categories do no more than describe discovered or admitted sexual behavior, and behavior is the most changeable aspect of human nature.

As men with homoerotic preference, gay men participated in the tidal wave of social liberation, they too were caught up in the "sexual liberation" that was a part of the experimental social change. Having been told for generations that we were set apart and scorned because of our interest in *sex* with other males, we naturally believed that homosexuality was the difference that defined us as people. It was inevitable that many of us would demonstrate our liberation by enjoying as much homosexual attraction and behavior as possible.

Sexually transmitted diseases flourished during the period of sexual liberation. They flourished among gay males in the more liberated parts of the world too, but that did not seem to be a problem since medical science had found treatments and cures for venereal or sexually transmitted diseases. The same diseases that had plagued both nobility and the commoners of the eighteenth and nineteenth centuries now seemed easily remedied. Enlightened gay men learned to seek medical assistance for such problems early.

But why gay men seemed particularly susceptible to AIDS infection still was a mystery. It was years before medical researchers realized that the phenomenon involved a very fragile virus that was easily transmitted during anal intercourse if a condom was not used. And condoms were not being used by gay men since there had been no reason to use them.

When AIDS became newsworthy as a presumed gay-related disease, people of prejudice were caught up in their own fear and meanness of spirit and tried to use the existence of the disease as further reason to isolate gay people, deny us civil rights, and cause us suffering beyond that inflicted by the disease itself. They made the too easy connection between our participation in the period of permissive sexuality and their assumption that we are bad people. They deduced that AIDS was a just punishment. In their fear it helped them to keep an illusion of distance as protection from the threat of the disease. Ultimately they were forced to see it as a disease that could and would strike anyone, regardless of erotic orientation. Prejudice is not rational and it is almost always harmful.

As the forward thrust of determined permissive exploration dominated the decade of the seventies, the struggle with the AIDS epidemic was to dominate the decade of the eighties. Gay men, lesbians, and the people who care about us have been forced to live with the horror of an AIDS epidemic set in a hostile environment, and meanwhile give as much of the needed care and assistance as possible, all the while trying to keep enough perspective to continue to struggle for civil rights and help the larger community understand that all people are caught in an urgent health crisis, both mental and physical.

Ironically, it was the advent of the AIDS crisis that helped the world to begin to see how diverse a group gay people are. Celebrities and other people of high visibility who had been assumed to be non-gay fell ill with the disease. Presumed heterosexual actors, priests, athletes, statesmen, and military people became ill. For some the secret was kept to the end, simply announcing that the person had died after a struggle with pneumonia, cancer, or whatever was the most prominent disease resulting from their AIDS. But some, like actor Rock Hudson, shocked the world with the public admission of AIDS and gay identity.

Though gay men did not invent or give this disease to the world, along with the lesbians of our community and the non-gay people who love us, we *have* given the world a model of how to care for one another in a crisis, even when governments shockingly fail to fulfill their responsibility, and bigots freely attack. We have managed to retain our sanity and remember that neither sex nor homosexuality per se are evil. We have been able to demonstrate that it is not necessary to yield to selfish fear and run from people in need.

Perhaps most important, we have been able to demonstrate that massive changes in a population's way of life can be effected in a short period of time when there is education and reason to do so. We altered our style of affectional/sexual relating

13

in so brief a period of time that observing social scientists were stunned. We put to rest, hopefully forever, the tired maxims that supported the idea that one cannot change that which represents greed and self interest in humans. Such belief systems and their resulting behaviors can be changed. We have shown the world how.

A physician friend who is not gay but has worked hard in the center of the AIDS storm from the beginning of the epidemic said, "You guys are something else. I have told many of the people I have worked with in my professional lifetime that their lives depended on changing eating, drinking, smoking or exercise habits. Most didn't change. They got sicker and died. I mean that was just food, booze, cigarettes and exercise! Imagine if I had told them they had to change their whole life style, including sexual practices and their way of looking for love, and do it right away! But you guys did it; now I wonder why the rest of the world can't follow your lead?"

Growing Gay

We have every reason to believe that homosexuality has been around at least as long as heterosexuality. There is not much reason to be excited about it as advocate or adversary. It is a fact of life and will continue to be so. People who are preoccupied with it are either researchers or live in a pitifully small world. There are many more topics that deserve our attention in this dangerous and rapidly changing world.

One item deserving attention in the evolving human world is gay identity, both for individuals and for the quickly developing sub-culture we know today as the gay community. The development of gay identity had its starts earlier but has taken root in these last dozen years and requires recognition. It is impossible to ignore the fact that there are Blacks, Jews, Arabs, and Asians in the world. Each group has a common bond, no matter how diverse its population. This is true for gays too. The person who does not understand this does not understand the world in which we live today.

Growing up as a gay male or lesbian is an experience unlike any other. In the past dozen years we have begun to understand that someone who is Black or Jewish wants to have the same rights and opportunities as any other citizen but has no desire to have other people pretend that he or she is not different from people who are not Black or not Jewish.

We gay people have grown up a lot in the past dozen years. We have had to do our growing fast. We do not want to be surrounded by pretense. We have had enough of pretense. It has harmed us and those we love. We want the same rights and opportunities that are granted to other citizens, but we do not want people to pretend that we are not gay.

We are like the black people who are citizens in nations far from the places where their ancestors were kidnapped and sold into slavery. It is difficult for them to piece together their whole identity, including the culture of the old world and their developing culture in the new world. We gay people are learning who we are. We are learning about our ancestors and what we have in common with one another. We know that it is more than mere homosexuality, though we have been forced to focus on it and have been punished for it as black people have been punished because of the color of their skin.

We know that like Jewish people, we have clung to a deep inner truth about our identity, though it has been costly. We too could, and sometimes have, "passed." That has been costly. We have learned that we cannot be whole unless we are who we are. That means that we must not only admit, but learn how to celebrate, our homoerotic desire and its consequent demand that we not exclude people of the same gender from our loving bonding. We must admit and celebrate that we are men who truly can love men and women who can truly love women, as totally as any human can love any other human. And we must live with the painful awareness that all of the suffering caused members of our tribe because of this ability to love was both cruel and unnecessary.

We have a new breed coming along now. Lesbians and gay men who have grown up in the last dozen years knew that they were not alone, and that has made a lot of difference. Not all of the news they heard about their fellow gays was good news, but they were able to see our pictures, read some positive statements about us, and know that we were everywhere, ready to be found by them.

Our new breed has the sureness and energy of youth, but it is more quickly tempered by the wisdom of our elders. Why? Because they grew up hearing lies about themselves and are eager to hear from their gay elders the gay truth. They will, of course, continue to evalutate that truth in terms of their own experience. They are quickly infusing our ranks with vitality as we grant them the best that we have of our accumulated wisdom.

It is a wonderful irony that we who have been persecuted because we are "different" are reaping the great advantages of diversity within our own gay community. Young and old, rich and poor, people of various ethnic backgrounds, mix more quickly and easily in our community than in any other. We learn from one another and we enrich one another's lives. It has been rapidly making us a very strong, durable group. We are generous in our ability and willingness to educate and support one another. Most of us know or sense that it is to our individual advantage to help another gay person grow stronger because it makes our home base stronger.

One of the reasons we are feared is because of our ability and willingness to overlook artificial lines that are so often used to separate people. That made us an international group before there was a League of Nations or a United Nations.

And, because we are unique in having loved ones from our biological families who do not share our identity, we have learned better than ever in these past dozen years the necessity of educating non-gay people. We are rapidly learning better ways of disclosing our identity to the non-gay people we care for and then taking on the responsibility of helping them to learn to abandon stereotypes and discover the good truth about us. We are good people who have been punished for our affection, and many people do not know that yet.

Our growth as individuals and as a group has been astonishing, so far beyond what might have been anticipated a dozen years ago that it is not possible to guess the extent and ways in which we will have grown and changed in another dozen years. We cannot foresee the joys and sorrows that lie ahead.

One truth is clear. In the past dozen years we have demonstrated beyond any doubt our willingness and ability to care for one another and for non-gay people also. We have helped ourselves and helped the people who have hurt us with their ignorance and prejudice. Our traditional enemies, be they a Hitler who interned and killed us in concentration camps, or the petty, ambitious politicians who persecuted us in witch hunts, do not rest easy in history. We do.

2
Gay People

I talked with the witty, spirited father of a lesbian recently. She and her lover had "come out" or made their disclosure to him only two days before, and there seemed to be little or no problem. He was, as he told me, a person who was interested and curious by nature and was more apt to ask questions than to judge.

"You know," he said, "you're the first gay man I have met. At least you're the first one who I knew for certain was gay, and you're not at all the person I expected you to be."

Before finding out exactly what he meant, I could not resist saying, "Would you believe that I am not at all the person I expected me to be?"

Everyone changes. But we gay people go through so many changes in our lifetimes that we usually manage to surprise even ourselves. In these current years of rapid change, attentive observers can see not only the individual lesbians and gay men going through the more or less anticipated ages and stages of adult growth we have come to expect from gay people. One can also observe us changing as a group. Like a tribe whose forest hideaway has been suddenly invaded by the bulldozers of "advancing civilization," we have had sudden, unexpected change thrust upon us.

We are a creatively adaptive people. The catalytic agent of the sudden change has been the AIDS epidemic. We would have changed without it but not as fast, and undoubtedly the changes would have taken some different forms. But here we are—exposed, shocked, and trying to piece our way of life together while dealing with the incessant, painful onslaught and somehow managing to build a stronger and more durable way of life. In our attempts to survive, we have found ways to prosper and become models for waiting places in the world that do not yet hear the bulldozers.

Who We Are

Rose and I had a nice chat. She was visiting her son and his lover who live on the coast, north of San Francisco. She is many years my senior but insisted I call her Rose. "My sweet man passed away six years ago and I don't feel like the other half of Mister and Missus anymore. My wonderful son is a grown man, and then some, so I don't feel like Mom anymore either. I'm back to feeling like Rose."

That reminded her of a conversation she had had with a long time neighbor at home. "We got to talking about me coming to visit my son and his lover, you know. She's not a bad sort. She tries to understand, but it's hard for some older people. She said to me, 'What I don't know is how to know for sure when somebody is gay.' Half the people on our block are Jewish. So I said, 'Same way you know for sure when somebody's Jewish.' 'How's that?' she asked me, 'You mean from what they eat?' 'No,' I said. 'When they tell you', I said. 'And if they don't tell you?' 'Simple', I said. 'If you want to know, ask.' We had a good laugh."

Unless you know someone fairly well, it is difficult to know if she is a lesbian or if he is a gay man. Our difference is not visible. We are people who are conscious of homoerotic attraction that is sometimes strong enough to qualify as homoerotic preference, meaning that it is then stronger than heteroerotic attraction.

There is some confusion about whether people choose to be gay, but the confusion is in the words and what the words mean. A person does not choose homoerotic preference. None of us choose our feelings. We do not choose to feel anger, sadness, joy, or sympathy either. Feelings come or they do not. Our choice is whether to willingly be conscious of our feelings or to try to put them out of conscious awareness. We have some choice also as to how willing we are to have our feelings influence our behavior.

Erotic feelings are stirred when they are stirred; one does not decide in advance who will stir them. The only decision you may choose to make in advance is whether you will act on those feelings with erotic behavior. You may choose to inhibit homosexual or heterosexual behavior.

Many people choose not to act on homoerotic feelings with homoerotic behavior. Most of these are people whose heteroerotic feelings are stronger than their homoerotic feelings. Some people choose not to act on any erotic feelings. Some choose to act on erotic feelings only with one partner.

Because this is the way we are arranged as humans, it has been possible in repressive societies for people whose deepest erotic and affectional attractions are for people of the same gender to block natural behavior and act as if their strongest inclinations are heterosexual. Just as prisoners whose strongest erotic feelings are heteroerotic often will make a homoerotic adjustment in prison, a person whose strongest erotic feelings are homoerotic often will make a heteroerotic adjustment in a society that is restrictive.

Homosexual and heterosexual are words that describe behavior, not the identity of a person. It has confused many people for decades because people with heteroerotic preference were described as heterosexuals and yet sometimes indulged in homosexual behavior. And, of course, the converse was true also.

In recent years, "gay" has gained in popularity as a word that describes identity because it eliminates some of the confusion. A gay person is someone who is aware of homoerotic feelings and is aware, at least sometimes, of homoerotic preference. A gay person is conscious of all sorts of feelings of attraction and affection, including sexual feelings, for some people of the same gender.

Gay identity is a step beyond homosexual behavior. A lesbian or gay man knows that she or he is capable of feeling love and sexual desire for someone of the same gender, is conscious of those feelings as an ordinary part of everyday life, and is willing to act on those feelings when the time is right. So it is fair to say that while one cannot choose whether or not to have homoerotic feelings, one can choose whether or not to behave in a homosexual manner, and one definitely makes the choice to be a gay person.

Choosing to be a gay person is not an easy choice. It is not a simple choice to behave homosexually. It is a choice that honors honesty and integrity of identity, but in a punitive world that shuns gay people as less than first rate, it is an act of real courage.

But Rose was right. The only way to know for sure is to ask. You cannot know unless we choose to tell you. Homosexual behavior alone does not mean a person is gay. We are a very diverse lot, and therein lies our strength as a community. We have only one thing in common and that is our willingness to be honest about our homoerotic feelings, our natural affections, and our loving even when that is unpopular or illegal.

Gay characters are appearing more and more often in films, television, and books. It is not because there are suddenly more of us but because audiences are more curious about us. We are more often being presented fairly than was the case just a few years ago, though we are still shown as exotic far too often. It is because audiences are more curious about us, I suppose, that very creative writers continue to portray us as a bit strange, thereby stirring more curiosity. We have an emerging culture as a community, but as individuals we come in all stripes, sizes, and shades of taste and persuasion, just like other people.

In the early days of gay liberation we worked hard to point out our good features to non-gay people. We do not have to do that as much anymore. There is no reason why we have to be better. We do not have to justify our existence. I think that our unique experience as invisible people growing up in a world that has treated us badly has awakened some remarkable and valuable facets in us, but I am eager to remind people that, as a group, we run the gamut of human characteristics.

Many of us are high achievers who are haunted by the feelings that one day it will be discovered that we are not as talented as people think we are. It is a common haunting disadvantage resulting from having grown up oppressed. If you have been told you are second class all of your life, it is difficult to believe wholeheartedly you are first class no matter how much evidence there is to support that fact.

Though it is much less true today than in decades past, gay people who are "coming out" or beginning to admit their gay identity still sometimes wonder how to go about meeting other gay people, where to find them, and how to recognize them. There are gay periodicals and various gay interest groups or clubs that help. But the most sound advice for the emerging gay person anywhere in the world is to be alert to people who show an interest in you. We are everywhere. You can meet someone on a hiking trail, in a supermarket, or simply walking down a city street. We have been noticing one another for centuries by the mere fact of our willingness and desire to maintain eye contact with someone who interests us just a fraction of a second longer than local custom permits. And, of course, the more willing you are to be honest about your interest in others, the more likely it is that you will discover when the interest is mutual.

Oppression Today

Talking with a group of health care professionals about the identity and needs of gay people today, an attractive young woman psychiatrist asked me a question that is frequently asked. "I don't understand why so many gay people are so strident in their determination to display a separate identity," she said. "Since it is your choice to announce gay identity or not, why isn't it better to simply assimilate and not appear to be different?"

Strident and different, I explained, are key words. As long as the general population sees the difference in our identity as being less than desirable, we are different in a disadvantaged way. People of an oppressed group can merge well into the surrounding larger society only when the oppression has stopped. You merge from a position of strength, not weakness. You merge because your difference is not only tolerated, but fully accepted and appreciated. You bring your unique goodness to the larger community. To merge when you are viewed as second class is to submerge, and that is not good for anyone's health. We will continue to become stronger in our separate identity until it is clear to everyone that we bring our gifts into the merger and expect our due share of gratitude.

And that which is considered strident, pushy, or otherwise offensive is often in the eye of the beholder. I think immediately of being seated at a symphony performance recently behind a young man and a young woman who slid down in their seats, kissed, nibbled earlobes, and looked at one another lovingly until it was time to applaud. They did not hurt anyone, though their behavior was a bit distracting for the symphony patrons seated near them. It was tolerated as an odd display of young love or lust. Yet I am sure that some of the people who witnessed that display of affection would have been upset if two men or two women had exchanged just one kiss and one nibble on an earlobe during the same musical performance. People continue to see any clear display of affection and/or sexual attraction between two women or two men in a public place as strident, offensive behavior when the same behavior between a woman and a man is viewed with pleasure. I thought the heteroerotic display at the symphony was strident, though it did not occur to me that they were trying to make some point about their particular erotic preference or identity.

By contrast, I was invited to a wonderful dinner party recently to celebrate a wedding that had happened thousands of miles away in the groom's hometown. It was a congenial group. Three of the people were old friends. In addition to the newly married couple, there were a woman and man who had lived together for several years but had no plans for marriage, one male couple, and the hostess who was in a temporarily suspended relationship with another woman. Only later did it occur to me that none of us were making any judgments about what was an appropriate way for anyone else to love. There was easy talk about our lives and easy, natural, unspectacular expressions of affection all around during the course of the evening. No one was pushing anyone else to notice their affectional identity because no one was judging. It is that easy. When the loving of gay people is pleasantly viewed as natural, it will no longer be an issue. The problem is less ours than the people who react to us.

We are better tolerated in the world today than we were in the last decade, but we are not much more appreciated. We continue to be more at risk in the long run from prejudice and ignorance than we are from the AIDS epidemic. Bigots are only too eager to use the AIDS epidemic to push for blood tests that could lead to quarantines and passport control, even though each year's experience with the disease increases the evidence that they need have no fear of being exposed to the disease by gay people unless they engage in careless sex with an infected individual or somehow take infected blood into their body, perhaps by sharing an intravenous needle.

The groups first identified as being infected with the AIDS virus were Africans, gay males, drug users who shared intravenous needles, and people such as hemophiliacs who had been exposed as a result of the use of blood products. A bit later there were children born to people with AIDS and the first showing of the disease among heterosexually active young adults. In the guise of protecting the health of the community, various punitive measures were proposed that would damage a person's ability to obtain health and life insurance, obtain or retain employment and housing, and restrict various other civil liberties such as the right to travel for business or pleasure. They were aimed at gay men, intravenous drug users, and Africans. Other people with AIDS were referred to in the media as "innocent victims," confirming the hidden prejudice that the three targeted groups were "guilty."

Not too long ago, the oppression of gay people varied greatly in different parts of the world. In some places it was less visible or absent. In nations like France, Great Britain, and Italy, for instance, there was oppression but homoerotic preference was worked more quietly into the fabric of the society with as little fuss as possible. A person's gay spouse or lover was referred to as "his long time companion" or "her friend." Not only is the world shrinking because of the revolution in communication technology, but the United States has exported much of its culture in the process. Along with Coca-Cola, blue jeans, and films demonstrating the gun slinging ethic of "might makes right," heterosexual superiority and its companion homosexual shame have been sold to the world as fashionably correct.

Yet there are signs of hope from the same nation. There are some enlightened communities in the United States that have begun to understand the need for affirmative action of all sorts. In the past decade there have been several police departments, for instance, that have grasped the wisdom and utility of recruiting gay police. These ideas are new but they exist, are working, and therefore will spread to other communities.

It is always more difficult for oppressors to recognize <u>their</u> own acts of oppression. Enemies of gay people are quick to claim that lesbians and gay men are not capable of forming loving, long-lasting relationships comparable to heterosexual marriages. Of course they overlook the statistics having to do with the failure rate of heterosexual marriages. They also overlook the legal roadblocks placed in the path of lesbians and gay men who would like to have marriages sanctioned by church and state. But most telling, they are the first to be furious at requests for spousal-equivalent benefits. The most frequent source of conflict are the fringe benefits offered by many employers to the husbands and wives of their employees, such as health insurance. Since legal marriage between two men or two women is made impossible, it seems only logical and fair that two men or two women who can prove that they are in a relationship that in all other ways qualifies as a marriage should be granted the same spousal-equivalent benefits. Opposition to such requests are simple, clear examples of oppression. The statement is: "You are different and not equal, not as good."

Our oppression is weakening, due to our determined efforts to combat it. Its costuming and language change with other changing fashions. But make no mistake, our oppression continues today.

Sex Now

Sex is a very important part of human life. It is a basic need like water and food. We are more sane in relation to water. We are troubled about drinking water only when there is not enough. We are more peculiar in the way we relate to our need for food. Some people eat too much, some too little. We feast and fear famine. People struggle to diet in communities where people are starving. And some people develop eating disorders such as anorexia and bulimia.

Neurotic as we may be about our food needs, we are even more neurotic in the ways we humans relate to our need for sex. Celibacy, monogamy, promiscuity, sexual compulsivity, prostitution, and rape are some of the ritual symptoms of the serious problem we have managing this simple need. Religions and governments try to control human sexuality with rules. Some very damaging, even life threatening, diseases have been and are transmitted sexually, thereby creating a conflict between erotic desire and fear. We must accept the fact that most people, in most places in the world today, are irrational in managing their sexual needs.

Gay people have handled the past two decades of increased sexual freedom with remarkable sanity. This is especially striking when one remembers that gay men have had lifetimes of training in which they were taught to compete with other men in subtle and obvious forms of sexual conquest and were taught also that insatiable homosexual desire was the core of their identity.

One gay man with whom I discussed this recently spoke for many when he said, "I was sure happy when they took the locks off the doors of the candy shop. I thought the gates of paradise had opened. I was so busy at the bars, baths, and private orgies that I hardly had time for my career. A lot of it was wonderful. I met people I would not have met who are good friends today. I learned not to be afraid of other men. But it took only a couple of years of gorging before I understood what other guys meant when they said there must be more to life than the next hundred sexual experiences. I started to slow down fast. The garden was great but the flowers were going by so fast they were just a blur."

His experience was typical. Many gay men and some lesbians made use of the period of increased sexual freedom to compensate for earlier starvation but then paused to take personal stock and realized that sex was one relatively small, though vital, part of their lives. During that period there was more than a little using and misusing of one another, and it hurt. But there was also a bonding that bolstered the feeling of brotherhood and sisterhood. There was nothing wrong with the exchange of easy affection with people who had been strangers.

The advent of the AIDS epidemic made people more careful and caring. The suspicion that AIDS could be sexually transmitted came quickly. The realization that AIDS was a life-threatening disease brought a remarkably fast determination to do what was necessary to make sex safe again. We had begun to find our way to sane sex. It became imperative that we not throw out the baby with the bathwater. It continues to be essential that we discover the most positive possible role for sex in our lives as gay people. We were wrongly taught that our sexuality made us bad. We have learned that our sexuality is a great asset. We have learned and will continue to learn how to increase self respect and enrich relationships by sanely meeting our sexual needs.

The gay community has every right to be proud of its self-help efforts in response to the threat posed by the AIDS epidemic. One model program that the non-gay part of the world is struggling in its attempt to copy was our educational campaign to alter sexual practices so that sex could be caring and safe. Many gay men first thought it would mean dreary prohibition. Some mourned a seeming loss of spontaneity and abandon. Most learned that it expanded their sexual range. As one man said, "Big deal. There were two or three particular sexual acts that were becoming as routine as the old heterosexual missionary position. I had to stop one, alter one, and use a condom for the other. And, by the way, I learned a hundred new ways to have sex. Some awful sacrifice!"

Perhaps it was because satisfying free sex was so new in our lives. Perhaps it was because we had only begun to realize the benefits of the bonding it helped to create. Somehow, we knew that we must not stop our sexual exploration. We knew that we must continue to make sex an increasingly satisfying part of our lives. Perhaps that is what gave us the motivation to find safe and caring ways to relate to one another sexually. Perhaps that intensity of motivation is missing in the non-gay world. We need one another. We need as many of us healthy and alive as possible. We will tend our wounded and make any necessary changes in the ways we relate to one another, but we will not abandon one another nor deny the value of our sexuality.

In some communities the baths are being closed since they are places where people meet for sex, and are, therefore, places where disease can be spread—unless guidelines for safe and caring sexual behavior are followed by the people who meet there. A resulting problem is that sexually active gay men are returning to meeting places that were available before safe bathhouses were opened. Parks, restrooms, and bars can be unsafe in ways that are not new. Thugs invade parks intent on queer-bashing; police decoys wait to arrest people in restrooms; and emotionally unbalanced thieves and murderers turn up in gay bars looking for prey.

Inventive as always, the gay community has spawned newer safe ways of meeting in addition to the shared interest group clubs that had begun to grow in number and variety before the advent of the AIDS epidemic. There are political clubs, hiking clubs, athletic clubs of all sorts, gay cruises, gay vacation resorts, and now a great variety of volunteer organizations that do their best to meet the needs created by the epidemic. In addition there are clubs with names like The Jacks or Stroking Together where it is safe to meet in an environment where sexual contact is limited to touching and masturbation. And there has been the advent of telephone sex with the advantage of non-visual imaginative stirring of erotic desires as well as the opportunity to meet people around town or around the world. Finally, there is a greatly increased market for sexually explicit higher quality video tapes to enhance masturbatory pleasures.

Gay men have continued to meet the challenge of finding ways to love rather than fear their brothers. They have continued to meet the challenge also of overcoming the programming that forbids yielding to another man. Whether or not a gay man practices anal intercourse today, with the safety of a condom, he finds some way in sexual lovemaking and play to communicate his willingness to yield and open himself to his partner. Some communication of opening and yielding precedes the opening of the heart, as always. Joy is still found in trusting. Honor is still found in caring and being worthy of the trust.

The difference between recreational sex and affirmational sex is still to be found. There is less recreational sex now since there is obviously less likelihood of passing along any disease, whether a venereal disease or a common cold, if one has fewer sexual partners. Yet the play of recreational sex serves a need, and it continues, whether in erotic massage or a meeting of a Jacks

Club. And each person still must learn for himself or herself to differentiate between recreational and affirmational sex. Affirmation is not often found in the playground, and marriage or meditation are not good forums for irresponsible play.

In the rapid learning that we have been doing about how to make sex a more satisfying part of our lives, sexual and emotional monogamy have come up for reexamination. I notice that gay people handle the issue of monogamy more creatively and with more allowance for experimentation than our parents and grandparents did. Many are discovering that sexual and/or emotional monogamy is a great asset during some time in their lives, depending often on such factors as level of security, health, sense of worth and age. Some people are discovering that they prefer a lifetime of monogamy. Monogamy is there as one possibility to be considered or reconsidered, to be used temporarily or as a permanent pledge.

One couple with whom I discussed this recently told me that they had discovered that one partner felt most comfortable when he made a commitment to sleep with no one other than his lover but that he wanted to retain the option of sex play now and then when it was only play and did not involve going home with anyone. His partner felt most comfortable when he made a commitment to have sex with no one but his lover, though he might want the body contact comfort of sleeping with a friend now and then when his lover was away. They had also talked about experimenting with a short period of absolute monogamy that would involve not sleeping or having any sort of sex with anyone but one another. They were finding their way to meet their needs, able to make use of monogamy without taking an eternal pledge or laughing it away as a preposterous idea. It is this sort of willingness to explore ways of meeting individual sexual needs that has saved us gay people and has helped us to grow.

Health and Education

Gay people have long had a deserved reputation as a group for being more attentive to being attractive and, hence, more interested in working at maintaining good physical condition. That has made us a health conscious group. Since the advent

30

of the AIDS epidemic we have become even more health conscious, eager recipients of relevant education.

In these remaining years of the twentieth century, we are bombarded with research findings, general information, and commercially motivated claims as to what contributes to good health. Some amount of education is required to be able to sort the real from the unreal information to which one is exposed. More education is required to evaluate the relative risks and potential gains of various proposed methods of enhancing or restoring health.

An excellent example can be found in the use and misuse of drugs. The number of drugs stocked in a pharmacy today is impressive. The number of drugs manufactured is amazing. Some are considered legal and some illegal. Governments vary in their opinion as to which drugs must be prescribed by a physician. For that matter, governments vary in their opinion as to who is a qualified physician. A vast number of drugs with oversimplified descriptions of their content, utility, and danger are attractively packaged and easily purchased in drug stores and supermarkets.

It is agreed that the world has a drug problem. Yet governments focus only on the purchase and use of illegal drugs—those not manufactured, packaged, and sold by pharmaceutical companies with government approval. It takes quite a bit of education to understand that every drug can help someone and that every drug is also dangerous for some people.

It is understandable that governments are most concerned about drugs that significantly alter a person's state of mind, level of consciousness, attitude, and point of view. Drugs invented for use in warfare so as to make the troops of another government feel less like fighting have found their non-government approved way to people who enjoy their effects, and that concerns a government very much indeed.

There is no doubt that drugs, including alcoholic beverages easily obtained almost anywhere, have the potential for ruining many lives. Alcoholics Anonymous, Narcotics Anonymous, Alanon, and other twelve-step programs would not be such a vital and thriving success if this were not so. Almost everyone knows at least one person whose life has been seriously damaged by the use of drugs, whether those drugs were considered legal or illegal.

31

Yet real education about drugs is hard to come by. It is an amazing fact of life that a well-intentioned government in the twentieth century could believe that the problem of drugs could be dealt with by trying to teach its people to "just say no" to any drugs that the government decrees illegal.

Drug addiction, drug dependence, and co-dependence are complex topics. A person can become addicted to an easily obtained "legal" drug. People by the millions have become dependent upon the use of drugs produced and advertised legally for profit. Co-dependent people have a problem with a damaged sense of self that predisposes them to be attracted to the problems of a person who is addicted or dependent. Yet the person with an ordinary, respectable school education learns little or nothing about any of this, though it affects the majority of the population.

It would be shocking if we did not know that we live in a world where some people who are believed to be professional educators would rather see their students die from communicable diseases such as AIDS rather than educate them truthfully about sex, sexual practices, and sexually transmitted disease. The same is shockingly true of the parents who support such non-educational practices, preferring to risk their children's lives than to have their own sensibilities jostled.

During the recent decades of social liberation, gay people and other searchers were happy to explore the so-called "recreational drugs" that alter mood, attitude, and outlook. The experimentation with such drugs coincided with the spiritual search that was taking root in the gay community. Some of these drugs are still used in the gay community and outside of the gay community. Most are used as a "temporary way out," much like the customary use of alcoholic beverages. Some are used in an attempt to expand awareness and spiritual understanding. Such use of these "mind-altering" drugs is an ancient practice in various cultures. The difference is that traditional, ritualized use of such a drug in a society that has institutionalized its use, has the benefit of supervision by elders with the cumulative experience of generations. It is an educated use of the drug. Freewheeling experimentation in a culture where education and guidance is not available is destined to produce some amazing growth and some tragic destructive mistakes. Mere humans do a much better job of educating when they are willing to do so than they can ever do in making rules about who can and who cannot take a bite of the apple.

The carefree use of recreational drugs dropped dramatically in the gay community with the advent of AIDS. Part of our task in educating one another was to help everyone to learn that most drugs tax the body's immune system, whether the drugs are legal or not. Some are more taxing than others. Since it had become very important to protect the healthy functioning of our immune systems, people learned to think about the possible cost of drug ingestion. People who could not easily regulate their drug intake were confronted with their obvious problem of dependence or addiction. Since then, gay people have swelled the ranks of the twelve-step programs. Had we not educated one another about the effects of drugs on the immune system, we would not have discovered how high is the percentage of addiction and dependence in the population—both gay and non-gay.

The prevailing morality and its representative government in any part of the world may prefer good news and a good image to difficult truth. Very reputable newspapers have insisted on propagating the belief that AIDS is a disease of gay men, Africans, and users of illegal intravenous drugs. They support the belief with statistics that demonstrate naivete and denial. The statistics are unreliable and misleading, of course. Priests, military officers, government officials, and other people who are heterosexually married and would be disgraced in the public eye if they were known to have had homosexual liaisons die of cancer, pneumonia, and a host of other diseases. There is no mention made or statistics recorded indicating that the disease was the result of AIDS. Bigotry hides truth, impedes education, clouds judgment, and ultimately kills.

It is the same bigotry that produces the invisible prejudice that leads mental health professionals to play a shell game with diagnosis when confronted with gay people. The professions have made public pronouncements clearly indicating that gay people are not, per se, in any way emotionally unbalanced, and that homosexual behavior is not, per se, symptomatic of mental illness. Practitioners who may or may not be aware of their own prejudice too often find sickness in a gay person, however, just as they too often find mental illness in a person who is black or otherwise culturally different. It is easy to lead a distressed, young, emerging gay person to say that he or she does not want to be gay and to conclude that the homosexual desires and behavior are therefore "ego-dystonic," or foreign to the real nature of the individual. How many young people would dare insist that they claim full membership in a group that is persecuted?

Health consciousness and education has improved rapidly within the gay community. Support groups are more in use than ever before because they are an excellent way of reducing stress. Money that was being spent on suntans now often goes for a massage because heavy exposure to sun is taxing on the immune system, and massage reduces stress and replaces some of the tactile reassurance and bonding once found in casual sex.

We continue to have problems with depression, naturally. We had enough trouble with it when we were swallowing our anger. We learned to speak out with our anger, but we are now having to endure the hurt and sorrow the epidemic has brought. In my first aid advice to people dealing with depression, I have found it helpful to add the fourth "N" of *nature* to the previous three of expressing negative feelings, finding nurture and using novelty. Visits to nature, whether ocean, forest, mountains, or desert seem to absorb the feelings that weigh one down, and the scale of nature dwarfing our human dimension helps give needed perspective.

Although I rarely conduct weekend groups now, many other people are doing various forms of gay weekend group retreats. The techniques used alter to fit the styles of the time and the talents of the group leaders. Many of them are excellent examples of education—a dedicated willingness to search for and tell truth, because it is only with truth that we can be healthy.

Maturity, Commitment, and Relationships

Witnessing the suddenly abbreviated lives of so many friends and loved ones has forced lesbians and gay men to reconsider most of our most basic beliefs and values. We have had to mature very fast as individuals, and, as a community, we have had to develop in ways that would ordinarily have taken generations.

A friend wrote recently, saying that he and his lover had been having long thoughtful discussions about their commitment to one another, sexual and otherwise. "We each are trying to get a clearer understanding of what we believe and feel and then say it out loud so it can influence our development whatever way it will." He said they had talked a lot about what sex meant to each of them, wondering to what extent it was an opening to intimacy and vulnerability. "I think it carries the implication of being desired, hence wanted, hence valued." He said he thought that it was possible for some partners to share sex with people outside the relationship as fun, comaraderie, friendship, and brotherhood, but that he could not seem to alter the feelings he had experienced when his partner had done that in the past. He had felt as if his lover preferred others at those times, and, therefore, that he was finding them of more worth or value. "Even though his pledge of himself and his intimacy was to me, and I knew he was coming from a different set of feelings, I still felt threatened."

One part of our learning is that we must beware of tender areas, the unspoken hurts that come easily in the areas of sexuality, intimacy, and privacy. The early twentieth century norms were painful shackles to the gay person. The sexual liberation of the second half of this century permitted the creation of another set of mandated norms for gay men. Some gay men found they were an equally isolating, painful prison.

Many, perhaps most, gay people grow up feeling worthless, perhaps unwanted. In a primary bonding relationship we seek and need some peace and security at last. We need to know that this precious other person values us above all others. There is a giving of self, each to the other, unfashionable during the early days of our current liberation. But it is a marriage of content rather than mere form. This noble marriage is in some ways as simple and primitive as that found in the bonding of other creatures. It requires that I place *our* welfare on a plane that is synonymous with *my* welfare. I am motivated to help us, protect us, and in all ways see to our well being. To do this, I must constantly learn about my beloved and what nourishes him or her. I must learn what makes this precious other person feel safe. I must learn to accept this person *as is* while knowing that he or she is also changing in his or her own ways, and I must concentrate on appreciating my understanding of him or her *as is*. Only then dare I hope for the same from him or her.

My friend said, "I think the way we develop our bond is in our building of our life together. I believe that I must find my way to abandon competition and the loneliness of simple self-protection." To do this requires a period of courtship and true engagement with one another. In that process the resolve can be tested, the ways found, and the strength developed.

But in a gay marriage we cannot say "forsaking all others." We need our brotherhood and sisterhood. We need to find our ways of appreciating our appreciation of one another, including our appreciative feelings of sexual attraction for one another that are both within and beyond the marriage. And we need to do this our own way, not in the stylized heterosexual manner that has failed. It is here that our newly heightened sense of humanity can help us to transcend the bonding of other animals. We can, must, and are finding our way to celebrate the truth of our eroticism while protecting *above all* the peaceful security and newly reassured sense of value experienced by our mates.

We are reconsidering our sense of commitment to lovers, partners, mates, the gay community, and our own individual ideals. Part of the process is learning to admit mistakes and go on to try out new beliefs and arrangements. In the original version of *Loving Someone Gay*, I suggested that a calendar by the phone helped some couples avoid jealousy and unnecessary feelings of hurt when one of the pair made individual, separate social plans.

In recent years more and more people are finding that arrangements such as that are simple, but they do not work. The partner who reads the calendar wants to feel safety in your affection. A noted evening out with someone else easily feels like rejection unless the person and reasons are known and comfortable. It seems now that long engagements are preferable to a calendar by the phone. It takes time to learn to be yourself with integrity and to care equally about not hurting your partner. A long engagement permits that process to happen.

Maturity involves the willingness to admit mistakes, the courage to search for new answers, and the inner security that permits you to consider that old-fashioned, previously rejected answers may be worth looking at again. Like many other people, I used to wince when I heard someone talk about "working on our relationship." It sounded like a house or an automobile that needed work before it could function satisfactorily. But one day a better image came into my mind. Someone was in my office talking about working on his relationship and I knew it to be a good, satisfying, treasured relationship. The image that came to me was of someone lovingly working on the making of a quilt. It was not repair, not a chore, but active, joyous creation that he was talking about. It was a nice old-fashioned sort of image.

There is some old-fashioned wisdom that is returning to current style. It was missed while it was missing. I think of how gay couples, particularly male couples, are learning to remember to say "I love you" more often when they happen to be feeling it strongly. People are remembering to say other private feelings that not long ago were considered too sentimental. A woman friend told me that she had been sitting in the living room with her lover with a thought going through her mind for a full four minutes before she brought herself to say it. "I was stupidly looking at the minute hand go around on the clock on the mantle and I finally had the courage to say, 'I really want to grow old with you. I hope we do.' It was the day after Chuck's memorial service. I guess that helped. We both had a good cry and a good hug and a wonderful kiss."

Those thoughts are best said aloud. They can help your partner experience a sense of well being and security. Of course, it is also a good idea not to say such things unless you are sincerely feeling them lest you "cry wolf" and ruin the chance of your partner's hearing the ring of truth when you are feeling strongly.

As we have learned to be more caring in these recent years, we have learned to be more careful. Humiliation and its connection to wounded pride and damaged self esteem is a particularly sensitive issue for us gay people. You must know your partner well if you are to avoid accidental humiliation. It is best, when in doubt, to refrain from possibly humiliating behavior until you can check it out with the person who shares your most valued relationship. Older and younger partners, for instance, may experience humiliation in quite different circumstances that are not too difficult to understand if some thought is given to it. The younger partner may be sensitive to any suggestion that his older partner is being patronizing about his relative lack of experience in life. The older partner may be particularly sensitive to any possible suggestion that his partner is attracted to another younger person. A monogamous gay husband can be humiliated by his non-gay non-monogamous wife making a casual reference to her other sexual relationships.

These particular examples are chosen in part as a reminder to us all to congratulate ourselves on the wonderful variety and mixture we have become in our gay community. Mixing older and younger people, for instance, has permitted our youngsters to gain wisdom more rapidly, and it has permitted our seniors to be bolstered by the enthusiasm of youth while knowing they need not fear being left alone.

Like too many other people in the world, we gay people still have our fear of intimacy. Knowing all that we have been through in recent years, I sometimes wonder why it has stayed with us so persistently. Perhaps it has something to do with our collective experience of betrayal by so many people in our lives with whom we assumed we had intimate relationships until they found out we were gay. We are less in danger of avoiding intimacy by distracting ourselves with random, casual sex, and quick infatuations than we were in years past. It seems to me that gay men have made great progress in getting past the visual training and the training for prowl and conquest. We are better at seeking satisfying nest mates thanks to having been forced to get to know one another better, in more ways, beyond sex.

But the fear of intimacy lingers. We can only hope that our quick maturation, and our evolving understanding of commitment and relationship will give us the faith in one another that comes with time, and the consequent security that will permit us to enjoy the intimacy we have earned in this process of helping one another to live and die.

Our Spirituality

Religions have treated us shamefully. There is not a lesbian or gay man alive who cannot tell you some ways in which she or he has been harmed personally by institutionalized religion. Yet we have been drawn to religions of all sorts. Today, as always, many of the priests, rabbis, ministers, sisters, brothers, and important lay members of all religious sects are lesbians and gay men. This amazing fact persists even though these same institutions have persecuted us and shown little understanding, compassion, or mercy for us. Many of us practice the doctrine that many of them merely preach. In a very real sense, we are their contemporary martyrs, yet they fail to recognize us.

By the middle of the 1970s, religious lesbians and gay men were trying to find alternatives and at the same time trying to build organizations that could communicate with the religious establishments. The Metropolitan Community Church, founded earlier by Troy Perry, had begun to spread from Los Angeles to other communities, other states, and other nations. It represented an attempt within the usual framework of contemporary religion to present a church that clearly welcomed lesbians and gay men in the congregation and as its ministers.

Roman Catholics had founded an organization called "Dignity," and other religious groups followed with organizations designed to speak for them in dialogue with their official religious leaders. Their work required persistent persuasion and a great willingness to forgive. Unfortunately, it has elicited little positive response through the years from the establishments it tried to reach in dialogue.

During the same period other less conservative groups looked for new forms of worship. There were "radical faeries" and even covens of lesbian "witches." They broadened the spectrum and helped increase the awareness of our too frequently unmet spiritual needs. As a result we have seen the establishment of some heavily gay congregations in particular churches and the creation of some openly gay synagogues.

The impact of the AIDS epidemic in our community brought with it a merciless confrontation with the fact of human mortality and increased the urgency of our collective spiritual search. Many people returned, some temporarily, to the religions of their childhood, though they knew any comfort they found there would be mixed with the psychological punishment they had experienced earlier in their lives.

Those members of our community who were the first to die as a result of the epidemic helped us beyond measure. Their need to suddenly place their lives in perspective before death combined with the awareness that there was no time to be wasted on half-truths and idle soul-searching platitudes.

Two of my friends who knew they were headed quickly toward death while trying to appreciate life and fighting to continue to live taught me a great deal. Both had been enrolled in religious establishments as children, and both had declared themselves atheists as adults, after realizing how shamefully they had been treated by their religious leaders. Though they had come from quite different religious backgrounds, both found a similar path in their final months of life.

One spoke to me shortly after an uninvited visit from a staff clergyman while he was in the hospital. "He asked me if I believed in God. It made me smile. I was dopey from the medication so I said the first thing I thought. I said I thought the question he needed to be asking was whether God believed in him."

Both friends told me that they had come to realize that they were aware that we live in an enormous, complex cosmos that is continually changing, expanding, and balancing. They came to see that all of it, All, is God, and that each of us is "of God." One of my friends said, "I'm just going home, elsewhere, with the rest of God. This lifetime has been okay. I could have done better with it, but I did okay. I tried to learn and to be honest. I am trying to be the best part of God that I can be. And I understand that most people, including people who work in religion, are too busy trying to accomplish something else to be able to relax and appreciate God. I'm appreciating."

It made me cry, of course. His theology was so simple and so direct. As I was leaving the hospital, I was asking in my mind "Why? Why can't our honesty and goodness be appreciated." Quite suddenly, I felt a sense of peace as I realized that I, too, and many others, know that we are "of God," and *we* appreciate the honesty and goodness we find both in our community and from those who truly love us. We are appreciated.

I had to tell him the last time I saw him that I was sorry he was dying and that I would miss him. He took my hand. "It looks like a bad thing happening," he said, "but who's to say? Let's say I'm getting off work early, but I'll be around." And so he is, still at this moment, very alive in my memory.

Though it was the men in our community who were the early casualties, the women quickly rallied, joining with the men in a manner that could only be described as spiritual. A close woman friend with whom I have had long discussions about these difficult years was one of the first women to be deeply involved. Her best friend was one of the first men to be diagnosed. She said, "It brought me to life. I think I was half asleep. I miss him terribly. He's still my best friend and I still talk to him. I wouldn't have missed a minute of it, including all the awfulness and pain. He taught me more than any other person ever has. I know now who I am and where I am—and I don't mean my name and address."

We gay people had learned that living with our intellect was not enough. We had learned that we had to become aware of our feelings and give them voice. We learned that our bodies were invariably included in that awakening of feelings. To reclaim our feelings we had to reclaim our bodies. Now we have become aware that we must reclaim the spiritual self and that it does not come packaged and defined by the local preacher. We have to work as hard at finding our true spirituality as we had to work to locate our true feelings.

Our foundation is stronger now. Any dairy farmer can tell you that a three legged stool is a lot more sturdy than a two legged stool. We now have our intellect, our emotions, and our spirituality. We are learning to integrate the three, and, as a result, we are once again a group to be watched.

So often I am impressed with how briefly someone speaks of some complex aspect of our new spiritual learning. A twenty-four year old man sat in my office, speaking from his heart just two days after his lover had died in his arms. "I thank God that Gene and I found each other," he said. "No matter how long we live, we're in this life a short time. He helped me to learn how to care about him and not take his life away from him by caring for him in the ways he could care for himself. We both had to face the anger and hidden loneliness we had been carrying in a world of strangers all of our lives, but now both the anger and the loneliness are gone. He helped me to see that we're here such a short time it just doesn't make any sense to give any less than the best you have to give. We did that for each other. We gave each other the best we had. Thank God."

Many more of us have found some comfortable concept of a power greater than human power, though it may not be possible to explain one's understanding in scientific terms or in an articulate, rational manner. It is no longer embarrassing to speak of God in a gay social gathering. And it is quite acceptable to ask for help in understanding and coping. I was amused recently to hear a gay bartender say, "Hell, I don't know how to explain God but don't push me to explain electricity or microchips either. But I thank God I found my way to A.A. and that I have a good job and a roof over my head. There may not be an old man in a dress sitting on a cloud, but it sure feels like I'm getting listened to."

At so many gay memorial services, one hears reference to the deceased person having moved on to another plane. It's a concept gay people can consider, having experienced more than one plane within this lifetime.

3
Loving Us

I was alone with a college student who is the son of a gay friend. It was getting late in the evening for me, but he was full of energy, interested in talking, and seemed intent on conversing about the basics of life. He had returned recently from a trip to visit relatives in Ireland and was affecting an Irish manner in his speech.

"Tell me something, honestly," I said. "You've met quite a few gay men and lesbians by now and you seem at ease among us and clear that you are not gay. What is your impression of us as a group. Is there one identifying characteristic to be found?"

He was thoughtful, then looked at me and smiled. "I'd have to say you're a loving lot," he answered. "You're a loving lot who love a lot."

And I must agree. I believe that it is difficult to say any one thing about such a diverse group of people, but, while there are exceptions to be sure, we are a loving lot who love a lot. Stereotype would have it that therein is the sly way of admitting that we are terribly sexual people. We are sexual people but not terrible. Most of us are as nicely sexual as you would wish any mature person to be. But our experience with love has been hard-earned. We appreciate love, and we put a lot into our loving, whether sex is involved in the relationship or not.

There are all of those tired jokes about people who loved well but not too wisely, usually resulting in unwanted pregnancy. Because gay people have had to find their own way without a lot of help from their culture, it may be fair to say that many of us have loved well and not too wisely at times, though that seldom resulted in unwanted pregnancy. But, in the final analysis, most people would admit that it is better to have loved well and not too wisely than to have loved wisely and not too well.

If you are a non-gay person reading this book, it is probable that the reason is that you want to love better, both well and wisely. It is the best that we can hope for, from ourselves and from others. In one of the letters that I received following the original publication of *Loving Someone Gay*, the person wrote, "My reason for reading the book was so that I could learn better how to love a special someone who is gay. Now I realize I was trying to learn to love better, period. And at least one of the people I care for is gay."

We are a loving lot with a lot of love. Try to offer that which you want. Give that which you need in your life. Learn about the person you love and let that person learn about you. We have mistakenly made loving more difficult than it need be for all of us, gay or not.

Knowing and Loving

"Where have I failed?", she asked in a parody of parental alarm. A lesbian was telling a group of eager friends about her disclosure experience with her parents. She had prepared carefully and done well. Both parents had listened quietly, looked at one another, and then the mother had said, "It doesn't make any difference. We love you just the same as always. You're no different to us now than you were before."

"You'd think I could get a little credit for all I've been through." She was only half joking. She was terribly relieved that her parents had taken the disclosure so well. And it was too soon after the disclosure to know all of their feelings. But she did want some credit.

Most of us have learned that being gay is wonderful. But all of us know that it has made our lives more difficult. Few of us would have had the courage to choose to be gay if the inner truth had not been there pushing us along. We want and deserve some credit for the cost of being different. We want our loved ones to appreciate that there is more to us than they had thought if they had not known already that we were gay.

A gay friend's brother asked him, "But how can I get your friends to like me and accept me. I'm not gay."

The truthful answer is that it is easy to be accepted and appreciated as a non-gay person in gay circles. All you have to do is be yourself and show that you like us. We make friends easily with people who want to be our friends. Our hostility is reserved for people who choose not to know us and/or who believe us to be inferior.

The relatives and friends of gay people who have the most difficult time accepting, appreciating, and loving us are the ones who never learned to love themselves. If you do not love yourself, it is hard to offer love to another person. It is the reason why non-gay people who have done the hard work of soul searching and getting to know themselves truthfully are more at ease with themselves and more at ease with people who are different from them. If you accept yourself, you are much more likely to take another person as you find her or him.

Ignorance is a barrier to any sort of relationship. Warring groups generally do not know one another well. They have been taught stereotypes. No matter what our seeming differences because of nationality, skin color, language, and customs, human beings are very varied but more alike than different.

Whenever a family member tells me they are worried that they will not get along well with a sibling, son, daughter, father, mother, or grandparent now that they know the person is gay, I say that they are probably right unless they value the person and the relationship enough to look forward to getting to know the person even better. Getting to know someone better when you already care is very enjoyable work. But biological families do not always function well. Just because two people are biologically related does not mean that they have enough in common to enjoy one another.

The same is true for today's chosen families, those developing networks of friends and relatives that become one's real family through the years of a lifetime. If you discover that someone in your chosen family is gay, and you want to keep that person in your chosen family, it will not work unless you value the fact that the person is gay. And in order to value that fact about the person you may have to learn a lot more about what it means to be gay. Books are available and so is the person. Most of us like it when we know that someone loves us enough to put some effort into understanding us better. We are eager to assist.

A psychologist friend telephoned me to ask my opinion about something he is writing having to do with gay people. He mentioned as an aside that he had recently visited with his eighty-eight year old father-in-law who had wondered aloud why there seem to be so many more gay people around today than there were when he was young. He wondered if there are more being born these days. The psychologist, with a possible bit of hidden homophobia, wondered if it was not because we had pushed people during the peak years of the human potential movement to "explore that part of themselves" and "sort of pushed people in that direction." It sounded to me suspiciously like he was talking about pushing people over some invisible line from which there is no return.

The plain simple truth is that there appear to be more lesbians and gay men around these days because it is easier, if not easy, to find the courage to "come out." All evidence indicates that we probably are the same percent of the population in all parts of the world and at all times in human history. When the social atmosphere is less punitive, and there are visible role models already "out" and staying alive with self-respect, it is easier to consider being truthful about your identity and to stop having to hide your true self, even if some people would like you better if you continued to pretend to be just like them. From what I heard, there was no reason to believe that the eighty-eight year old man was complaining. He was probably reviewing his friends or perhaps remembering a dim secret of his own.

Another perennial that comes up when family members learn that someone is gay is the fear that they may have inherited it, too. It seems quite likely that the predisposition has a hereditary basis as does preference for left handedness or right handedness. But we accept easily the simple fact that some members of the family are left handed and some favor their right hand.

When asked, I like to look the person in the eye and tell them that if they have a homoerotic preference they are aware of it already. We all know whether it is males or females that more often turn our heads on the street or in television commercials. It is an automatic and involuntary physical and emotional response. If the preference is there, one may choose to hide it or exercise it. If it is there, it is healthier in the long run to exercise it if the environment is not too punitive.

I hasten to reassure people that you cannot catch homoerotic preference any more than you can catch heteroerotic preference. Neither is contagious. If they were, strongly heterosexual societies would not have to bother with the constant suppression of homosexual desire and behavior. But if you are related to someone who is gay, you *can* catch some acceptance and appreciation. Gay people have worked hard for it and will be glad to help you gain it also.

It is too bad that many families have learned of a loved one's gay identity only at the time he developed AIDS or an AIDS related disease. It is very difficult to hear the gay identity as good news when it is combined with such bad news. But once the truth is out in such a situation, families, more often than not, quickly realize that they are much more concerned with helping a loved one who needs their help than with passing judgments as to the goodness or badness of which people he finds attractive and loves.

It is not always true that to know someone is to love them. But it is true that you cannot love someone unless you know them. Only foolish, unfounded fears stop non-gay persons from wanting to know a gay person they care about better so that they can care more.

Prejudice

One of the most serious social diseases of contemporary times is prejudice. As information is more and more easily obtained and attractively presented around the globe, there is less and less excuse for its existence and for the terrible toll it takes in human suffering.

Prejudice is a matter of pre-judging, making a decision about someone or something with insufficient evidence. Often it is a matter of actively ignoring evidence. The damage is done when one acts on the basis of prejudice rather than reality.

No one is immune from this disease. The most respected citizens in most parts of the world carry it in some form and willingly spread it to other people. It may be as innocent as a belief system that concludes in advance that all cooked vegetables are tasteless. It may be as dangerous as the untested belief that all people with a certain skin color, language, or erotic preference are untrustworthy and second rate. It is the latter sort of prejudice that causes people to be beaten and killed for war or sport.

I made a similar remark in passing while discussing another subject at a professional meeting. A non-gay colleague turned on me with considerable anger and said, "You're a fine one to talk. When are the homosexuals of the world going to clean up their act. I am sick and tired of being the recipient of their prejudice."

I answered that there might be something in the behavior of gay people whom he had met that he did not care for but that I doubted very much if it was prejudice. Prejudice breeds on ignorance. In order to keep your prejudice intact you must be sheltered from too much information about the people who are the targets of your prejudice. Almost every gay person in the world grows up in a non-gay family and in a non-gay community. She or he is exposed regularly to non-gay school mates, merchants, neighbors, teachers, employers, and co-workers. "I think it is safe to say that we know a lot more about you than you know about us," I told him. "We have lived very close to a wide variety of people whom we knew were non-gay. Some we have loved and some not. I doubt if you have lived very close to a wide variety of gay people whom you knew were gay. And I doubt if you were aware that you loved some of us."

It is curious but true that some people who are not naturally predisposed to prejudice will follow the prejudiced perceptions of their leaders. A clear example is religious leaders who, at their worst, justify holy wars by promulgating stereotypes about "the enemy" that could not possibly stand the test of getting to know one hundred different people who are being lumped into that category. A less vivid example is the parent who passes along the stereotypic images of prejudice that he or she received from parents and grandparents.

It is extraordinary to think that half a century ago many people believed that Jews had horns on their heads. Some sadly sheltered people probably believe it still. But then some people today still believe that gay people are those "dirty homosexuals" who lurk in darkened alleys waiting to prey on "innocent heterosexuals."

In the early days of gay liberation, we used to suggest half jokingly that prejudiced people "take a lesbian to lunch." We were trying to suggest that it is hard to keep your prejudice about us when you get to know a few of us.

I am sorry to say that I continue to hear stories regularly of patient sons and daughters whose parents have "accepted" the fact that their offspring is gay but absolutely forbid the son or daughter to bring any friends into the family home. It is almost as if they sense that they would receive evidence that would destroy their prejudice.

But then people cling to old beliefs as they sometimes do to comfortable old shoes that are no longer doing their job well. A mother, who had refused to meet her son's lover or any of his friends for fifteen years, met them when she visited her son in the hospital in the last weeks of his life. "I am so ashamed," she told me. "They showed him more love than I did and they were more wonderful to me than I deserved." Now her son is dead and his lover and friends are welcome in his mother's home.

Prejudice is no one's fault. It is a disease of the mind and spirit. The existence of a disease is no one's fault. But it is the responsibility of every sane human to do what he or she can to fight any disease that threatens human life. It may be hard to challenge a prejudiced statement the first time, but it gets easier.

The same mother told me about someone at her place of employment who did not know the circumstances of her son's death, saying casually at the lunch table that one thing good about AIDS was that it was cleaning a lot of the undesirables out of the population. "I just couldn't speak. I knew I would cry. But another woman at the table said, 'If they make you a judge, be sure to let me know because I want to live in another county where it's safe to have somebody think I'm undesirable.'"

The first woman laughed and said, "Don't be silly; I'm talking about queers and drug addicts. Everybody knows they're undesirable."

The second woman said, "You'll have to introduce me to the ones you know. On second thought, don't. I think I'd still like the ones I know better. The ones you know must be some kind of weird."

Point made.

If you care about one of us, you will have to do what you can to combat the prejudice about all of us. Look in your own heart first. If you think you know one thing that is true about all of us, you are wrong and you are pre-judging.

Communication

In a world full of chatter, most of us have difficulty in expressing that which matters most to us. We can talk about the weather or the news, but—though you may want to do it very badly—it can be most difficult, even frightening, to anticipate talking about feelings with the people who matter most in your life. We fear judgments, misunderstanding, and loss of love.

There is always more to learn about another person, and there is always more to tell about yourself. It is very tempting to try to shape someone you care about into the person you think he or she should be. Since the other person cannot oblige and be exactly the person you would wish him or her to be, you are apt to do some trimming, adding, and altering in your perceptions. Learning more about the person you care for means daring to rid yourself of false perceptions. Telling someone for whom you care more about you means helping that person to see you more truthfully, without their own false perceptions. It feels risky because we know we do not like to have our privately manufactured perceptions evaporated in the light of truth, and we are apt to fight it one way or another.

When I am consulted by loved ones who want to know how to improve their relationship with a gay man or a lesbian, I state the obvious. I advise that people say what is on their minds, ask the questions that are hidden inside, and say their emotions aloud, too. You can do all of that while retaining some sensitivity to the other person's feelings. Talking out your feelings is much less hurtful than acting them out in some behavior that is a code you expect the other person to understand.

Sometimes it seems impossible to know where to begin. I think of three people who told me of sending a copy of *Loving Someone Gay* to their families after having made the disclosure of gay identity. Each sent the book with a letter saying that they hoped it would give them a starting place in being able to talk about being gay.

The first was a lesbian who had sent it to her mother, father, and teenage brother. One week later they were on the telephone, telling her that they had all read the book and had a lot of talking they wanted to do, asking if she could come home the following weekend.

The second was a young man whose parents made no comment at all. He asked if they had received the book and his mother said they had. On his next visit home he noticed that it was at the bottom of a stack of books on his mother's side of the bed. Twice he tried to begin talks, and made mention of the book but there was no response. Clearly, his parents were not ready to communicate, for reasons unknown.

The third was a man who sent copies of the book to his widely scattered grown up siblings. He had a variety of reactions from his brothers and sisters but never recovered from having been told by one sister that another sister's husband had burned the book in the living room fireplace without anyone in the household having read it. Correctly reported or not, correctly decoded or not, it hurt him deeply. It had taken a lot of courage and caring on his part to try to open communication. The violent response was an unhealed wound that hurt him to the day he died, a year later. His family mourned deeply, perhaps more deeply because some of them had been unwilling or unable to communicate with him about who he was.

If you love someone who is gay, tell him or her that you do. Then back up the words with actions by trying to learn as much as you can about the person, about what it means to be gay, and about your own feelings in response. Remember to say it out rather than act it out. Words can be confusing until the meaning is untangled. Behavior meant to take the place of words can be even more confusing. Show that you care by being unwilling to give up on the effort to sort things out by talking even if you have only negative thoughts about homosexuality. Remember that no matter how many seemingly appropriate greeting cards you send, you do not love another person until you are willing to give up your false perceptions and improve your understanding of that person.

For many people, communicating love is the most difficult. Some have learned to say "I love you," with such regularity that it has lost most of its meaning. Others are stingy with the words. When you mean it, say it. It is very reassuring to hear it when you sense the other person is saying it because they feel it. This is especially difficult between men. Men are not trained to say "I love you" to another man. It can become a monumental problem between father and son, between brothers, or even between male lovers. Because of cultural training, males may have to force the words until they come more easily. Women may have to check themselves on too easy, and, therefore, relatively meaningless use of the words.

When I think of communication, I like to think of one middle-age lesbian who fell in love with another woman when she was just past forty years of age. "Those first weeks were wonderful and awful," she said. "I didn't know what I was feeling exactly, how to say it, or if I should say it. But she helped me. She used to hold me quietly sometimes and say she wanted to speak from her heart. One day I understood the difference. There was all the usual talk and then there was our heart talk. When she spoke from her heart, all I had to do was listen and love her, and care. Sometimes I would feel hurt or angry or whatever, but if I spoke from my heart, no matter what it was, she was always there listening, caring, and loving."

True communication comes before all else in a loving relationship. Telling is only half of it. Listening with care is the other half.

Acceptance

A striking moment, still vivid in my memory, happened while seeing a nineteen year old young man and his parents. He was trying his best to explain his gay identity. His parents were uncomfortable about and critical of many aspects of his life. He was not turning out to be the person they had hoped, planned, and dreamed he would be. He stopped abruptly in the middle of a sentence of explanation and burst into heart rending sobs. When he could speak, gasping for breath, still sobbing, he said, "I'm trying to be the best person I can be. Can't you just accept me now as I am?"

It is a question that goes to the heart of the matter. Each of us wants and needs that acceptance from the people in our lives who matter. The problem is that most of us have trouble granting that acceptance without conditions. It is difficult for us to accept another person *as is* though experience should have taught us before the end of childhood that we cannot change another person. Nor can we change many of the events that come along in life and impact on us. We must learn to accept that which we cannot change, or we will know no peace in life and will miss the opportunity to give those we love the most precious gift we are capable of giving.

For a non-gay person to give the true gift of acceptance to a gay person, it is necessary to learn as much as possible about what it means to be gay and to unlearn the negative stereotypes that are so plentiful. Sooner or later, sex must be confronted. It is unfortunate, but true, that all of us, gay and non-gay, have been trained to focus on homosexuality as the core of gay identity. Homosexual desire is always involved; homosexual behavior of some sort usually is involved.

You must come to terms with all of the reasons you have heard in your lifetime that are supposed to prove that homosexuality is bad. If you are successful in your quest to honestly reexamine your learning, you will come to the conclusion that sex is sometimes hurtful and often wonderful. The difference has to do with what is happening between the people involved in addition to the sexual act. You will find that it has little or nothing to do with the gender of the people involved.

Because gay people have been exposed to the same training in their lifetimes, there is a sharper focus on sexuality. We pay attention to it. As a result, as a group, we tend to be more frank and honest about its good and bad aspects. To a non-gay person, trained to think about sex but to mention it only in certain *acceptable* ways, it can be shocking to listen in on gay talk about sex or to hear the sexual innuendo in general conversation. Sometimes it is exaggerated. Young gay people are particularly likely to emphasize it as they try to find their way through the thicket of fiction and facts about gay sex and what it means in their lives.

If you love us, you must try your best to accept us as we are. Like the sobbing, wounded, nineteen year old, each of us is trying to be the best person we can be, whether that fits your idea of how a good person should be or not. Most of us spend all of our lives trying to get more free of the oppression in which we have been bathed since birth. We continue to try to be worthy of our own respect and love. Your acceptance can help a great deal; your conditional acceptance can slow us down.

Gay or non-gay, most of us are so inexperienced in giving the gift of unconditional acceptance that we think we are doing it when we are not. Being neutral about gay in an anti-gay environment is not quite enough to qualify as accepting. A neighbor once said to me, "As far as gay is concerned, I'm neither for it nor against it. It's up to you whether you're gay or not." It sounded almost right. I know that my gay identity is my business and not my neighbor's. It would have helped more, though, to hear something like, "I think gay is just as good as not gay. I like you. And being gay is part of you, so it's part of what I like about you."

The message you need to try to get across, once you feel it, is that you support the person's gay identity. Often the word is used with no meaning. Many times relatives will tell a gay person, "I accept the fact that you are gay but I don't like it." There is no acceptance in that statement other than the word. Real acceptance has a bit of appreciation in it. Either you accept the person, or you do not. If I tell you that I accept something about you but I do not like it, I have done no more than admit that I cannot find a way to change you into the person I want you to be.

It is difficult. You must be who you are and hope that the gay person will accept you too. All of us are changing. We can only hope and try to change in better ways while hoping that the people we care most about appreciatively accept us as we are at any given point along the way.

I met a man recently who told me that a few years earlier he had been gay for a year. That interested me since I know that all the professional and unprofessional claims to "cure" people of gay identity are, at best, false advertising.

It happened that all of his best friends in college were gay and involved in the same attempts to win social change that interested him. He knew that he found several of his male friends attractive and so he reasoned that he, too, must be gay. He had a boyfriend for a few months and then a serious lover relationship for some months. It was one of his gay male friends who helped him to recognize that while he was capable of sharing affection and enjoyable sex with a few males, the people his heart went out to more strongly were women. He had gone overboard in his attempt to be accepting of gay identity. He had correctly located his own gay feelings but ignored his stronger non-gay feelings. He laughed when he told me about it but also admitted that it was not at all funny at the time. "I had to go through a long period of coming out to my gay friends as being basically straight."

Whatever our erotic orientation, each of us can be no more than the person we are. If you love someone who is gay, try your best to learn about us and about that person in particular. Try your best to offer the gift of unconditional appreciative acceptance and you may find yourself the recipient of that same wonderful gift.

Unanticipated Loss

Certain kinds of loss are almost always unanticipated. A thought of it may have crossed your mind, but it was too unacceptable to be held long in imagination. This is particularly true with the death of a child. It is true when any young person dies, seemingly before her or his time. It is also true when a love dies.

Relentless unanticipated loss began to haunt the gay community when the AIDS epidemic began. I remember sitting in a group of twelve gay men when someone said what all of us had thought, "A year from now, probably one or more of us will be sick or dead." One year later, one person had died and another was in the hospital, nearing death. Nothing could have prepared us for it. Both were young, vital people, eager for life, maturing well.

Though gay people have been saturated and worn by the toll of this awful epidemic, it has seriously touched non-gay people as well. I heard a friend, in the last months of his life as a result of AIDS, say more than once, "I wish we could get the idea across that we are *people* with AIDS. We are dealing with a disease but, first and foremost, we are no better and no worse than other people. I am a person. If you want to help me, treat me like a person, like myself."

There are training courses for professionals and volunteers who work with people with AIDS. Most relatives and friends, when they discover that someone they love has AIDS must begin to learn fast without the assistance of a training course. Many are able to do most of the right things intuitively because as one man's brother told me, "He's somebody I love and he's sick and probably dying and that's all I need to know." Another man's grandmother, who had had more experience with death, said, "Very few of us choose our time to go. I'm here to love him and let us comfort each other as long as we're both alive. We'll do the best we can for each other, step by step."

There are AIDS hotline telephone services staffed by wonderful volunteers who can help with suggestions or just by listening as you think out loud, finding your own answers. Often the best person to help you is the person you are concerned about. It is an intensification of the experience of helping one another through life day by day. When a disease, particularly a terminal disease, is discovered, we learn to pay as much attention to helping each other through what is left of life, day by day, as we can manage.

If you are concerned because someone you love has AIDS or you fear that someone you love may be diagnosed with AIDS in the future, talk about it. Get it out in the open. You may need more information about the disease and how it is passed from one person to another. You may need more information about the life-style of the person you love. You run the risk of asking an indiscreet question. But that is far less harmful than operating on assumptions that are not true.

A young woman, who was in the final months of life because of a disease that was not AIDS-related, said, "One of the most awful things is feeling like I have to bring it up with people. I can talk about it if someone needs to talk about it. But I see them choking back questions and thoughts, and so I bring it up to get it out in the open. I wish they'd do their part of the work."

A person with AIDS, or anyone who has a life threatening disease needs love and support, as do we all. That does not mean false love or support that only clutter the remaining time. You must find the love and support that is genuinely yours to give, and give it. The recipient will be the better for it, and you will be the better for it. So often people say, "I feel so helpless. I want to do something and there's nothing I can do." That is far from the truth. You can listen, love, care, and be willing to help in other ways that the person indicates he or she wants help. We are not born alone, we do not live alone, and most people would prefer not to die alone.

The other most frequent unanticipated loss that enters the lives of gay people and the people who love them is the end of a marriage or other close relationship. Sometimes the relationship is based on the understanding that both people are not gay. When one of the people discovers or becomes able to admit that he or she is gay, it may mean the end of the relationship. At the very least it means a change in the relationship.

People choose to work at keeping the relationship strong and alive sometimes, altering it as little as possible, making it better where possible. This happens sometimes in a heterosexual marriage. It is difficult. It takes enormous willingness to try to help one another meet needs. The gay partner in the marriage, after the disclosure, often experiences a drop in heterosexual desire. It may be a compensatory reaction to years of having overworked heterosexual desire. Usually it does not mean that the spouse is loved less, only that the sexual desire has shifted. It may be possible for the relationship to accommodate the change. It is only one of many hurdles to keeping the marriage going. But it is possible for some people.

If one or both partners in any relationship decide that it is time to part, it is very difficult to do so and keep mutual love and respect. We become understandably dependent on a secure, loving relationship. We know it must end someday, with the death of one of the partners, but that is always in the future.

It is often too difficult to find the way until after a period of spent fury and hurt. A former wife of a gay man told me, "Now that we're getting to know one another again, some of the old solid love is there. At least I have that and the memories to show for those years. It didn't all just die and go away. We mean something to one another and still care about one another."

A former husband of a lesbian said, "She was willing to try to work things out so that we could stay together. I've wondered, but I think it was right to part ways. She could not be monogamous. It was okay with her if I had affairs. But I need monogamy. It makes me feel safe, I guess. I still love her. It's too bad, but there was a basic flaw in the match."

Whenever there has been an unanticipated loss, or when one is confronted with imminent unanticipated loss, it is a good idea to seek counseling and make use of a support group if possible. The loss, or the prospect of it, opens up the nightmare world of fears that we have brushed aside, out of conscious awareness. We humans are marvelously adaptive, but we need help getting through dark places, and, more often than not, the help is there if we let it be known that we need it and are not too proud to take the offered hand.

In this unique period, I have seen many non-gay people find the help they needed from both gay and non-gay volunteers or friends of a loved one who is sick. Invariably, there is the surprise that the stereotypes once believed are not true and the solid gratitude for new found awareness. I always wish it had been possible for it to have come sooner, under easier circumstances.

We cannot dwell on all of the possible unanticipated losses in our lives. It would cause serious emotional imbalance. We can accept the fact that it is likely that there will be some sort of unanticipated loss and try to be prepared to ask for help to get through it. We can also do the best loving we can do in our important relationships, treasuring rather than wasting the days we have.

4
Helping Us

I was standing in a line in an airline terminal. There had been many cancelled flights for all airlines the day before. There were many people with unexpectedly changed plans and insufficient sleep. When the man in front of me stepped up to the counter, the tired clerk who was trying her best said, "How may I help you?" He looked at her blankly and said, "I don't know."

The truth of the moment combined with my own fatigue caused me to laugh, not at him or her, but for us all. "Isn't it the truth," I said, and we all laughed. Sometimes we know we need help and don't know what help we need. Sometimes we want to help and do not know what help is needed. At least we have our foot on the first step. We know that help is needed, and there is a willingness to help.

Twelve years ago, it seemed to most of us who were gay activists that gay people needed a lot of help. It was true. We did need help. And we got the help we needed, mostly from one another. Now there are many gay people out in the open, and the world sees us. Many people in the world think we need help. And we do. But now we gay men and lesbians see that the world needs our help too. We are willing to help. Our foot is on the first step.

I overheard two gay men in a restaurant talking. The first said, "When you were a little kid and people asked you what you wanted to be when you grew up, what did you tell them?"

His companion said, "Well, mostly I used to say I didn't know. As a matter of fact, I still say that sometimes. But I know parts of it now. If I had known then what I know now, at least I could have said 'gay, and I could use some help getting there!'"

We could all use a little help getting there even when we are not sure where "there" is. Maybe the human world is learning that we must help one another. Certainly we gay people have learned that. Like everyone else, we may not be sure where we are going, but we are willing to help one another along the way. We are trying for the next step.

Being Professional

Our perception of professionals and our expectations of them have changed and are changing. We have a rapidly increasing variety of trained and respected helpers called by a variety of names such as professionals, paraprofessionals, assistants, interns, staff volunteers, etc. We have come to expect less magic from the professional and a respectable amount of dedication and responsibility from all official helpers. There are minimal guidelines that we expect any designated helper today to follow.

As understanding and communication have increased, it is reasonable to demand that officially designated helping persons be familiar with the values, customs, and ceremonies of the people they presume to help and that the meaning of these values, customs, and ceremonies is understood. If you intend to help someone who is a member of a sub-culture, you are of limited help, at best, if you do not understand the world in which that person lives.

A hospital may have a rule that friends are not permitted to visit a very sick person, or stay beyond limited visiting hours, a "family only" rule. If that is the case, everyone on the staff who may be expected to enforce the rule must know who is "family" for a gay person. We do not have licensed wives and husbands. It is insane to expect the sick person's spouse, often called "lover" by us, to wait in the hospital lobby while an unimportant cousin who happens to live in the geographical area is permitted to visit. Such behavior on the part of the staff is unprofessional and inexcusable today.

Though it is difficult for those mental health workers who cannot or do not admit their own homoerotic feelings into consciousness, nonetheless they must honor the homoerotic feelings of people they presume to help. It is a matter of professional responsibility.

A lesbian, who was supposedly receiving counseling from a woman social worker, dared to admit that she was sexually attracted to her counselor and sometimes had sexual fantasies about her. The social worker became flustered and then angry, shouting, "That's not what I'm here for. We'll have to assign you to a male case worker." That was wrong. She could have smiled, said "Thank you," and gone on with her work. Not only did she not help, the social worker did some harm.

There is no excuse for responsible helpers daring to dishonor homoerotic feelings in a situation in which they would honor heteroerotic feelings. I was told recently about a police cadet handling a squabble in a restaurant in an admirably professional manner. The cadet was with his girlfriend. He was not yet on duty, but in uniform. A restaurant worker was threatening to assault a patron who had winked at him. The cadet intervened quickly. In response to the worker's saying, "He said I'm cute and I'm gonna rearrange his face," the cadet said, "So he's wrong. You're not cute. And you're wrong. You're not going to hit him. You're not the first person who's been winked at in this restaurant and you won't be the last. That's allowed. Rearranging someone's face is not. Relax. It's all in a day's work. I get winked at too."

We are becoming much more aware of the subtle and not so subtle ways in which people have used and do use positions of presumed authority to intimidate and misuse other people. We are becoming particularly sensitive to sexual misconduct by official superiors in the workplace and in professional settings.

A presumed helper must be very careful in this area in work with gay people. As mentioned earlier in the book, sexuality has been made into a major issue for gay people. It is important for the lesbian and gay man to have self esteem enhanced and homoerotic orientation supported whenever possible. It is impor-

tant, therefore, that professionals and other professionally designated helpers continue to make appropriate appreciative remarks.

But it must be clear that the helping person is not inviting
seduction or sexual intercourse. This is most clear in psychotherapy. The psychotherapist must state clearly that she or he will be
responsible in upholding a contract that prohibits actual sexual
contact with the patient. This is important today because people
have become sensitized to the issue. The psychotherapist has the
professional responsibility to uphold the contract so that the patient is free to verbalize openly all erotic and sexual feelings, including those feelings that have to do with, or seem to have to do
with, the therapist. There must be no shame or inhibition and no
worry that the therapist will use the revelation of feelings in order
to initiate sexual contact not truly desired. Sometimes patients
and therapists become friends, some have sexual affairs, and some
marry. This happens after the therapy is absolutely finished, after
there has been a cooling off period of sufficient duration for the
therapist to shrink down to life size and be no more than herself
or himself. We are increasingly concerned that it must be clear
that neither person is taking unfair advantage of the other.

Yet appropriate support and appreciation must be there.
A gay man I met socially told me, "My therapist is a great guy.
And I think I'm sexually attracted to him. I was telling him one
day how ugly I feel when I walk into a party, and he told me he
thinks I'm really good looking. Do you think it would be wrong
if we had sex with one another?"

I hastened to tell him I am not a judge but suggested that
possibly his therapist had already made it clear that sex was not
part of the psychotherapy contract. People sometimes forget these
things said early in the process when they did not seem relevant.
I told him it might be a good idea to check that out with his
therapist since that is the usual clear arrangement nowadays. I
said also that I thought it would be wonderful if he could tell his
therapist about his sexual attraction and feelings for him as soon
as he felt that it was safe to do so and also that I hoped he could
enjoy his therapist's admiration of his attractiveness and feel safe.
Psychotherapy is an appropriate place to explore your attractions
and attractiveness and how they operate as part of your life.

I hope there will come a day when it is no longer necessary to caution people about the devious ways in which prejudice is apt to operate covertly in the guise of professional judgment. That day is not here yet. As awareness of the potential magnitude of the AIDS epidemic penetrated professional circles, there was increasing discussion of possible plans for quarantine and relocation centers, at the very same time that evidence was accumulating that the disease was not spread by casual contact. It was an excellent and sad example of unconscious prejudice at work, fueled by fear and ignorance as usual. The person who is prejudiced may be a trained professional. Prejudice must be identified as what it is and disarmed before it does more harm. Prejudice running rampant in professional groups can do enormous harm in a community.

Fear and Failure

Anyone who has chosen to work as a person who helps other people has had the experience of failing to help at some time because of fear. Fear makes failure more likely. More often than not, it is the person or people we are trying to help who help us to overcome our fears. We fear that which is unknown or unfamiliar. I recently spoke with a physician who is not gay who said, "It was difficult for me to have to admit that when AIDS patients began to be admitted to the hospital, I was afraid to deal with them or walk into their rooms, not because I was so afraid of the disease, but because I was afraid of them." She told me several stories of patients who were "so kind and understanding. They knew the trouble I was having before I knew. They were my teachers. They even helped me through my shame when I did realize what had been going on."

Sometimes professionals and other helpers need special help to rid them of ignorance and fear. In the early years of the epidemic there were police, firemen, paramedics, and others who failed to offer appropriate professional assistance when it was needed if they thought the person might be gay—because they were afraid that any gay person might have AIDS, and that any person with AIDS might transmit the disease to them in some mysterious manner. The information that would have eliminated their ignorance and fear was available, but before it got to them, lives were unnecessarily damaged and lost.

Professional helpers are people who have had special training, but they are only people. Fear can cause a person to put as much distance as possible between himself or herself and that which is feared. Mental health professionals, for instance, continue to invent new diagnostic categories that are not used in the best interest of their gay patients or clients. Too often the utility of the diagnostic category is that it comforts the practitioner because he or she does not feel described by it and it thereby puts gay identity at a seemingly safe distance. But once again the maneuver unfortunately prevents the mental health practitioner from getting closer to gay people and learning more so that ignorance and personal fear could be reduced.

We rely on professionals to use their education, compassion, judgment, and to take risks when they believe those risks are justified. We admire professionals who take personal risks that they believe are in the best interest of the persons they are trying to help. If they are good at their work, the risks they take are more often right than wrong, and the risk is more often to themselves than to the person they are helping.

We must have that trust in professionals to make judgments that involve risk. No set of rules can cover all circumstances. Most of these risky judgments go unknown because persons not there at the moment might come to incorrect conclusions and judgments. I think, for instance, of how important human touch is and how styles of what is permissible change from decade to decade.

It was not considered extraordinary during the time when interest was highest in the human potential movement for a professional helper to use various forms of touch and body contact, including full body massage, when doing psychotherapeutic work. Today it is much more likely that the practitioner will be cautious in touching, for fear that the touch will be misinterpreted as a major or minor form of molestation. Undoubtedly the style of permissiveness will shift again. The professional must ride these changing tides, trying to use good judgment as to what is permissible, how it will be interpreted or understood, and what is in the best interest of the person being helped. The usual guiding rule is to attempt to judge whether the procedure honestly is designed to help the person who is seeking help or the practitioner.

One out-of-the ordinary story I was told deserves repeating. The person who told me this story is no longer living. I was in a hospital doing a bedside psychotherapy session with him. He was very sick as a result of AIDS. He had been denying the gravity of his condition. He told me that in the middle of the preceding night, the awareness of impending death had come to him. He was in pain. He was terrified. He could not sleep. Pain-reducing medication and sleeping pills did not help. He felt chilled and continued to shiver. The gay male nurse on duty understood what was happening. He stayed with the patient, holding his hand, but the patient could not stop shivering. He cried, telling the nurse that he felt himself to be more alone and lonely than ever in his life. He knew he was near death and would never be held in another man's arms again.

The nurse took off his wristwatch and told him he had to go and make some arrangements with the other night nurse. He told him to watch the minute hand until it reached a particular spot, fifteen minutes away. Within fifteen minutes the nurse had returned, removed all of his own clothing and got into the bed with the patient holding him close and warm until the patient fell asleep. "It was the most wonderful thing anyone ever did for me in my whole life," the patient told me.

Unprofessional or professional? Judge that as you may. The nurse went beyond fear, took a personal risk, and did what no medication or conventional nursing care could do. He helped.

Different Problems

With the constant change experienced in any society, there is a shift of focus and priorities in viewing problems. Changes in the perceived strength and value of the biological family lead to a more intense focus on the problem of young runaways, battered wives, abused children, and mistreatment of the elderly. Increased crime and incarceration leading to overcrowded prisons bring the problem of homosexual molestation and rape into sharper focus. A much wider range of familiar types of drugs used brings into focus the problems of drug misuse and abuse, along with the awareness of the problems of drug dependence and co-dependency. A new disease epidemic, AIDS, brings increased concern about sexually transmitted diseases that could be decreased or stopped by education that is opposed by some church groups.

Along with shifting focus, there is an increase in the tempo of changing priorities in perceived social problems. People who work as helpers are being forced to bypass the simple and inadequate answers of the past that enabled them to pass the problems along to the next generation. Just saying "no" to a worldwide problem of misuse of drugs and the misuse of the drug problem itself by various special interest groups does nothing more than divert attention from the complexity of the social problems involved. Primly stating that all homosexuality is wrong and immoral does nothing to solve the complex societal problems for which the murder of innocent gay people, rape in overcrowded prisons, and juvenile prostitution are no more than symptoms.

Professionals and other helpers who are willing to face complex problems and do what small amount they can to solve them, together, do the real work toward curing the ills of the world. One start in that direction is the recognition that homoeroticism and heteroeroticism and the resulting sexual behaviors are different but equal. Once that is accepted, there is work that can be done to help house the homeless, manage sexuality in all institutions where people are warehoused, and work within religious institutions to alter the teachings that force desperate people to seek escape.

Silly, false modesty is a societal affectation we can no longer afford. Helpers must be able to do their work. A sign of the change is in the universities. More doctoral level research is being done now on the causes and cures of homophobia and prejudice. Most academics are no longer titillated by genteel research on people known to enjoy homosexuality. They are more interested in the role that sex plays in maintaining health or the ways in which sex is used as a competitive power ploy.

Educated and unprejudiced police people are less likely today to be concerned with one's gender preference in sexual partners than in learning whether a person has been sexually victimized. Enlightened police are seeing the value of outreach programs to recruit lesbians and gay men for police work, knowing that they may not like a particular lesbian or gay male co-worker just as they have disliked particular non-gay co-workers in the past.

Teachers can speak more freely with colleagues and with their students about the differences in lifestyles of public people who are more contemporary, ranging from Rock Hudson to Liberace and including people who are gay and still alive. Just as there is more awareness of the educational damage that can be done by licensed teachers who might call someone a "nigger lover," there is a growing awareness of just how dangerous teachers are who might call someone "a queer." Conformity training and education are incompatible.

Our focus on problems will continue to shift. And the shifting view of problems will continue to accelerate as worldwide communication continues to improve. While this dangerously increases the potential for hysteria and fear within a generation, it also greatly improves the chance to see the underlying problems that face us and to work toward eliminating them. There are problems facing humans living on this planet which we do not have any idea how to solve. We do not know how to contain the surprise damage of volcanoes, earthquakes, floods, and famine, though we are learning how better to help the victims of these natural disasters.

We can and must come to terms with the damage we do to one another. There are grave, basic social problems that we humans create. They spawn all manner of human misery. We can teach one another how to stop hurting one another.

At This Time

We have the misfortune or the good fortune to be living during that time in human history when there is a disease epidemic threatening the lives of an unprecedented number of people around the world. It is not possible in the late twentieth century to contain such a disease epidemic within the boundaries of a nation or a continent. It also happens to be a time when the entire world is threatened by the possibility of a nuclear holocaust of our own making. If the resources that we allocate for defense against possible aggression by one another in this paranoid world were to be used to fight this disease epidemic that is certain to kill an unprecedented number of people around the world, we would witness a contemporary miracle. The question we are living with is whether we humans have yet come to terms with a desire for power that permits us to rationalize as blameless the passive taking of another's life.

Whether we witness a miracle or a major tragedy, we are being forced to learn one of the most difficult and rewarding lessons to be found in various philosophies. We are being forced to live each day, one day at a time, and find our fears, faults, sorrows, joys, and peace within that day. Gay men, the first people to make news headlines by being infected by the AIDS disease, suffered scorn and prejudice as if they had invented the disease and set out to murder one another. Unique among the people who have suffered from this epidemic, we have had to learn to help the people who used our misfortune to further harm us. Because we found our ways to help one another during this awful crisis, we are able to help other people find their ways now in the crisis.

Recently I talked with three people who were living with life-threatening diseases. I asked what they feared most. It was not death. They most feared the careless violence that is now so evident in the world. I asked also what they were most proud of in their lifetimes. It was not civic honors or material success. It was that they had been able to fight against the moral wrong of social oppression in a non-violent manner.

Non-violent resistance to social wrongs is still fairly new in our world compared with the many centuries of human blood spilled in the name of a glorious ruler or a religious belief. It seems to be an idea whose time has come. An army with weapons can be defeated. A simple truth cannot be defeated. Brave people who speak it may be badly treated, sometimes killed. That does no more than assure that the same truth will be spoken by more people who clearly do no wrong because they refuse to retaliate with violence.

Gay men and lesbians have been punished unfairly for centuries. Today, we confront those people who would wrongly harm us. Our clear visibility in increasing numbers and our clearly stated non-violent truth will not vanish. A lesbian speaking at the memorial service of her friend said, "It is sad beyond saying that there are people who are happy to see gay men die because they are gay. The intellect and imagination of these people are so small that they believe this may be a plague that will remove all gay people. These people do not understand that they are our parents and will continue to produce generations of us as long as there are people. The world needs us more than anyone knows, but God knows."

These years of change in our lives test everyone's imagination. Yet the variety and force of the change helps us to transcend our usual limitations and see the difference between that which is basic and vital to human life and that which is no more than changing style.

I find that I deal with some different issues in psychotherapy now more than ten or twenty years ago. People are more concerned with exploring religious and spiritual beliefs as they influence the development of their lives. There is more reflection on emotions related to sickness, death, dying, and stress. There is more unembarrassed attention to which particular sexual practices are the most caring, satisfying, and safe, as well as to the value of bodily expressions of affection and the value of eroticism in life. Beneath these changes that are appropriate to the time, I see people searching still to understand their lives in a broader perspective, finding ways to satisfy basic human needs for affection and mutual support while living life well.

I find myself changing in my work, too. My weekly on-going psychotherapy groups are smaller and more intimate. I rarely work in the weekend growth group format now, except when the people have some way of continuing their learning together so that they can depend upon one another for continued help as a small community. I see more than ever how much we need the continuing comfort we can offer one another in an intimate community.

I am more interested than ever in that which happens and cannot be explained. I had no difficulty in understanding a man recently when he told me about having experienced a "revisit" twice from his lover who died months ago. He wrote about the experiences in careful detail and shared his notes with me. Both times his lover reassured him of their lasting love and the man was enormously comforted.

I was with a friend not long ago who was half-jokingly talking about an article he had read about phone calls from the dead. Two days later we were together again when a telephone instrument that was not in any way connected to its wire rang twice.

There was a time when I would have had to follow seeming scientific dictum and explain such events one way or another. I am content now to absorb information and not know the why until and unless I do learn a clear explanation. Perhaps this change helps to explain my renewed interest in writing fiction, since it is an acceptable way of sharing a range of truth that is less acceptable to educated people when presented as non-fiction.

I continue to feel blessed by my identity as a gay person. It has brought wonderful people and an amazingly expanded horizon into my life. When I wrote the first edition of *Loving Someone Gay* I said that I was grateful for having rediscovered my gay identity. I said that it was like coming home except that there never had been any home before. Today I can say also that my reclaimed gay identity has made it possible for me to find my family in that home that never was before, and to have caught a glimpse of our own place in the majesty of this changing, expanding universe. That glimpse has humbled me while giving me strength and willingness.

PART TWO
Loving Someone Gay

1
Being Gay

At a costume party last Halloween I met a man dressed as the invisible large rabbit named Harvey. It inevitably led to jokes about his being a bunny of the Playboy variety, and that led to jokes about Gay people. Then I told a joke about straight (non-Gay) people and "Harvey" looked at me with a troubled expression from under his large floppy ears. "Why did they have to take a perfectly good word like gay and ruin it so that my mother now has to be careful when using it?" he asked. I told him that I would just as soon we were called jolly or delightful but that the roots of the word usage had to do with people who deviated from the straight and narrow, first theatrical people and then prostitutes who led "the Gay life." He still thought it sad for mother to have to be so careful and I told him that I, as one Gay person and as one professional helper of people, hoped that we could work toward the day soon when his mother could ask anyone if he or she were Gay—at once inquiring as to mood and orientation—without insulting any one. By then we will understand that being different does not necessarily mean being bad.

Five years ago, a man joined an ongoing weekly Gay group that I was leading in San Francisco. He said that he felt desperate. He looked around the small living room at the group, all of us Gay, and said, "I feel as if I've been running away all my life. Meeting Gay people like you here in San Francisco gives me a little hope that I can stop running. I've only been here a few weeks but I hope I can stay. I can't find a job and I'm so lonely it hurts, but I want to stay. None of my friends know I'm Gay and I'm afraid of what would happen if my family found out, but they're back East."

We could feel his fright and his fatigue. We tried some words of comfort and then gathered around him and held him. We touched him without words, trying to tell him that we knew those feelings and that, while we could not make promises, we wanted to help. He cried and cried. We knew that those tears were for the broken dreams of the past, the endless hurts, and the risk of beginning to hope once more.

I cannot bring myself to assign him a fictitious name; he was a beautiful and real person and his name fit him perfectly. He came to two group meetings and then the everyday pressures of money began to mount. He had no income except for a part-time menial job. He wanted to be an actor but theater work was hard to find, though we suspected he had the talent. Actor friends urged him to go to New York and try to find work there. His family wrote and begged him to return home. The group wanted to keep him in San Francisco until he could build more strength as a Gay person. But he was only human. The job and money pressures of the moment added to the pains of the past and he lost strength. He went home and, in a last try to get his footing, he told his family he was Gay. They committed him to a mental hospital and a month later he was dead. He killed himself, alone.

This sad, true story is too common. It need not happen. Gay people can support one another, survive, and grow stronger. People who love someone Gay can help.

The word Gay is not defined in the same way by everyone. For me, being Gay is an asset, not a liability. It means there are additional options open to me, things I can do. Being Gay does not mean that I am unable to have satisfying heterosexual relationships but that I am able to have satisfying homosexual relationships. All of the evidence that we have about human sexuality suggests that the human infant is flexible and inclined to seek experiences that produce pleasant sensations. It is in the growing-up years we learn about the cultural code that limits recognition

74

of some feelings and forbids the expression of those feelings in behavior. The very young human is not sexually judgmental and has yet to go through the personal learning that will shape his or her sexual preferences.

So, in a sense, we are all born Gay, capable of moving toward pleasant homosexual sensations, unconcerned about the gender of the person who is the agent of our gratification. It is a gift given to each human at birth, but because it is discouraged in our part of the world, only some of us keep the gift.

I am Gay and that means that I know that I am able to involve myself emotionally, sensuously, erotically and intellectually with someone of the same gender. He and I can interrelate in a whole and satisfying way without having to create dishonesty and diversion from fear of possible sexuality. Being Gay means that I know I am capable of this range of relating to another male and that I am willing to act on the capability and translate this potential into behavior.

I was speaking to a gathering of mental health professionals a few months ago and had just issued a similar personal definition when a woman who had been listening intently, offering encouraging smiles and making copious notes in her program raised her hand, stood, and spoke in a cultured Viennese accent. "I agree with all which you say," she began. Then turning to the audience she consulted her notes and said, "I also must agree that we should examine our working assumptions, and that even our teachers and genius master teachers could have been fooled by their times of living and made some mistakes which we follow. This nice man up there," she continued pointing to me with shaking hand as her voice gained emotion, "is to us saying that he could even sexually love another man. Why should we not let him? Why should we think less good of him or that he is not such a good psychologist if he one day gives in to these impulses? Maybe nobody gets hurt. Maybe it is we who hurt ourselves!"

I told her that I truly appreciated her words and her sentiments, but I had to point out that she (and probably many others present) had misunderstood part of my statement. Being Gay means not only that I am aware of my sexual and affectional feelings for other men, but also that I am quite able and willing to translate these feelings into behavior, given the right time, place

75

and person, and that I need no one's permission to do so. It is my choice—to be made in freedom.

At this point a younger male colleague leapt to his feet. "I don't believe you," he said, glaring at me. "The Gay people I know are totally preoccupied with the pursuit of sex and incapable of controlling themselves, just as anyone would be if they gave in to sexual feelings the way you say you do. Besides I know some people who know you and I hear you lead a pretty straight life. You're not out cruising the bars and parks!"

All in all, it was an interesting meeting. Once again I was surprised, if not astonished, at how easily my words were misunderstood in at least two different ways once I presented my Gay identity. Everyone hears through his or her own screen of prejudice. I had to admit to the young man that I lead a fairly quiet, ordinary life and that "cruising the bars and parks" would not be for me—at least not at this point in my life.

Much of the hearing problem has to do with all of us having been born and raised in an environment that has turned natural human sexuality into a paranoid, fear-laden phenomenon. We are taught to be secretive about our own sexual feelings, yet hyper-sensitive to any innuendo that might have sexual implications, and to distrust anyone's sexual interest in us as well as our own sexual interests in another person unless those interests are sanctioned by religion and licensed by state. We grow up learning about sex in phrases like, "took advantage of. . .," "cheating on. . .," and "gave in to" accompanied by paranoid watchful eye movements, hushed tones, and salacious laughter. Magazine racks overflow with sexually provocative pictures designed to sell books and periodicals, and sell they do (though few show up on the coffee table in anyone's home).

There is constant pressure to attend to sexual words, pictures and actions. There is also constant pressure to disown sexual feelings. It is nearly impossible truthfully to integrate one's personal sexuality with any sort of developing self-esteem. One lives with constant secret shame, most of which mercifully sinks from awareness.

In this background, the phenomenon of *homophobia** has developed. Woman/woman and man/man sexual feelings are for-

---

*This word was first used by George Weinberg in his book *Society and the*

bidden and we learn that such feelings "should be" experienced as loathsome and disgusting. It is a hotly defended pillar of sexist dogma and the foundation of homophobia. Without it the sexist programming begins to crumble. Women might begin to view other women as desirable, and therefore not inferior or justifiably kept in their place. Men might see other men as desirable, and therefore not enemies to be tested and conquered.

But the seemingly shameful homoerotic feelings that sank from awareness are always ready to resurface. The discomfort that would be associated with their re-emergence into awareness acts as an efficient guardian of sexist training. The secret shame of these hidden feelings is the dragon at the gateway of full self-awareness. Beyond the dragon-guarded gateway are the treasures of simple human feeling that give life a sense of zest and worth. Fortunately, each of us has created his or her own dragon, and can therefore learn to tame it. Unfortunately, most of us settle for the seemingly easier life of conformity to sexist homophobic dogma. Were it not for the sexism and homophobia, each of us could be an individual who grew into a satisfying self in all ways, including sexual gender preference. That day may yet come.

Being gay, as I stated earlier, can be a great joy. Prejudice, misunderstanding and fear, however, create a burden that too often smothers the joy and replaces it with great pain. Like other "social inferiors" who are punished for their identity, some of us Gays are destroyed by the thoughtless cruelty of neighbors, friends and family. Some are damaged but manage to survive. And some grow strong, building emotional muscle in the struggle to survive.

This book is an offering of love for Gay people and the people who love them. It comes from my two decades of experience as a clinical psychologist who, for the past seven years, has specialized in working with Gay people. It also comes from my own personal experience, being Gay on my own terms.

At that professional meeting described earlier, a distinguished-looking man who spoke with the assurance of one accustomed to hearing his own voice in public said, "I must tell you,

---

Healthy Homosexual, St. Martin's, 1972 (later published in paperback by Anchor/Doubleday).

Dr. Clark, that your remarks are interesting but suspect. Since you are an admitted homosexual, we must discount your views on the basis of subjective bias. We need objective observers in this area as in all other areas of the social sciences. But your views are interesting."

I had to tell my distinguished colleague that I was unwilling to be so summarily discounted and that his attempt to do so filled me with anger and with distrust of the evidence accumulated about real human beings by investigators who claimed objectivity. I am not an objective observer. There are no objective observers in this area. Distaste or disinclination for the Gay experience easily mask prejudice. At best, the scientific observer without Gay experience is certain to miss subtleties apparent to the "native." I am an interested, experienced observer who, like my non-Gay colleagues, has been trained in the discipline of social science, the art or craft of the clinician, and who works toward objectivity while studying human phenomena. Unlike my non-Gay colleagues, however, the terrain, language and customs are familiar and comfortable for me.

Hopefully this book will remove some of the mystery that surrounds Gay people. Comedians tell jokes about us and fail to see us sitting in their audience. Family members create hurtful slurs about us and fail to see us in their own family. Mystery and misinformation about the unknown breed fear. Fear feeds prejudice and cruelty. This book presents ideas and suggestions for changing attitudes and behavior so as to aid Gay people and the people who love us. My hope is to help remove unnecessary oppression and reconstruct the simple pleasure of Gay identity.

Just as it is difficult for a non-Gay person to explore and understand the subtleties of Gay experience, I know that there are subtleties in the experience of being a Gay woman that I cannot fully understand. For this reason most of my work has been with Gay men, and I apologize for any inadequate representation of the Gay woman's experience. It will be for Gay women to say how well the ideas presented in this book fit their own experience.

Growing Up Gay

There are as many different kinds of Gay people as there are different kinds of people. The one thing we have in common is an awareness that we are attracted in all ways, including sexually, to some people of the same gender. What we do with this awareness varies, as the following anecdotes will show. But in any anti-Gay society such as ours, a lonely emotional struggle is predictable.

Let us take a true example. The man, whom I know, was born on a farm in the Midwest in the early forties. His family and friends knew him to be a youngster with a gift for school work and a good sense of humor. His strong hands and back were appreciated on the farm during his growing-up years. His father was the strong, silent type and his mother the cheerful healer of wounds. His older sister was an independent person who had little to do with him. He had a male cousin the same age. When the two families got together, the two boys always shared a bed. They were good friends and playmates; they also enjoyed one another's bodies. Somehow they knew it was to be kept secret. As he grew into adolescence, he was sexually interested in both women and men, but found men more exciting. It worried him, so he talked to a trusted high-school teacher about it. The teacher told him it was something he could overcome with clean thoughts and self-discipline. In the army he was afraid to let anyone know his feelings, though he always hoped that someone would guess and make the first move toward him. After the army he went to college near home. He signed up for a psychology course and read whatever he could find in the library about homosexuality. He learned that he had a psychological maladjustment and so he sought counseling as the books recommended. He remained celibate for fear of compounding his problem, lest he discover that homosexuality was as attractive in fact as in fantasy. In two years of counseling his turmoil increased as he tried harder to overcome his attraction to men but found that it was still there.

Or let us look at another man I know who grew up in a socially prominent family in a small eastern city. It was a large, devoutly Catholic family heavily interested in sports and politics. From the time he was four years old he knew he found his father, his older brothers, and some other men bodily attractive. But from the beginning he fought to push away these feelings because he suspected they were sinful. Certainly no one else in the family talked of such feelings. In his early teen years, he went on camping trips with his friends. They would complain about the unavailability of girls and invariably work their way into a mutual masturbation session. He enjoyed the sexual contact enormously but no one else was openly enthusiastic and he felt guilty. He worked up his courage to confess one day, and the priest told him that it was sinful and he needed help. His priest instructed him to talk it over with his family, and when he said he did not think he could do that, the priest told him to come back later in the afternoon for counseling. He feared that if the priest saw his face he would tell the family, so he never went back for counseling and never again confessed homosexual thoughts, feelings or behavior. Today he is a compulsive seeker of anonymous sex in men's rooms and parks. He questions his religious training but still fears that he may be doomed to Hell, since he sees little likelihood of repentance.

And there is the woman I know who grew up in a popular middle-class family in a large town in the Pacific Northwest. Her father was a middle management executive and her mother was active in the community. Her childhood affectional feeling for girl friends moved easily into erotic feelings. When she spent the night with friends at her home or theirs, they usually slept in the same bed. Some friends were more responsive than others. When she was thirteen, a new friend accused her, half jokingly and half seriously, of being a Lesbian, and added some lurid details about this variety of "freak." She was upset by the accusation and told her mother about it later the same day. Her mother blushed, seemed angry, and told her not to talk about such things, adding that if she had any of those feelings she would be better off keeping them to herself and not sleeping in the same bed with her friends. Her mother even implied that it would be better, if necessary, to start becoming sexually involved with some boys, but made it clear that this was the end of the discussion. The daughter was shocked and hurt. She never again spoke of her feelings with her parents until, at age twenty-four, she told them that she was Gay and settled happily in a monogamous relationship with another woman. The parents disowned her and she has not seen them since.

And there is the man I know who grew up in a Chicago slum. Both parents worked and both drank. He saw little of them in his childhood. He and his three brothers and two sisters took care of one another. He remembers that he was afraid to act friendly toward another boy on the street for fear of being called a fag, queer, or homo. He knew he felt attracted to other boys and men but felt ashamed of his feelings. He never acted on those feelings until he was thirty years old, had been married ten years and had three children. At that time he gladly allowed another man to pick him up at the gym where he worked out. The sexual experience felt right—and long overdue—but he feared that his wife or the men at the auto plant where he worked might find out so he told the other man harshly he did not want to see him again. Now he feels guilty about that because he liked the man and he feels indebted to him for a much desired tender experience. He is hoping that it will happen again, yet is afraid to let it happen.

The Gay person, like everyone else, begins his or her life being open and interested in the body, mind and emotions of all other nearby people, regardless of gender. The culture encourages us all to tune out awareness of sensual and erotic interest in people of the same gender. We do not know why some of us refuse or are unable to follow the cultural instruction. Social scientists who assume that such interests are abnormal and therefore wrong, have looked for causative factors. The search for causes makes as little sense as looking for the reasons why some people do follow the cultural dictum and actually tune out their same-gender feelings.

Last summer I attended a large and colorful wedding held in a beautiful house in an inspiring sunny California mountain setting. The ceremony had been written and staged by the woman and man who were joining their lives. The guests had brought a wonderful variety of food and the wedding punch was assisting the pervasive mellow mood.

A woman in her forties, dressed in a gossamer gown that reached to her bare feet approached me with a smile and handed me one of several flowers she held. "You don't know me but I asked Joan to point you out. I know that you're Gay and work with Gay people and. . . I hope you won't be offended but I want to ask you a question." I said that I loved the flower, her gown, her smile, and that I also hoped I would not be offended.

"Well, what I want to know is what makes people grow up that way?" She paused, her smile still radiant. "I have three children I love and if they turn out Gay it's OK, but if I can do anything to help save them from it, I'd like to know so I could be doing it now." She sniffed at her flower, smiled again and said, "Is there anything I could read: I'm sure you don't want to give a lecture in the middle of a party."

I had to tell her that she seemed like a nice person and a good parent and that I was, as feared, offended. I agreed that it was a poor setting for a lecture but I did need to say she could be most helpful to potentially Gay offspring by trying to change a toxic society and raise her own consciousness, and that what offended me was the assumption that children might be "saved" from being Gay like me, since I am glad I am Gay, as I hope that she is glad to be the person she is.

The reasons why some people grow up Gay and some non-gay are varied and numerous. Nor are they of much interest unless one presumes it desirable to alter one condition or the other. As long as we assume that in the future, as in all centuries past, some people will continue to retain some amount of their sensuous and erotic interest in people of the same gender, we know that we will always have citizens of all ages, ethnic background and socio-economic status who are Gay. Some of these people would be happy to disclaim the label Gay or any other label, but it will be used throughout this book to designate those of us who have refused our culture's instruction to rid ourselves of sexual interest in people of the same gender. We need our separate identity until we are perceived as full equals who can integrate with heterosexuals in a pluralistic society.

Most Gay people are aware of their forbidden interest early in life—some as far back as they can remember, some with awareness beginning at age eight, nine, or ten. I can remember, for instance, being in Florida at age four and watching an attractive male neighbor go into his outdoor shower stall wearing a bathing suit and carrying a bar of soap. I could see his head, arms, chest and legs as he turned on the shower and started to sing while he lathered himself. I thought he was quite handsome and jolly, was enchanted by the happy scene, and felt a sweet strange feeling in the pit of my stomach. When his bathing suit was thrown over the top of the wooden shower stall door and he continued his singing and lathering, I had a terrific urge to join him and help with the soaping. The sexuality of the feeling is perfectly clear even as I remember it today. And the scene reminds me of some of today's TV commercials designed to sell soap, shampoo, and underarm deodorants to men. (I presume either advertisers believe women do all of the shopping for men's cosmetics or they understand that men do have some sexual attraction for other men.)

We do not know how or why the awareness of sexual attraction to some people of the same gender comes into focus or why it is not abandoned. Perhaps it is the ostentatious silence or absence of outspoken support for such feelings that sharpens the self-aware focus. One becomes emotionally aware that boy-girl interests are a matter of constant comment while boy-boy or girl-girl interests are played down, considered appropriate in young children only, laughed about, or condemned.

Just today I noticed that phenomenon in action. Both my son and daughter had friends visiting for an overnight, since school let out for the summer last week and everyone misses everyone already. A visiting boy's mother dropped by to bring some forgotten necessity and the boy said to his mother, "I like Andy's bathing suit—it's really sexy." His mother knew that "sexy" was more a general statement of appreciation than an indication of sexual interest and said with feigned fatigue, "I suppose you want one just like it." There was a nod of happy agreement, an inconsequential discussion of how he had not yet outgrown the one he was wearing and then a moment of silence. Something seemed to be tugging at the mother's awareness. Then she brightened and said to her nine-year-old son, in a tone hearty with presumed joking, "Listen, if you want to start looking at something sexy in a bathing suit, you'd better start paying attention to Vicki or Sarah!" It was a joke and not a joke. The mother seemed somewhat relieved but I felt bothered by the homophobic tension in the room.

For some of us there is an awakening in adolescence, perhaps set off by a sexual experience. Looking back, people often report that they can see the interest was there earlier but dormant

83

because of a reluctance to face up to it or because they simply never thought about such things. Adolescent memories of camping trips during which two boy friends had to double up in one sleeping bag because the other bag got dropped while crossing a creek, or two girls who rolled into one another's arms during a slumber party while each pretended to be dreaming of the world's current male singing idol, are numerous. Not infrequently, there is a tale of an attractive cousin, neighbor, young aunt or uncle who is pursued by the youngster until the moment of passion is achieved. The youngster sometimes later disowns responsibility on the basis of being a few years younger, but honest remembering more often brings back memories of the longing for intimate body contact that had a sexual component.

For a smaller number of Gays, the awakening comes in the twenties, or even the thirties or forties. Again, looking back, they usually admit the interest was there earlier but that they either guarded against their own awareness of it or feared acting on it because of the assumed dire consequences.

Whatever the age of awareness (and for most it is quite young) there follows a long period of quiet, internal, emotional struggle. It is a lonely secret. Consciously or not, you become an alert gatherer of information. You listen for news of others who have the same feelings, and most of the available news is bad. Rarely is there a truly respected friend of the family or truly loved relative who is openly Gay. There are few, if any, apparent respectable models. You feel caught, pulled in the direction of your impulses and feelings, yet held by the repugnance of becoming an outcast.

You try cautiously talking to a friend but there is rarely support, because all too often the friend is secretly doing battle with some of the same feelings. If you are brave, you may try talking to a relative, parent, school counselor, teacher, priest, minister or family doctor. You risk at least a negative reaction or the visible retraction of respect and good will toward you. You also risk outright censure and persecution. You are usually cautioned to mend your ways, repent, get well, confess, pray for forgiveness, or at least keep silent.

Gay youngsters grow up in a lonely, unfriendly world. Older Gay people are reluctant to become involved even when invited because of the very possible harsh legal consequences. A Gay adult can spend a lifetime behind bars for trying to give aid and comfort to a Gay child.

It is during these years that Gay youngsters often build an invisible wall between themselves and their parents. It is built as a protection. They have listened carefully and seen no sign that their parents are likely to be supportive if their Gay identity is discovered. The more open and sharing they are with parents, the more likely is the discovery. Hence, the transparent wall is erected and parents wonder why their offspring has suddenly become so uncommunicative.

Some youngsters immerse themselves in religion, devote themselves to being good twenty-four hours a day, and/or have inexplicable emotional breakdowns which are the result of having carried too large an invisible emotional strain. Some become equally inexplicable suicides. Families and friends mourn sincerely without having any idea that they have contributed to the youngster's misery. The usual refrain is "————— had everything to live for, why this?" They speculate that someone slipped a mysterious psychodelic drug into the unsuspecting youngster's food or drink. It does not occur to anyone that the noxious agent was the socially approved, seemingly natural, conspiracy of disapproval.

Invisibility, Oppression, and Damaged Self-concept

During the past ten years most of us have been made increasingly aware of the subtle ways in which Blacks, women, and other unfavored groups of people are oppressed. Yet it was not apparent to us earlier, though the oppression was then more rampant. Few people noticed the absence of Blacks in TV commercials or top executive positions. Few people noticed how guilt was used as a potent weapon to keep the "little woman" in her place in the home, or that those women who escaped and dared a career in the man's world were paid a smaller salary than that paid for the same work done by a man.

Today there are still few people who are aware that there are Gay people in prison and in mental hospitals because they are guilty of crimes such as kissing on the street or are suffering from such emotional disabilities as a desire to be open and public about their full identity, including Gay thoughts and feelings.

Family and professionals usually warn against public pronouncements of such non-conforming feelings and certainly forbid public display of Gay feelings, such as two men walking down the street holding hands or two women kissing with true tenderness. Such unusual expressions of simple affection are "not done." They are considered offensive to public decency. Family and professionals reason that if the Gay person persists in breaking such written and unwritten rules for human conduct, it is surely a signal or a symptom indicating that the person is "asking for help." Such "help" is more likely to help the embarrassed family since it means removing the Gay person from the community and placing her or him in an institution such as a mental hospital. The non-Gay community is thus reassured that such feelings and behavior are indeed "wrong."

If we had the perspective to view this social phenomenon as science fiction it would seem incredible. I ask non-Gay readers to consider your own feelings for a moment without attaching emotionally loaded labels. if you are a woman, imagine that you are dining in public with a woman friend. In the course of conversation, your friend touches on the recent death of her child, and sobs silently for a few moments. You speak the few words of compassion that you can find and your friend tells you how very important it is to her to be able to share with you this way. If she were a man, your natural impulse might be to ignore other people present and to move closer, perhaps taking his hand or kissing him. But, because you are both women, you are likely to feel restrained and unable to express yourself as fully. You know other eyes in the restaurant watch, and years of training cause you dimly to fear their disapproval. It is because you are two women. Your gender has cheated you. It is pure sexism. You are the victim of your own gender training instead of being simply two human beings in a moment of closeness.

I would ask the non-Gay man reading this book to fantasy himself in another scene. Imagine that you and a trusted male friend go off on a day's fishing trip. He is unusually pensive and finally blurts out that he has had a physical checkup and was told that he may have a terminal disease. He has not shared this information with anyone because he does not want to cause worry. He grips your arm and closes his eyes to contain the tears that begin to escape. You are alone. There is not even the fear of eyes that may disapprove. If your friend were a woman you might gather her into your arms and hold her tight, trying to share her burden and fear. But your friend is a man, like you. It has taken a lot for him to touch your arm and cry in your presence. For the two of you to embrace, press bodies together for comfort, and feel mutual tears on the soft skin of your faces is nearly unthinkable. What stops your natural human impulse to share and comfort with body contact at such a moment is the sexist gender training reminding you that you are two men together alone. You can talk but not touch. Again, it is pure sexism.

Neither of these examples includes any sexual thoughts or behavior. They involve simple deep human feelings which our sexist training discourages, thereby leaving us all impoverished. For the Gay person, feelings of affection for a person of the same gender come easily and need not be stirred by such dramatic events; but are they any less respectable because we find them with less provocation?

Near the end of 1973 the American Psychiatric Association removed homosexuality (and Gay identity) from its diagnostic list of emotional disorders. The organization declared itself ready to view homosexual interests as "different from" but not better or worse than heterosexual interests. It was an admission that the belief held throughout this century that people should be considered emotionally disordered and in need of treatment and/or be institutionalized because of Gay identity was a mistake. The organization deserves respect and credit for admitting its mistake, though the enormity of human suffering brought about by that mistake is breathtaking.

And then a truly unbelievable thing happened. Some of the physicians who are respected and politically powerful members of the profession caused the issue to be reconsidered by the entire membership of the American Psychiatric Association. Each member was asked to vote on whether he or she believed it was natural and normal to be Gay or whether it was a mental disorder. The membership voted, using professional experience and personal prejudice. Consider how unusual that event was! It was a close vote, but we Gay people are now removed from the "sick list" unless we give the same cause as non-Gay people to have a psychiatrist believe we are eligible for a diagnosis.

Meanwhile some of us psychologists had formed an organization more than a year earlier and called ourselves the Association of Gay Psychologists. One of our primary objectives was to force the American Psychological Association to see us as responsible, if oppressed, members of the profession and to support us in our struggle for the full civil rights due any citizen.

In January of 1975 the American Psychological Association issued the following statement:

The governing body of the American Psychological Association (APA) today voted to oppose discrimination against homosexuals and to support the recent action by the American Psychiatric Association which removed homosexuality from that Association's official list of mental disorders.

The text of the policy statement, which was submitted to the Council of Representatives by APA's Board of Social and Ethical Responsibility for Psychology and recommended by the Board of Directors, follows:

1. The American Psychological Association supports the action taken on 15 December 1973 by the American Psychiatric Association removing homosexuality from the Association's official list of mental disorders. The American Psychological Association therefore adopts the following resolution:

Homosexuality per se implies no impairment in judgment, stability, reliability, or general social or vocational capabilities;

Further, the American Psychological Association urges all mental health professionals to take the lead in removing the stigma of mental illness that has long been associated with homosexual orientation.

2. Regarding discrimination against homosexuals, the American Psychological Association adopts the following resolution concerning their civil and legal rights:

The American Psychological Association deplores all public and private discrimination in such areas as employment, housing, public accommodations, and licensing against those who engage in or have engaged in homosexual activities and declares that no burden of proof of such judgment, capacity, or reliability shall be placed upon those individuals greater than that imposed on any other person; Further,

88

the American Psychological Association supports and urges the enactment of civil rights legislation at the local, state and federal level that would offer citizens who engage in acts of homosexuality the same protections now guaranteed to others on the basis of race, creed, color, etc.; Further, the American Psychological Association supports and urges the repeal of all discriminatory legislation singling out homosexual acts by consenting adults in private.

The council also amended the Association's 'Statement of Policy Regarding Equal Employment Opportunity' to include sexual orientation among the prohibited discriminations listed. APA's employment practices in its various professional placement programs and advertisements in all Association publications will comply with this policy.

Now that the American Psychiatric Association and the American Psychological Association have officially stated that we are as emotionally respectable as anyone else, one might expect the oppression to die away. But it has been ingrained in our society and will not vanish so easily.

People still do not notice the absence of openly Gay people in TV commercials or in top executive positions. The telephone company, after being repeatedly picketed and hauled into court will now hire openly Gay people to work as operators in some states but they are still not ready to hire openly Gay people for top management positions. There is an assumption that Gay people—like Blacks, women and Chicanos—are to be kept in their place. (After all, who would expect a worker to follow orders from such an inferior person?)

And as to TV commercials, I had an interesting personal experience. In June 1974, in connection with a massive effort of Gay organizations to attract the positive attention of the news media during Gay Pride Week, I spoke at a televised news conference. One of my points that caught the interest of the interviewer from the San Francisco educational television station was the absence of openly Gay people in TV commercials. I pointed out that Gay viewers also have need of laundry soap and pet foods. I asked why two women or two men portrayed as living together and discussing their concern for the poor appetite of a beloved pet could not as charmingly sell the pet food.

The interviewer was so captivated by the idea that he interviewed advertising executives, who mostly thought the idea had merit though it was "unusual." He then did street interviews of men and women who nearly unanimously had positive reactions. My favorite was a preoccupied older woman who seemed disgruntled at being stopped on the street and unbalanced the interviewer by snapping that "Of course, they should give Gay people a chance the same as anyone else"—her irritability to me seeming to imply the foolishness that such a question need be asked in this day of supposed respect for individual differences.

There are other institutions in our society that still continue active efforts to oppress us. Most churches are willing to receive our financial and participatory support as congregants but insist that we are sinners who are ineligible for leadership as priests, clergymen, or policy makers. Most states have legislators who drag their feet, fearful of what their constituents will say and therefore uneasy about changing the laws that make us criminal. And educational institutions, a hundred years behind the social times as usual, in their eagerness to parade tired old customs in "innovative" costume, continue to deny the presence of Gay children. Some colleges are "permitting" Gay Unions to meet on campus but there is little, if any, official support and sanction. And administrators of elementary and high schools pale at the mention of "Gay students."

The armed services, which would probably cease to function if every homosexually inclined career military person were to go on strike, still officially harass, punish, and excommunicate any openly Gay person. The same can be said for the YMCA, YWCA, YWHA, YMHA, etc.

Like Blacks, we Gays must become more visible in our variety before the average citizen begins to notice how invisible we have been. Only then can people of good will begin to consider the nearly silent acts of guilt induction that have been used to keep us in our place occupationally, socially, and emotionally.

People become desensitized to the violation of civil rights for a non-favored group if the violations happen so regularly that they seem normal and therefore morally right. That is why it took so much trouble for Black and women activists to have people notice such wrongs. Gay people are regularly stripped of civil and human rights and it happens so regularly that most people do not notice it. It is difficult for two men to rent a one-bedroom apartment together if they are too old to pass for college room-mates. It is difficult for a Gay couple to will property to one another without risking having the will contested. It is impossible for a Gay couple to marry and enjoy the same tax benefits as married non-Gays. It is extremely difficult for a divorced or legally separated Gay person to retain custody of children if the ex-spouse charges moral unfitness. It is impossible for a Gay person to be sure of keeping a security clearance or any employment dependent upon such a clearance. In most cities and towns a Gay person who dares patronize a Gay meeting place risks being arrested at the whim of the police.

But though they are not noticed by the average citizen, these scandalous facts of life are merely the open forms of oppression. They are the visible club held over the heads of Gay people, urging them to stay in hiding, threatening punishment for those who get out of line. This is only the tip of the iceberg. Most oppression is more subtle.

Some of it is the same variety used against other non-favored groups. There are the put-down jokes, the social ostracism, fewer raises, fewer jobs, less advancement, and outright verbal abuse heaped on the heads of openly Gay people. Marauding gangs of thugs still attack visible Gays, and most policemen look the other way or at least fail to pursue the attackers.

A friend of mine stopped off at a late night eating establishment with his lover to buy a pack of cigarettes and was accosted by five neighborhood youths who probably were bored or looking for an opportunity to prove their manhood. He was asked for and gave cigarettes to them. A few minutes later, on the street, he was hit in the back by a beer bottle and one of the five then knocked him down and kicked him in the face. He spent weeks in the hospital, and more weeks with his jaws wired together facing a possible operation to remove bone from his hip to place in his jaw.

The manager of the restaurant saw it happen and did not call the police. A bus driver saw it happen and drove away. Then my friend saw his assailant in the neighborhood and called the police to demand legal action. The police questioned his assailant, who repeatedly used the term *lousy faggots*. They did not arrest him, but in the process of questioning gave information that would make it easier for him to locate my friend's residence.

Lawyers advised against building a case because of unreliable witnesses, expense, and the likelihood that the defense would suggest that two "fags" had made some sort of sexual advance, thereby justifying in the eyes of the jury the understandable, if perhaps "excessive," reaction on the part of five respectable, red-blooded American youths. We are one of the last minority groups to pay taxes while not enjoying the protection of life and property. These things happen to visible members of our group every day.

Most of us are, or have been for many years, invisible. This is an important fact to remember. It is during these years that the real damage is done. Scalp wounds heal. Irrational hatred and abuse can be understood when it comes from socially damaged people who are trying to vent blind anger. But when the wounds are inflicted by family, friends, trusted counselors, and civic leaders, the wounds go deep and damage self-esteem. A scarred and seriously damaged self-concept is the result. Almost every Gay person has been invisible for some years and some Gay people remain invisible all their lives. Contrary to popular mythology, most of us do not fit the stereotypic "pansy" or "dyke" image.

We know we have loving feelings for some people who share our gender and that we sometimes want to express those feelings sensuously and erotically. We see men and women set up as heterosexual models for expressing those feelings to one another. We see it in the family, on the street, in magazines, movies, and on TV. Thus do we shape our idea of what is right, normal, natural, and good. Never do we see loving expressed by two men or two women. Our inner truth is not validated visibly; we have no models. It is as if other people like us do not exist. We hear stories and see fictional portraits of deranged, depraved, and defective people who grotesquely act out our feelings, and we wonder if that is who we are. There seems to be an obvious choice to be made between honesty and respect.

Consider some of the sex education films shown to youngsters in supposedly enlightened communities. The homosexual is portrayed as an ugly man in rumpled, too-large overcoat who lurks under the pier hoping to attack delicious young boys who dare take a shortcut home from school, or the "emotionally disturbed" older woman who sneaks about darkened movie theatres buying popcorn for young girls who will think she is friendly and maternal until she touches them with perverted desire. I have reviewed these films in print and do not exaggerate their portrayal of the "homosexual." There is no way to identify with the person so presented on the screen and still maintain self-respect.

Because we are not visible, we hear the pointed derogatory jokes and stories about people who share our feelings, and these hurtful messages issue from the mouths of fathers, mothers, aunts, uncles, brothers, sisters, teachers, counselors, and friends. Few would think of telling a story or joke that is anti-black in the presence of a Black person or one that is anti-Jewish in the presence of a Jew. But if by chance the Black or Jew is exposed to such an insult, that person has the comfort of family and the inner community of relatives and friends. Not so for the Gay. She or he is invisible. Not only can we not turn to family or friends, it is these very people who insult and traumatize us throughout the years of invisible development.

The Gay person begins to think of himself or herself as wrong, bad or defective. The one hope is that no one knows, no one sees. The secret must be protected—sometimes with lies that reinforce the bad self-evaluation. "Not only am I sexually perverted," one reasons, "but I am also a liar." Energy goes into a personal civil war fought against natural Gay feelings.

Privately we grow up during the invisible years suspecting that there must be many basic things wrong about us. Why else would loved ones say such things about people who share our feelings? And the seeds of self-doubt and self-hate grow and grow. They live with us every day. Only the lucky few, so far, have found ways to excise them.

Pressures and Attempts to Conform

With the bombardment of negative messages telling us what Gay people are supposed to be like, the resulting injuries to self-esteem, and the energy that goes into hiding true feelings, it is small wonder that most Gay people yield to the massive pressures and try to conform to the popular image of the "normal" person. The first effort to conform usually goes on for years.

More often than not, the Gay person is aware of Gay feelings long before he considers himself or herself eligible for the label. Much effort goes into explaining to oneself why the feelings are there. The attempts at explanation are usually extracted from the anti-Gay myths of our culture. I may decide that the Gay feelings are stemming from having a strong mother and a weak father, or a cold mother and a loving father, or an absent mother and a disagreeable father, or any other psychoanalytic caricature of my true family situation. Or I may believe that the feelings come from having been infected by evil and that Satan has a grip on me. Or I might believe it is an inherited defect, just like Uncle Charles or Aunt Ruth who got put away or committed suicide. Or I may believe that I am losing my mind because I have been masturbating. Or I may simply believe that I have been hanging out with the wrong crowd.

Whatever the presumed genesis of the feelings, the next effort in the struggle to conform is to guard against these Gay feelings being translated into behavior. This is a time for active use of will power. But will power is sometimes not sufficient, and more vigorous efforts to disown the feelings are called into play. A common maneuver is to announce one's own intense anti-Gay feelings and behavior. The person who puts the most energy into baiting and hating Gay people is doing battle with unacceptable feelings inside himself or herself and these feelings are probably homosexual.

While this war to disown feelings rages, the control over having those feelings translate into behavior is ironically apt to be least efficient. The openly Gay person is able to decide when to translate feelings into behavior but the person torn with internal conflict cannot. He or she is like the person obsessed with a weight problem who is constantly confronted with cakes, candy, and other irresistible but fattening delights. He is the serviceman who gets drunk, wanders into a Gay bar—accidentally on purpose—and swears he remembers nothing the next morning when he awakens in bed with another man. She is the woman who arranges a weekend away with a woman friend whose admiring glances have supposedly gone unnoticed, picks a motel room with a good view and one bed, and awakens during the night outraged to find that the other woman has just finished committing a rather lengthy sexual act with her. He is the man who manages to get himself on hunting expeditions, long boat trips, or in other places where there are no women and then lets a "queer" have his way with him because he must have release from sexual tension, having mysteriously forgotten how to masturbate. The Gay feelings are there, the inefficient controls fail, the distorted feelings are translated into not very loving behavior, and rationalizations are called upon in an attempt to hold off the guilt. The guilt is coming from having given in to the unacceptable feelings on the one hand and having distorted them and made them bad and ugly on the other hand.

Homosexual rape outside of prisons is rare. A person involves himself or herself emotionally and sexually with someone of the same gender usually because the involvement is desired. In Gay language such a person is said to be "in the closet" (if Gay feelings are not admitted to self and others). Since almost all Gay people started in the closet, we are sensitive to the symptoms. We may react with sympathy or irritation, remembering our own days in the closet, but we are apt to spot the phenomenon quickly. There is a fading bit of Gay folk wisdom to the effect that "today's trade* is tomorrow's competition." It simply recognizes the truth that someone who invites sexual attention or seduction is eager for homosexual experiences. It is fading now because the raising of Gay consciousness has made more Gay people aware of how self-degrading it is to get involved with a person who devalues Gay experiences. The Gay person today is more apt to offer a helping hand to the seductive "straight" when he is ready to come out of the closet.

The openly and comfortably Gay person is able to decide when to translate erotic feelings into sexual behavior, just as the person who does not have a serious weight problem is able to decide when to have a sweet by testing the strength of the desire and checking reality factors for appropriateness of time and place. If there are no complications of self-concept, one can de-

---

*"Trade" is a self-defined *heterosexual* who seeks or "permits" homosexual sex.

cide whether it is apt to spoil an upcoming meal or increase the likelihood of indigestion when it is a matter of sweets. One can also decide whether it might complicate current interpersonal relationships in some way or add demands to an already satisfying and sufficiently taxing sexual life when it comes to erotic temptations.

Nor do I mean that all Gay feelings are sexual feelings. That is one of the myths that has been perpetuated in our anti-Gay society. Gay feelings run deep. They encompass love, compassion, sympathy, respect, understanding, and altruism. Sexual interaction helps to express these feelings in ways where words fail. But Gay people do express Gay feelings non-sexually as well. The internal struggle with Gay feelings is apt to focus on sexual feelings and sexual behavior because sex has been made the all-too-visible center of the sexist taboo.

An interesting by-product of this difficult internal struggle is increased creativity. Necessity being the mother of invention, the desperate need to find some new patterns of understanding and/or behavior to alleviate the awful anxiety accompanying the struggle can easily push the person to try on new ideas or juxtapositions of ideas viewed from a variety of unaccustomed intellectual and emotional vantage points. Like the prisoner of war, obsessed with the hope of escape, the new and unusual are entertained in a manner that could only be understood by a psychologist as an increase in creativity. For those who survive this period of attempted integration, the increased creativity is likely to be an added asset for life.

During the inner struggle with Gay feelings, it is easy to lose a sense of balance and perspective. I have already pointed out the usual reactions one gets if he or she seeks professional help. But before seeking professional help, one is likely to turn to loved and trusted family or friends. Family usually becomes fearful and guilty knowing the community may place blame for having fostered development of this "deviant." Friends become fearful of guilt by association. In more rational moments, family and friends are apt to fear that their loved one will be treated harshly in an unsympathetic world and urge outward conformity at least, and inward conformity if possible.

Sometimes the loving friends and relatives waver, sensing the human responsibility to encourage integrity. A male client recently told me about the valiant efforts of his woman friend. They had been together for several years starting in high school, had a sexual relationship, and each assumed they would marry one day. Increasingly facing his Gay identity, he sought counseling with me. He gained strength and was able to present himself more fully, including his Gay feelings, to his woman friend; she said she knew that the added information did not make him a different person, and that she still loved him, but she felt afraid and wanted to check a few objective sources for support. She called two sex information counseling services and received the same advice from both. "Drop him and get out of the relationship now before you get pulled down with him." She was distraught and he was distraught; their worst fears seemed confirmed. Both began to see him as "one of those people" because of some words uttered on the telephone confirming the culture's dogma of bigotry to which they had been quietly exposed for a lifetime.

When the internal war against Gay feelings is being fought, the controls against translating these feelings into behavior are unreliable, as stated earlier. The controls slip more and more often. After repeated homosexual experiences, the person must eventually choose a somewhat schizophrenic existence with dual identities or begin to view himself or herself as one of "those people." Very often the self-confrontation is harsh and the person is apt to apply ugly labels in a hurtful way: "I am a queer" (or dyke, or fag, or lesbo, or homo, or pansy). It is a step toward personality integration, but at the price of admitted self-hatred.

With the failure of this first prolonged attempt at conformity, more than a few commit suicide. Having cut deeply into an already injured self-esteem with the hurtful self-confrontation in which ugly labels are self-assigned, a part of the previously valued self is murdered. Feeling more alone and less worthy, the person is then easy prey to the unflattering anti-Gay bigotry which he or she may have actively supported and perpetuated in earlier attempts to maintain distance from homosexuality. Having murdered a valued part of self and being haunted and weakened by visions of a distasteful future, it is not too difficult to imagine the final giving up.

Hope for self-respect may be relinquished. One may well feel that the only hope for peace lies in completing the process of self-murder that began with the confrontation and self-assigned pejorative labels. The final completion of the self-murder draws on the energy of the non-conscious rage at a world that seemingly makes it impossible to be one's true self and have self-respect. But the rage turns inward, believing in a mad final moment of loyalty to one's society that "they" are right and I am "bad." The misdirected rage provides the energy for the emotionally drained person to finally pull the trigger or tie the noose. Their act of self-murder is a shame that we who represent their society must bear. It should be cause for any professional helper of people to examine his or her personal conscience and past professional behavior very carefully.

Gay people who do not kill themselves after this awful self-confrontation and attempt at integration are likely to seek professional help. We turn to counselors of all sorts. Once again we try to change ourselves. We try harder to conform. We pray, take pills, enter psychotherapy, or yield ourselves up to the painful electric shocks designed by behavior modification professionals to "recondition" our feelings. Brainwashing and atrocities of medical experimentation are words used to describe phenomena that have taken place in far away times and places. Yet the ingredients of these distasteful anti-humanistic phenomena exist today in expensive private offices and well-staffed hospitals. Some Gay people make considerable sacrifices of time, money, and emotional suffering and willingly expose themselves to these experiences because of hope. They have been told by authoritative, respected professionals that there is hope that these experiences will change them into socially acceptable heterosexuals or at least rid them of part or all of their shameful homosexuality.

The first massive effort to conform is motivated by the reluctance to admit to a deviant identity. It ends in failure. The second struggle to conform is motivated by hope that the deviant identity, while true and privately accepted, can be changed. After this second long stage of trying to change has drained emotional and financial reserves, most of us are left with seriously lessened self-esteem and confronted with despair. It is at the end of this second try that another large number of people seek rest by turning their rage inward and completing the process of self-murder. It is a harsh weeding out of those with less than superior emotional stamina and reserves. The strong and well-defended will survive. It is a quiet war not required of conforming heterosexuals. The self-inflicted final death of those who choose suicide at the end of this second try confront the conscience of all of us who remain.

The surviving wounded Gay must cope with anguish and despair and make some choices. It is now that some people settle for a zombie's life of work, food, TV, and sleep. Some give up only partly and enter an institution that will take care of them for life. Some try to kill the pain with drugs and/or alcohol. Some give in and become the devalued, laughed-at eccentric. The males lisp, mince, giggle; the females cut their hair, put on work boots and talk tough. They do what they can to live out the stereotype. The other good citizens laugh at them but are willing to be more tolerant, to permit their existence now that they have fitted into a proper niche. If the good citizen is made somewhat uncomfortable, it may be because these eccentrics in their angry despair have chosen a kind of integrity that brazenly flaunts the lie of the stereotype in the face of the bigot. The behavior says "You knew me once as a person like yourself. I know you too have bottled up Gay feelings but I have decided that my honesty about my Gay feelings is more important than any respect that I might get from people like you by pretending that I am like you." These are hurt and brave people. They are surviving and refuse to go under or to go unnoticed.

Miraculously a small but increasing percentage of the Gay people are able to choose a path of integrity and truth without giving in. They are able to find their anger and use it as a key to freedom. They are the ones who have managed to grow stronger in the struggle. Most of them are young but they come in all ages and from all walks of life. These survivors who have not gone back into the closet with their TV, bottle, or needle, have decided once and for all to come out of the closet and be self-respecting.

Consciousness and Community

My repeated experience in conducting weekend growth groups for Gay people is the pleasure of seeing a dozen strangers, who distrust one another and are prepared to see anti-Gay myths acted out during the weekend, come together into a varied, non-conforming but mutually respecting community.

I am writing this the day after having finished such a weekend group. The faces are fresh in memory, as are the pain and joys we shared. Laughter and tears become the truthful warp on which the fabric of our community is woven. When we were closing yesterday, a young architect looked across the room at an older physician and said "I hope I don't have to go through everything you've been put through and carry as many scars, but I look at you here still slugging away and making your life better and I just want to say 'thanks.' Thanks for keeping the road open when I was too young and dumb to know I would need it to find my way to other Gay people and thanks to you and everyone else here for reminding me how different we all are and how strong we are together." Then a student looked at the architect and said, "That's how I feel about you and the others too."

Gay growth experience groups and Gay organizations are growing in strength and membership. We are beginning to understand that our loneliness is not required as the only alternative to conformity or self-destruction. Gay people who survive and grow strong in the struggle for integrity and freedom from oppression are able to do so by increasing consciousness and developing a sense of community. Increasing one's consciousness is a matter of increasing awareness, alertness or sensitivity to facets of oppression.

If you do not see the arrows coming it is easier to get wounded. Much oppression is perpetuated by decent people who do it, not out of malice, but from insensitive habit. The Gay person who increases consciousness is able to help other people who are unthinking oppressors open their eyes and see what they are doing. Once aware, most people are willing to alter their behavior so as not to offend or disadvantage another person.

Increasing consciousness and developing a sense of community often go hand-in-hand. It is possible to increase consciousness through thoughtful exchange with a trusted friend, through reading or observation, but the most efficient method is by participation in discussion groups. Research on small groups dating back to the Second World War has consistently demonstrated that attitudes change most easily in small groups. Changing attitudes help pave the way for possible new awareness of feelings and new behavior. Groups referred to as CR (consciousness-raising) groups facilitate increased awareness of previously unquestioned assumptions. Open, honest discussion of feelings with other Gay people can be a liberating experience in itself, but it also lays the foundation for honest feedback (the verbal reflection from other group members of your own words and behavior as a means of helping you see your own attitudes, feelings and behavior more clearly). You begin to watch yourself more closely and you begin to watch other people more closely.

As Blacks raised their consciousness, they helped all of us to be more sensitive to how words like "boy" and "girl," when applied to adults, are used to promote the image of a dependent, irresponsible, immature and unreliable child-like person who must be cared for by a superior "adult." It provided the psychological excuse for exploitation. As women raised their consciousness, they helped us all to see how the use of words like "chairman," "man and wife," or "man-made" facilitate the exploitation of women with the psychological assurance of male superiority and male right to power. As Gay people increase consciousness, we are helping others to see the even more subtle use of words and images to support the ideal of the limited heterosexual male and female image. Contrary to our habitual language, one may consider the possibility that a he-man (real man) can kiss another man or hold hands with him, do needlework, cook a meal, and appreciate art. Or the possibility that a real woman can fill another woman with desire, change a tire, balance a checkbook, or even bring home the bacon. Some hints of this new consciousness are beginning to peek through in films and TV, but not yet in ways that forcefully challenge the strong prohibitions against same-gender demonstrations of affection.

But increasing consciousness is not only a matter of becoming more sensitive to words and pictures. The Gay survivor learns to be wary of people who seem solicitous and ask if you "have any idea why you have had trouble developing fully satisfying relationships with members of the opposite sex?" Such a line of inquiry reinforces the myth that Gay people are running away from half the population—which is more likely to be true of the exclusive heterosexual, since homophobia is much more the style of the day than heterophobia.

In Gay CR groups we can learn to laugh at the person who offers us tolerance or acceptance. That person is coming from a position of presumed superiority. We learn compassion for the person whose life is so limited that she or he is astonished to meet a Gay person who is a steel worker or a psychologist because she or he honestly believed all Gay men were hairdressers or interior decorators and all Gay women were taxi drivers or military personnel. We learn to express our anger and indignation when Gay people are arrested for frequenting a Gay establishment, beaten with impunity, fired as security risks or undesirables, excommunicated from churches and disowned by families. We become aware that no one has the right to treat us that way.

By raising consciousness we become sensitive to the myriad ways in which anti-Gay myths are perpetuated. We begin to see that if we do not take the time and trouble to expose and block each of these attempts, unwitting though they sometimes are, we are cooperating by tacit agreement in our own victimization. It is unpleasant to be a guest at a dinner party and have another guest make passing reference to "the fag who lives upstairs." It is unpleasant to have to interrupt the story and say that you find the derogatory word offensive. It is unpleasant to find all eyes focused on you while you counter the explanation that "no harm was meant" since the speaker "really likes the guy" with the obvious retort that he would not have said "nigger" when talking about a Black friend or "kike" when talking about a Jewish friend. It is unpleasant, but the alternative of silence is actually a statement to everyone present, including yourself, that such careless bigotry is justifiable or excusable. A Gay person soon begins to see that the road to one's private Hell (feeling tortured by alienation and lack of self-respect) is indeed paved with such social tolerance. We learn not to participate in our own victimization.

As Gay consciousness increases, we see the need to protest victimization of other Gay people, though we are not involved directly as individuals. We see the need to write a letter to the editor when a slur against Gays is printed as part of a news story. We see the need for a phone call to the TV station when the villain of the story is Gay and the hero is heterosexual for no apparent reason. We see the need for pickets outside the offices of the telephone company when a top executive has announced a policy of employment discrimination against Gays. We see the need to mourn openly and send money to help survivors of an arsonist's fire in a Gay bar where thirty people were incinerated. No Gay person has the time and energy to fight all these battles, but we can learn to fight as many as we can, because each time we are making a statement of our right to be and of our determination not to give silent assent to habitual victimization.

Consciousness-raising and a sense of community go hand-in-hand, not only because so many of us begin to raise consciousness in groups but also because the process of increasing consciousness helps a Gay person to see how we are all related and that we cannot survive without mutual support. We are another in the long line of oppressed groups to understand "united we stand, divided we fall." This does not mean that because you are Gay you must love all Gay people. We are too varied for that. It does mean that each of us must honor the bond of Gayness and offer support to other Gay people who are threatened with oppression, whether they happen to be individuals we might like for friends or not.

The ultimate reward from developing a sense of community with other Gay people is that you are no longer alone, and that is of great importance in the life of a Gay person. The nightmare ends. Each of us grew up in isolation. Unlike other minority groups, we were not reared in a Gay family. We grew up feeling alone and different. As your vision encompasses a wider and wider spectrum of the Gay population you are not alone any longer. There are even heroes and heroines. There are people who share your values and lifestyle. There are people to learn from and models to emulate. It is a sense of coming home, familiar only to other minority groups who have been separated from their people for a long time. And today there is the pleasure of watching more and more Gay people emerge from the closet, pulled by the magnet of liberation and community. Since most of us have been invisible, the emergence of someone you know, an army sergeant, a football player, a politician, or an actress, may come as a surprise and delight. "You, too?" There is a sudden extra warmth in the kinship. But beyond joy, there is the assurance of people who care and understand—people who can share familiar feelings and offer mutual support.

The Pleasures of Being Gay

The foregoing attempt to portray the experience of being Gay from an insider's point of view as well as discuss some of the psychodynamics of Gayness and oppression has presented more of the sorrows of being Gay than the joys of being Gay. Hopefully, it is clear that the sorrows need not be there, since they are the result of interaction with a hostile environment. When the hostile environment changes, most of the sorrows will go. It is a testimony to the good sense and goodwill of today's surviving Gay people that our joys are able to flourish amid the pollution of rampant oppression.

Understandably, some people are apt to ask, "If it's so much trouble, why do you stay Gay?" And well they might ask. But why continue to be a Christian, to have blue eyes or to be Black? Because it is natural. To try to conform to some non-Gay image is an impossible affront to integrity. It is unnatural for us. And the unhappy consequences of such efforts have been detailed earlier.

But what do people enjoy about being Gay? It is impossible to generalize. There are so many different kinds of Gay people. I like knowing that other men are potential love partners rather than competitors or enemies. I like it that we Gay people really know it is better to make love than to make war. I like walking down the street and exchanging a glance and a smile with another Gay person, acknowledging that we are related and we know it. I like the camp humor that we have developed as a means of spotlighting the insanity of most convention, the hidden oppression, and our ability to laugh and keep afloat in spite of it all. I like the sharing of tenderness and compassion that is largely denied to non-Gay men. I like the easier democracy that permits people more often to flow across the usual social barriers of income, education, color, and religion. I like the way Gay women relate to me as a person, an equal, and not as the "opposite sex" to be flattered, feared, or manipulated. One of the unsought fringe benefits of being Gay is that you are an admitted outcast who in any new situation is invisible once again. You can materialize as Gay at any time you choose to reveal yourself (to the considerable discomfort of any bigot present). When I was a child I listened to "The Shadow" on radio and sometimes I remember that force for justice when I hear evidence of bigotry as my invisible Gay self and then confront the bigot-villain as a suddenly visible Gay. As invisible Gays we do not usually intend to mislead. It is the bigot's own blindness that creates our invisible condition. He or she deserves embarrassment when we respond with honest indignation.

The problem we present to conformists can be a boon to us. Since we are already non-conforming puzzles to the Establishment, we have nothing to lose, and some hope of improving self-respect, by questioning the sacred moral tenets of our society. This provides more flexibility in sorting one's personal values and establishing a satisfying code of ethics than is available to the non-Gay person. For instance, I must decide for myself under which conditions, if any, monogamy and fidelity are suitable and satisfying options for me. I must decide whether it is satisfying and right, or hazardous to my emotional health, to retain contact with my biological family. In any serious Gay relationship I must see the value of it day by day in order to continue, since the state has not licensed the relationship and makes it all too easy to dissolve it. The flexibility inherent in status as an outcast is at once a privilege and a responsibility, though it is a gift most of us would not have chosen since it is born of pain.

Perhaps one of the greatest joys in being Gay is that it permits you to be a full human. By definition, you do not fit society's picture of the real man or the real woman. Once the program is thus flawed it makes it much easier to go ahead and explore options supposedly reserved for "the opposite sex." As a man you can be tender, intuitive, warm, sensitive, spontaneous, uninhibited, colorful, emotional, or even flirtatious. As a woman you are free to be strong, determined, reliable, forbearing, dependable, tough, smart, and even aggressive. Nor is there any need to give up any of the attributes ordinarily reserved for your gender when and if you find them attractive and satisfying. The same holds true for behavior. A Gay man can cook and a Gay woman can patch the roof and not fret about what the neighbors will say. They are saying it already, anyway. The Gay man may continue to be the home handyman just as the Gay woman may continue to find pleasure in sewing. I must add that some heterosexual women and men (thanks largely to the women's liberation movement) are exploring non-sexist roles these days and enjoying the widened horizons offered Gay people.

And the range of relating is increased for Gay people. You are free to relate in depth to anyone, regardless of gender. Of course, popular anti-Gay myth decrees that Gay men do not like women and Gay women do not like men, but it is not true. Most of this heterophobia is the projection of homophobic heterosexuals. Gay men are likely to relate to women more fully without dragging along the male chauvinist oppressor games played by most heterosexual men who have been programmed to dominate women. Gay women can and do relate to men as friends and equals without any need to play "dumb broad" or subservient coquette. They are not trying to capture a man, nor are they interested in following the programming that dictates the strengthening of any nearby male ego. From such depth and equality in relating can grow fine friendships and loves. Nor is heterosexual sex excluded. The Gay person may be more attracted to persons of the same gender in general but a particular sexual relationship is based on individual attraction, not general attraction. Some Gay people, of course, have not yet questioned the myth and have kept their distance from people they were trained to see as the opposite sex. Consciousness-raising is helping to expose this myth finally, however.

Being Gay is not anti, it is pro. We are not against people, we are for them. We have learned to appreciate individual differences the hard way. We have a stake in everyone's freedom because it is the only way we will be assured of our own. And we cannot survive without our freedom. We have been hated because we are people who dared to follow our own truth in times and places where our love has been forbidden.

There are so many advantages to being Gay, and most of them are difficult to communicate joyously because they have been earned at considerable cost. The Gay person is apt to have had more experience with both reality and fantasy than he or she

106

would otherwise have had. The realities may have been as harsh as hearing your own daughter say, "You know, Mom, lesbians are so disgusting that I think it would be the one time it would be all right to round up a particular group of people and take them to the gas chamber." The pain of such a moment is hard for a non-Gay person to understand. The reality is, however, not new, and a Gay mother can understand that her daughter has learned to hate an image, does not fully know her mother, is struggling with her own sexual impulses, and can be helped to develop tolerance for self and others. And all of this while bearing the pain and not missing a stroke with the hair brush.

And the experience with fantasy can be as intense as spending six years in the army surrounded by other men under battle conditions that churn up raw emotions, developing true love for one or more of your comrades and listening to them talk about the girl back home while you stay emotionally alive with fantasies of your comrade discovering his love for you and celebrating sexually together on a three-day pass, then settling into a quiet life on the farm you will buy together if you are both still alive when the war is over. And all of this while cleaning your M-1 rifle and encouraging your friend to be patient with his girl for not writing often enough.

This daily experience with intense reality and intense fantasy builds a wider and deeper internal emotional capacity, though it may not be visible to everyone around you. It is a quality that some sensitive non-Gay people feel and wonder that they are so often drawn to people who turn out to be Gay. It is an asset also in terms of flexibility. Our increased experience with reality and fantasy makes it easier to take life's surprises in stride, maintain balance, and take care of responsibilities in everyday life.

Then there is physical attractiveness. Gay people are not born with genes that make them more attractive, yet they do seem to become more attractive with the self-admitted awareness of Gay identity. Partly it is the result of released tension. Partly it is self-destructive hypersensitivity to the media's concept of beauty and the money and time spent to conform to that image so as to be found worthy. But mostly it is the advantage of awareness. In this case one is aware of the physical attraction to some people of the same gender. Unlike the non-Gay man who is supposed to not notice other male bodies, the Gay man does notice other men and sees what is naturally beautiful about a body that is cared for with self-respect. The Gay man is more likely to watch his food intake and less likely to get paunchy. The Gay woman is less likely to preen with a palette of paints and devices to disguise her true form since she is appreciative of the natural body beauty of a woman.

We Gay people have had to develop a benign, self-protective alertness that can be viewed as a positive form of "paranoia." We must try to be aware of how other people are seeing us and reacting to us emotionally. It is necessary lest we be hit unexpectedly with a stroke of bigotry based on someone's suspicion of our Gayness. This Gay "paranoia" is benign because it acts only as an early warning system that helps us to make social adjustments that smooth social interactions. It is not the malignant sort of paranoia that keeps you tense with the suspicion that the whole world is out to get you and makes social intercourse tempestuous or impossible.

The Gay Early Warning System is costly in energy, but it pays dividends. It provides plenty of practice in noticing words chosen, posture, voice intonation, and facial expression. In other words, it provides the experience that increases sensitivity. It builds not only greater sensitivity but also greater self-awareness. When you are constantly alert to how other people are responding to you emotionally, you cannot help correlating it with your feelings and behavior at the moment. Gay people are more likely than their non-Gay counterparts to know that a fixed smile will not cover unsunny feelings and that it is better to stay home when you are feeling unsocial (or at least to let your social companions have some clues as to what's bothering you so they need not feel responsible). The combined sensitivity and self-awareness, though costly, is a strong social asset.

There is also something wonderful about being part of a group that has insistently survived and brightened the world under the most adverse circumstances. We're like that beautiful orange flower called the California poppy. We are apt to pop up anywhere—beside a railroad track, in the wilderness, in a pampered floral display, or in a long forgotten garden covered with weeds and trampled by careless footsteps. We keep blooming with a beauty that is there to be seen by anyone willing to appreciate it.

Most of all, I suppose, from the long list that could be drawn of the pleasures of being Gay, I like being able to be myself, to respect differences in people, and to look on the human world with a sense of compassion.

It is not easy to be Gay in our society today, though it is easier than it was a decade or two ago. Once you realize you are Gay you know that you are in for plenty of pain and struggle. The cards are stacked against you. You face discrimination and prejudice from people who supposedly love you. The emotional pressures are enormous. You are apt to be tempted at one time or another by suicide as a way out. The painful wounds increase your chances of falling into drug or alcohol abuse. But all of this is due not to your Gayness but to the prejudice and bigotry of a society that has unthinkingly used Gayness for scapegoating. In spite of the enormous weight placed on you by an oppressive environment, it is possible to join hands with people who appreciate Gayness, especially other Gay people today, and celebrate the pain of the past and the potential of the future. While most of the rest of the population struggles with the half-lives assigned them by their stereotypic gender roles, we are released by our Gay identity. We know we can love anyone worthy, including people of our own gender. We know that we can be whole as humans. For those of us who survive—and there are more and more of us who do—the world is rich and full. And we know enough to appreciate its richness and its fullness.

2
Glad to be Gay

I recently attended a dinner party in honor of two Gay male friends, one Jewish and the other of vaguely Spanish heritage, who have declared themselves a couple. The hostess raised her wine glass in salute and said, "Here's to the two of you. May you live gaily forever." As one of the partners responded with "Olé!" the other said "Oi vey!" while the rest of us choked in surprise.

"Was that a bad toast?" the hostess asked. The Jewish member of the team, who had been responsible for the "Oi vey" said, "It was an involuntary response. First, please understand that I love this man more dearly than I have ever loved anyone, the dinner party is superb, and you are a wonderful friend. I think it flashed through my mind that I now had to be Gay in a new way because we have become a couple. It's like starting all over again, again! I grew up with a lot of weird ideas about the sort of person you had to be if you were a homosexual. I fought that identity and stayed in the closet for twenty years. Then, as I tiptoed out of the closet, I got the Gay Liberation party line about the sort of person I am supposed to be if I am Gay and I tried on most of that costume. But now that we two have found one another it feels like starting all over. We're beginning to feel safe enough in our mutual respect and love that each of us can dare to present ourselves to the world as the individuals we are. It feels good and more than a little frightening—like I forgot my clothing or mask. It was scary and exhilarating enough to appear in the Gay Freedom Day march for the first time last June, but this runs deeper. I am responsible to myself and this other beloved person sitting here to be the individual I really am and not pretend to fit any prefabricated image, straight or Gay. So forgive the 'Oi vey,' because I know no one in this room wants to put me in a mold. It was just a reflex."

It was well said, I thought, and as I picture my friend's face, wrinkled of brow but glowing with new-found confidence, reflecting the effort and the reward, it is a moment I treasure in memory.

This part of the book, as its title suggests, has to do with unlearning negative associations so that you can relax and enjoy your *self* as the Gay person you happen to be. The ideas and suggestions have grown out of my years of professional work with Gay people, the real-life experiences of my Gay friends, and my personal experience in being Gay. It took time and effort for me to become Gay, to own the wholeness of that identity.

It took more time and effort for me to become a Gay-oriented professional. Gay-oriented is used throughout this book to designate the professional who, whether or not choosing to act on his or her own Gay feelings by translating those feelings into behavior at any given period of life, truly values being Gay. This is the professional person who has experienced the oppression to which Gay people are subjected, has an understanding of how that influences individual psychodynamic development, and celebrates any person's self-respecting behavioral expression of Gay feelings. For the Gay-oriented professional the task is clearly to be of assistance in helping the client become more herself/himself, and that means helping the Gay person to become more Gay and self-appreciative. The non-Gay-oriented professional (though he or she may be homosexually involved in private life) is not appreciative of Gay identity as a gift and is likely to subtly reinforce the covert belief that heterosexual is better, even if "Gay is OK." Gay-oriented professionals understand and appreciate the richness of Gay identity.

Those Gay people who come to me and my Gay-oriented colleagues for clinical service come for the same wide variety of reasons that people everywhere seek professional help. When the precipitating factor is an affair of the heart, a man may have just broken up with a man, or a woman may be depressed because "her" woman is having a fling with another woman instead of a man, but gender matters little at such a time. Humans are apt to be more influenced by their culture's training as to how one is supposed to experience and cope with such passions and will have nearly the same sorts of troubles regardless of gender. Beyond matters of romance, sex and love, people have the same sort of human troubles whether or not they are Gay. But in addition to these ordinary human troubles, Gay people can be better helped to grow if they work within a framework that appreciates Gay identity and is sensitive to the experience of being a Gay person in today's world.

There is some special learning that comes to the professional person who chooses to work with Gay people, and I feel fortunate to have been exposed to it. We Gay people are the same as other people, and we are different. We have grown up in the general culture and been influenced by the Gay sub-culture. And both cultures are changing. In order to grow strong, we Gay people have some special coping to do to balance the influence of two changing cultures in a sometimes subtly hostile environment that has taught us to think badly of ourselves and people like us. We may well be better off for having had to make the efforts in response to these special challenges to our integrity. The resulting learning can help us become more alert, sensitive and strong, but the struggle is long and difficult and deserves to be respected, not minimized. You are no less worthwhile for feeling the need of a helping hand in assimilating your Gay experience.

Becoming Gay

A heterosexually married woman came to see me in my office on a wintry day last year. Through the women's movement she had recaptured many of her feelings and a goal of self-respect. She had also met another woman who reawakened Gay feelings that she had hoped had been put to rest after college with the aid of five years of therapy, a loving marriage to a man, and a career as housewife with three children.

"I don't want to go through that hell again," she said, referring to her previous years in therapy. "But I also don't want to be Gay. I know it's wrong and that everyone will get hurt, including my husband and the kids. And yet I know the feelings I have toward her are good and honest."

And last week, an eighteen-year-old man and his woman friend consulted me. He had confessed to her that he was sexually attracted to a male friend. During one interview he found the strength to tell her that he was often attracted to other men and feared that he was homosexual. He told her he loved her and wanted to be most attracted to her, but he knew he had been mostly attracted to males since he was a child. Many cleansing tears were shed, though we have work to do in making their communication clear and honest. And they have decisions to make about the kind of relationship they want with one another right now.

If you are currently struggling against your Gay identity, know that almost all of us have gone through the same struggle. One day, hopefully, you will be proud of yourself as a Gay person. There are outstretched hands in many parts of the world today, ready to help if you will ask. Many universities have a Gay Students' Union or Gay Students' Association that can put you in touch with local Gay groups or individuals who are willing to talk and help. Some cities have a Gay community service center or a local Gay information service listed in the telephone book through which you can also find help. A Gay-oriented newspaper can also help with Gay services information.

But if you are as uncomfortable and shy as most of us are during the struggle to find identity, chances are you will not contact any Gay organization yet. You are more likely to contact a professional counselor whose group is non-Gay (because there are more of them and because you have been led to believe they will be more objective). In truth the non-Gay-oriented counselor is *not* more objective and is likely to be *less* knowledgeable unless there has been enough personal concern to take some extra training in Gay-oriented counseling. The non-Gay-oriented professional is likely to want to help you down the path of conversion to conformity. He or she may, if more enlightened, advise you to stop resisting your identity. Beware of help designed to change you, no matter how many degrees are hanging on the wall. And remember that actions speak louder than words. If the counselor *says* he or she thinks its okay to be Gay, but brightens and seems more enthusiastic when happy heterosexual events are reported, *run—do not walk* to a Gay-oriented counselor. This one is giving double messages, and that can really cause you more trouble. If you are emotionally, intellectually, and bodily attracted to people of the same gender, you know it. You may be far from wanting to admit it, but you are Gay. Efforts to convert and conform will be costly in time, effort, and money and are likely to leave you scarred, lonely, and feeling less good about yourself.

For the time being, until you are ready to reach out for some Gay-oriented help, the best thing to do might be to read. Go to the library and find what books you can having to do with being Gay. If anything describing the book or in the book itself suggests that being gay might be bad, close the book. You have been exposed to a lifetime of that poison already. Look for good news about being Gay, preferably written by a Gay person who knows from first hand experience. Reading can help you begin to free yourself of the belief that you are bad if you admit to your Gay identity.

Once you begin to see that you can be even more yourself and create a life of dignity and warmth, you will be ready to contact Gay people who may be a little farther down the path. At least they can listen and know what you are talking about. Some of these Gay people have their own problems, of course, and bear their own particular scars from the past. I do not mean to present all Gay people as angels and all non-Gays as devils. Some Gays, having swallowed a stereotypical picture complete with anti-Gay myths during their developing years, may now act out the stereotype by being bitchy and irresponsibly offensive as they leer at you, hopeful that you are the next item on their promiscuity menu. But this sort of Gay person is disappearing in our massive effort to reeducate and reclaim our individual identities. Gay organizations make great efforts to be staffed with counselors who are there to help you rather than to use you. They are people who have traveled some thorny paths and are interested in helping you to travel your path more smoothly. If you happen to run into a Gay person who is set to misuse you emotionally or sexually in order to meet his or her own needs, the problem presented is no greater than in a comparable heterosexual interchange. You need only sense that you are being set up and you can say, "Thanks but no thanks," and move on to a different and more sincere counselor. You cannot afford to believe the advice that comes from one person anyway. But if you expose yourself to a number of Gay people you can begin to put the advice pieces together in ways that make sense to you. We can help one another to avoid the self-destructive stages of coming out described in the first part of the book, and more and more Gay people are interested in reaching out a helping hand for new Gays coming along behind them.

Becoming More Gay

He yelled the words at me. "All right, God damn it, I accept it!" Then, staring at me wide-eyed and a bit unsteady through the thick lenses of his glasses, he said quietly, "But accepting your identity as a Gay person may still be quite a ways from rejoicing in it." These immortal words were spoken to me a few years ago by a man who had escaped from an academic job among the intelligentsia of New York City and who had used his savings to trip across the country with the aid of acid, mescaline, some amphetamines, hash, and a goodly supply of dope. He had hoped for sudden clarity that would rid him of the spectre of his homosexual desires. What he got was sufficient clarity to see that he was seemingly stuck with some sort of homosexual identity, though his mind was still dizzy from the recent kaleidoscope of closely packed drug experiences and he could barely understand that I had said some words about one day being Gay in all senses of the word and grateful for a Gay identity. He could not register what possible basis in reality such words might have. Today he is more relaxed and smiles more. I have not seen him in almost two years, but I still get a note once in a while. He does indeed rejoice in his Gay identity, and he is now able to help others to do so.

But his path, like yours and mine, was not always smooth or pleasant. For one thing, he had to be reminded to be patient with himself. Once he caught the scent of liberation, he wanted it all right away. He had to learn that he had been programmed to misunderstand himself in many ways, and that each piece of misinformation had to be unlearned so that he could change attitudes toward himself and other Gay people. And that takes time, because the unlearning can only take place as life experiences present opportunities to behave differently.

This man had learned to think of "homosexuals'' as people who were not very bright. He pictured them sitting about at endless parties, overdressed and overperfumed, discussing people not present in unflattering detail and tossing pseudowitty barbs designed to hurt those present. In the course of psychotherapy, he met another man at the baths. Ordinarily he would have used this man for sex and then been rid of him as quickly as possible. Instead, they talked before sex, and he found a bright, alive, intellectually oriented anthropologist who has become a lifetime friend and sometimes sexual partner.

My client had also learned to think of himself as not fitting his stereotypic homosexual image because it would cut him off from contact with women, and he had several close women friends. As he opened up about his true feelings, he discovered that one of his women friends was discovering her own Gay identity and the mutual disclosure brought them even closer.

A Gay woman friend of mine had an interesting relearning experience at a faculty meeting. Her stereotypic pictures of lesbians were many and varied, but excluded some possibilities. She had been a member of an interviewing committee to admit graduate students to a Ph.D. program. Everyone had been quite impressed with one woman candidate. She appeared bright, interested, capable, and responsible. She was divorced, lived with two young offspring, and had stated in her interview that she considered it a personal disability that she yielded too easily to dominant men but that she was "working on changing that." My friend liked the woman but saw her as "another housewife on the way up." She decided to take a stand and told her fellow members, "This woman seems fine but we have only a few vacancies and I'd like to see at least one filled by a Gay woman."

The white-haired male chairperson suggested my friend refer to page 3 of the applicant's papers, where it said, "My interest in alternative life styles has been stimulated by my acceptance of my lesbian identity."

"How could I have missed it?" my friend asked rhetorically over a drink. "Don't answer that—let me tell you! I still expect a lesbian academic to have short hair and want an M.A. in physical education. Put that in your book and I'll deny it! This one had blonde curly hair, a pink dress, and an IQ better than mine. I will do penance with twelve Hail Sapphos!"

The process of relearning can be quickened by such means as participation in Gay support groups, Gay-oriented psychotherapy groups and Gay organizations, but de-programming and relearning will still take years. You must imagine that you are reaching toward infinity, gathering more of yourself as you continue to try, but never getting all of yourself. Most of your relearning happens in the first months, but it never stops. It decreases quantitatively as time goes along because there is less to relearn and less pressure to do so quickly, but by then the process has become so valued that you treasure each new piece of relearning.

After all of these years of relearning, I was hit by a small but blinding flash of understanding just a month ago. For a long time something had bothered me about the standard phrase that appeared regularly in quick phone conversations or social encounters with one member of a Gay couple. The standard phrase to a man was, "How are you and Rob doing?" or to a woman, "How are you and Susan doing" It was invariably said by another person who cared about the well-being of each member of the Gay couple and cared about their relationship. Then one day I musingly turned the phrase around to fit it into a comparable conversation with one member of a heterosexual couple and it was suddenly clear. With a heterosexual pair one simply inquires as to how the other person is, not how they are doing. The inquiry about how a couple is doing carries the implicit assumption that they may not be doing well together. It is the unquestioned assumption that a Gay couple will have trouble staying together, but that the bond in a heterosexual couple is sacred and it would be presumptuous or rude to question its possible continuation unless invited to do so by some specific piece of information offered by one of the couple!

In the long process of recovery of self, the first place to look is at the unquestioned stereotypic portraits of behavior, attitudes, and feelings of Gay people that you have been taught to regard as truth. You must begin to question, observe real Gay people, and decide for yourself how much is truth and how much is destructive fiction. In order to do that, you must get to know some real Gay people. In the process you can find the Gay people you like and respect as individuals.

Deprogramming

Computers are complex "thinking" machines that behave or produce results in a variety of ways. Each type of machine has its own character and personality, dependent upon its design and construction. But the thinking and behavior of the computers is shaped by the program. The program is the set of instructions fed into the machine, telling it to operate (think and behave) in certain ways that are good or bad, right or wrong, according to the definitions of the persons who constructed the program. Should the program be fed to a machine which cannot, because of natural limitations or differences in design, follow the instructions, the computer will not compute. Should its design permit it to handle similar tasks but not exactly those on this program, it will behave in a "neurotic" fashion or fail to function at all. Computers, complex as they are, were designed as simplified copies of how humans think and behave.

All of us are programmed from the day of birth to the day of death. We are told what is right and wrong, good and bad. We are told how to think and behave. These instructions come not only from parents, teachers, religious leaders, and other influential friends and relations but from cereal boxes, TV programs, billboards, political campaigns, newspapers, magazines, movies, and even menus. We are bombarded with instructions. From them we build a general program that is harmonious because its parts fit together. Dissonant instructions are usually discarded or not taken seriously. Unlike most computers, we humans can screen our instructions and decide which ones do not fit the overall program.

But that overall program, made up of the thousands of bits and pieces of instructions that fit together, is forced upon us. We do not select it; it happens to us. If the program does not fit your individual nature, the way you are personally put together psychologically, you are apt to behave neurotically or fail to function. The program for each of us is unique, since we have fitted together the thousands of pieces personally, but the overall programs we have picked up in this society are very similar. And the overall program produced in this society today does not fit the Gay person. You are instructed to follow a strictly heterosexual path that ignores feelings of attraction to people of the same gender. This is against your nature. What to do? We can try taking the computer apart and rebuilding it so that the program will fit, or we can find a new program. For too long we have been attempting to take Gay people apart and rebuild them. It is time to look for a new program.

Futuristic novels such as *Brave New World, 1984,* and *Stranger in a Strange Land* portray how difficult it is to break one's programming. The guilt and anxiety are intense. It can be done more easily with the aid of a support system made up of similar people who are also working to deprogram themselves. Their support helps allay the guilt and anxiety. Their ideas point to possible directions for a more personally satisfying and responsible program. I'll have more to say about selecting your support system later.

If it is necessary, with near superhuman efforts the deprogramming and reprogramming can be accomplished alone. Parts of it must always be done alone. And the near superhuman effort must be made if help from other people is not available, because your life depends upon it if you are Gay. You cannot trust your life to a program based on the assumption that your most natural loving feelings are wrong and make you a bad person. A lifetime of reinforcement with that program almost guarantees a short, narrow, and unhappy life.

If there is one available in your area, or if you can find enough Gay people to start one, you would do well to begin your deprogramming and reprogramming with a Gay discussion group, Gay support group, or Gay therapy group. Such a group usually picks a different topic for each evening's discussion. Each person shares personal experiences and feelings related to that topic—often saying things he or she has never said aloud before. There is a feedback time during which people give you their feelings about you and what you said during the evening in the group, and then the group picks a topic for the next meeting. After only a half dozen meetings, you will find you are beginning to be more aware of the ways in which you have been taught to think and behave. You will begin to see the thousands of "rights," "wrongs," "goods," and "bads" that you accepted without question.

Choosing between a Gay support or discussion group and a Gay therapy group has to do partly with whether you will feel more comfortable knowing that a qualified leader is "in charge" or whether your goal is simply to increase awareness or to make difficult changes in your life pattern. If you choose a Gay therapy group, make sure that the professional leader is Gay-oriented and not simply a professional who has assembled a Gay group, with covert or overt assumptions that heterosexual conformity increases mental health.

Reading is another helpful source that can stimulate you to question your privately unquestioned basic assumptions. Of course, standard magazine rack reading does not help, it only reinforces the old program. But books and articles coming out of the Gay movement, the women's movement, or the Black movement are all apt to make you think and reevaluate. These books can be found in bookstores in most cities.

A vital help, especially if you are trying to do it alone with no support group or CR group, is to write a detailed autobiography, pointing out to yourself the values you have accepted along the way. Weigh every value located and do it on paper so that you can catch omissions and dishonesty. Then write an autobiography of the future and specify your new, more personally satisfying values as well as the old ones you have decided to keep. Use your future biography to show yourself how you can make your life more satisfying and how you can increase your feelings of worth.

Another necessary project is to examine your stereotypes about Gay people. You can use paper and pencil, or it can be done in a support group. Put out every generalization you have ever heard and even partly believed to be true of Gay people. When they are all out on the table you may see why you resist being Gay. Who wants to be like that? Understand that for years these stereotypic generalizations acted as self-fulfilling prophesies for many Gay people because they thought that was how they were supposed to act, think and feel if they were Gay and knew they were Gay. People, including Gay people, have been all too willing to try to squeeze into a mold if told it was the right and proper mold.

Now that the stereotypes are out on the table, think about whether you have to fit that picture in order to honor your attraction to people of the same gender. Then construct an ideal—another set of generalizations about the super-good Gay. How close can you come to living up to that ideal? This gives you a running start at building a picture of who you are and who you might become as a Gay person. Your road to change lies comfortably somewhere between the two.

Once begun, the deprogramming and reprogramming is never done. Each day brings a fresh insight about some behavior or feeling that comes from the old program. After some practice, you look forward to such discoveries because each one offers another opportunity to change yourself in the direction of the new program, designed by you to fit your own personality, character, and needs, in the world as it is and as it changes. You might try keeping a notebook in which you record old hidden assumptions that pop up and contrast them with newly learned information and personal hopes for the future. Looking back through such a notebook after a few months can give you a lift by reminding you of how far you have come in the cause of your personal liberation.

In a recent social evening spent with Gay friends, we rediscovered a recurring phenomenon that has to do with deprogramming and reprogramming as a Gay person. We were sharing stories about ourselves, searching, laughing at ourselves as one only can afford to do with friends. One man said, "You know, the first three people I involved myself with to any extent were as unlike me as day and night. Now I find I'm more interested in people who are like me."

A Gay person often starts the love-search being attracted to people who are opposite of the self, as if seeking some sort of integration or completion. This phenomenon may have to do with anti-Gay training that taught you to de-value yourself; the irrational inner assumption would then be that the more different the other person, the less bad the other person. It may also have to do with a lifetime of training which told you that you should be attracted to the "opposite" sex. Whatever the dominant facets of programming are, they are almost certainly related to our society's obsession with seemingly polar opposites and dualities.

As the deprogramming and reprogramming proceeds, the facets of self that have been held out of awareness or invested in opposite love objects come more clearly into awareness and demand integration in your self-concept. As the integration continues you find yourself feeling stronger and more worthwhile. The strong person is not a half-person but a whole person, rounded and androgynous, able to draw on the full range of human feelings and interests, able to choose to exercise those facets of self that are most satisfying in any given situation. One learns that even "male" and "female" attributes are a figment of human imagination based on a few anatomical differences and a mania for opposites.

As the Gay person deprograms and reprograms, becomes more whole and self-respecting, he/she is apt to be increasingly attracted to people who are similar and lovable as one's newly evolved self. There are always sufficient individual differences to assist in achieving momentary distance or perspective and even this experience can be used to better understand the self and the loved one.

My friend who made the observation that the first three people with whom he had seriously involved himself were as different from him as day from night, and who recently found himself interested in men more like himself, feigned horror later in the conversation. "Where will it lead? I'll be looking for someone with my exact wardrobe!" But that is where it does not lead. It is the internal qualities of character, personality, and values that are appreciated in their whole variety. It actually facilitates overlooking differences in age, for instance, since the two loved ones can appreciate they are at different points on the same life path, both able to see yesterday and tomorrow a little more clearly.

My friend ended the evening saying, "And the ultimate joke is that there is no 'us' or 'them' now—no 'our team' versus 'your team.' I've found new parts of me to add to the old, and love the people like me with this wide range, but I don't have to be scared of the people who aren't like me. I can look at them with real interest and appreciation—one of them might even be sporting one of my personality facets of tomorrow!"

Finding Your Feelings

"I feel terribly sad and yet I have no reason to feel that way—everything is fine." When that sort of statement is made in a psychotherapist's office it is an invitation to search for the roots of the feeling of sadness. In reviewing recent events and the person's associations it is not difficult to find how and when the sadness came to be. More likely than not, there is no reason for the sadness. It cannot be justified on a rational basis such as "I feel sad because my pet bird died yesterday." Feelings are not that connected to a simple rational cause-and-effect relationship. Feelings have their own logic and exist when they are needed.

Surely the most frequent question asked by a Gay-oriented psychotherapist is "How do you feel right now?" The answer may be, "Oh, I feel okay, I guess." The next question is apt to be something like, "How would you name the emotion you are experiencing? Would you say you feel mad, glad, bad, sad, happy, erotic, surprised, secure, inspired, terrified—what?"

The client may then say, "Well, I guess I feel something like uncomfortable—maybe a little irritable." It is a beginning. The search for feelings is on.

As people grow into adults, we usually become less and less aware of our feelings. We know what we think more often than what we feel. The intellect is efficient in problem-solving, but we need the balance of our feeling side as humans if we are not to end up imitating the computers that were built to imitate us. It is our feelings that add depth, beauty and color to life, that make life flow with living. It is our feelings that can warn us away from the externally imposed ill-fitting program of our culture and guide us in building new, more personally satisfying guidelines. Feelings are of little use without intellect, and genius is of little use without feeling. So the loss of awareness of feelings is a problem for all adults.

Gay people have an additional problem imposed by the non-Gay world. We are likely to have lost awareness of our feelings to a greater extent than the average adult because our feelings were invalidated from the first day we were aware of Gay feelings. It is not just the Gay feelings that were dulled, but all feelings. It happens by way of a process of generalization, usually when we are too young and/or unsophisticated to fight it. You become aware that you have feelings of attraction for some people of the same gender. No one around you speaks well of such feelings. Hardly anyone speaks of such feelings at all. People who are portrayed in advertisements do not show such feelings, nor are there any visible live models around you expressing such feelings. If you hear anything about feelings similar to yours, it will be that they are bad. More likely you hear and see nothing relating to your earliest Gay feelings. You do not sit down and think about it, but a shift happens inside you, beyond your conscious awareness. You assume that your feelings are so unlike other people's that they must be wrong. But these innocent early Gay feelings do not disappear. Each day the emotional conviction grows that you are not like other people, you have strange/wrong feelings, and you must try to change them and be like other people. After all, you do want to be a good person like Mommy and Daddy.

Now the process of generalization begins. Once you have begun to view some of your feelings as wrong, the others become suspect. It is guilt by association. You begin to dislike your feelings. You do not trust them because they might get you into trouble. A few minor episodes in which your feelings do get you into trouble (and this happens to everyone) is all you need for proof positive. You are now severing diplomatic relations with your feelings and paying as little attention to them as possible. Feelings are necessary to life, however, and they have sufficient strength and authority to reassert themselves in consciousness now and then. Their reappearance is disturbing, but you learn to pay as little attention to them as possible, to disown them in the vain hope that they will go away. They do not go away, but live underground, beneath awareness, more and more, causing unexpected trouble when they erupt in seemingly inexplicable behavior. "I don't know what's gotten into me," you say. "I can't imagine why I did that." Had your feelings been living in the light of consciousness where they could be honored and accepted, you would have known why you did that and had far more choice about whether to do it.

So we Gay people are apt to lose sight of our feelings because we associated them with discomfort and tried to disown those that were Gay. The process of generalization spread the alienation to the rest of the family of feelings. Add to this the realization that we need access to our feelings more than the average person because we need their help in getting free of our programming and establishing new guidelines, and you can see our dilemma.

Once the Gay feelings are accepted and begin to accumulate some self-respect, the rest of the family of feelings begin to reappear. But it all happens slowly. The feelings have been in hiding for years and are apt to remain timid about appearing in the daylight of consciousness. Sometimes it is useful to speed up the process of their reappearance.

The key to the reclamation of feelings is one of the feelings that went underground almost immediately when you first discovered your Gay feelings and suspected they were wrong. This key feeling is anger, and it probably has been submerged almost every time it has reappeared since then. Some people are able to divert it and express it in other areas of living, but most of us who are Gay have been busy pushing it under for all our Gay lives. This presents an added danger, because swallowed anger is notorious for contributing to depressions as well as to various physical ailments such as ulcers, severe headaches, high blood pressure, and colitis.

The anger appeared naturally in the early days of Gay feelings because you were being told that your most natural loving feelings were wrong. You were being told that what was natural for you was bad. This phenomenon is guaranteed to frustrate, and hence generate anger. You then tried to kill this natural part of your feelings and the anger that was the predictable reaction. Since the Gay feelings were presumed wrong, the anger against the world for declaring these feelings wrong and against yourself for the mutilation of your feelings also seemed out of place or wrong, and you joined the world in denying the validity of both the Gay feelings and your anger.

A sensible program for regaining awareness and ownership of your feelings involves self-recognition of all Gay feelings and anger feelings and public recognition of at least some of the anger. The public recognition of anger acts as an announcement to the world and yourself that you are entitled to your feelings. It is a request to your feelings to come home because all is forgiven. The public anger need not be a temper tantrum or a great dramatic production of any sort. I suspect, actually, that dramatic portrayals of anger tend to generate additional unrelated anger. Only in violence-prone cultures such as our own is it assumed that anger must be expressed in a frightening manner. All that is required is a very brief, very quiet, very sure statement such as, "That makes me angry" or "I am angry." As you become aware of your anger and do not express it you will begin to be aware that you are swallowing emotional poison.

Once your anger is quietly announced you are in the clear. If anyone wants more information about the probable cause or circumstance related to your anger, and if you feel comfortable sharing that information, you may choose to do so. But your task, for the sake of reclaiming your feelings and steering clear of depression and physical ailments, is the simple announcement of anger. When to share and when not to share your other Gay-related feelings publicly is more complicated. There are risks involved if you have not fully come out as yet. Also, we live in a part of the world where one does not casually disclose any erotic thought passing through the mind. Failure to observe this social taboo can result in social ostracism or institutional incarceration.

Of course, before you can honor and express your feelings you must begin to find them. You may be so accustomed to tuning out on awareness of feelings that the initial search is difficult. One device that helps is a "feeling diary." You make an agreement with yourself to write in the diary each day for ten minutes—no more, no less. During that ten minutes, you write about any feelings you are aware of having right then and any feelings you are aware of having had since the last writing. If the key feeling of anger is especially elusive you may want to start by making it an angry book and spending the entire ten minutes each day looking for angry feelings until that feeling flows easily, and then you can branch out and make it a general feeling diary. Once a month you can review the diary with a colored magic marker and draw a line under each word denoting a feeling and rejoice in how many there are.

Another technique that can help you to locate feelings—particularly anger and other feelings that you are shy about expressing—is to learn to write an "unsent letter." It is a technique that I have used in psychotherapy but it can be used out of psychotherapy just as well. You know that you have a lot of feelings in relation to someone, but you are not sure what they are. You make a contract with yourself to write a letter that will absolutely not be sent or shown to anyone. You sit down with a typewriter or writing tablet and begin the letter with no rehearsal of what you are going to say. You continue to visualize the person to whom you are writing and remember moments throughout the duration of your relationship and just write whatever thoughts and feelings come to mind. When writing the feelings you can risk exaggerating them a little since they will never be seen by anyone but you. The reason for the exaggeration is to help you get increasingly in touch with the dormant feelings. If you did not like something the other person did, you say in the letter that you hated it. If you felt some slight stirring of erotic desire you say that you wanted to have sex, etc.

You continue to work on the letter for hours, days, or weeks until you are sure that you have nothing more to say. Then put it away for a day or two before reading it to yourself. Chances are you will now be in touch with many more of the real feelings you had in the relationship and still have for this person.

Some days after reading your unsent letter, you may wish to put it away or destroy it and write a real (to be sent) letter to the person. Knowing it will be read, you will probably tone down many of the feelings, but you will know more clearly what you are feeling and how much of it you wish to communicate. But you must never send the original not-to-be-sent letter or your nonconscious mind will record the betrayal of trust and be more guarded if you ever try to use the technique again.

Yet another technique in investigating your feelings is a game that can be played with a friend. Take turns describing as many details of your day as you can remember. As you are recounting your day, preface each statement with: "I felt. . .," "I thought. . .," or "I judged. . .." See how many times your friend can catch you in an inaccurate description of what was going on inside you. "I felt embarrassed" earns a plus in the game because it is a description of an emotion. "I felt that he was being an ass" is a minus in the game because that is a judgment rather than a feeling. "I felt that he could lend the machine because I knew he didn't need it" earns a minus because it is a thought rather than a feeling.

Before you can become familiar with your feelings you must learn to identify them, and part of the identification process is not getting them mixed up with thoughts or judgments. More often than not it is simply a matter of confusion or mislearning. I had a roommate in college who thought he was color blind until we discovered that he could see each color as a different color but had learned wrong names for some of the colors.

Gay discussion groups or Gay consciousness raising groups are other good places to try out locating and expressing feelings, provided that everyone in the group is willing to follow the same ground rules about expression of feelings. It can help you to see that someone telling you a feeling he or she is having, even a negative feeling connected with you, is sharing a part of self with you. It is an offering. If the person did not care about you, there would be little or no feeling to share and certainly not as much wish to bother sharing it.

We have learned to view some feelings as "good" and some as "bad." (That's how we got into all this trouble in the first place.) Sympathy, for instance, is usually seen as a good feeling while anger is seen as a bad feeling. In reality, there are no good and bad feelings. All are equally valid and all are needed for survival.

Sometimes there is confusion in placing a name on an emotion, even when it is experienced clearly. Remember that most emotions were experienced and learned before you were taught language. The words you learned to use as labels may be inaccurate when compared to the manner in which other people around you use those labels, and this can be confusing. Parents are notorious for teaching children to mislabel feelings such as vexation or frustration. "You're just tired, dear, why don't you take a nap." The nap often lessens the frustration or vexation, but the name of the emotion was not "tired."

Because the experienced emotions predate the availability of language with which to label them, there are other confusions also.

A participant in a weekly ongoing group recently described his mother's visit. They had spent time with an aunt and uncle and with the man's brother and the brother's fiancée. He was not yet ready to disclose his Gay identity to his mother, aunt and uncle, but his brother and the fiancée already knew. The threat of accidental disclosure hung in the air during the visit, since he had already determined not to tell any lies about himself. At one moment during a gala social evening, for instance, his mother had said, "I feel so gay!" She then quickly followed by saying, "I'd better be careful how I use that word. There seem to be a lot of Gay people in San Francisco." The brother covered a guffaw while the fiancée, with overdetermined blandness said, "They're everywhere—all around, that's for sure."

In trying to find his feelings about the visit to share with the group, he was able to identify some anger, hurt, and a feeling of being scared. But no one of these three emotions rang entirely true, even though he had already learned they need not be rational. He finally found his way to the compound feeling (which, by the way, is a common one associated with imminent disclosure of Gay identity). It can perhaps be best characterized as "a belly full of tears." He felt the tightening in his abdomen and the heat there along with a desire to cry. The tears were an expression of hurt and anger and being scared. Add a touch of loneliness and perhaps you can vicariously experience this "belly full of tears" that is a pre-verbal compound emotion inaccurately described by any single word in our language. Recognizing it as an integrated emotion, one can understand the roots of its parts in present and past and welcome it into awareness to join the family of personal, useful feelings.

As you become more adept at identifying, understanding and expressing your feelings, you find ways to unlock your grip on them and their grip on you.

Depression is a major problem for Gay people. It comes from denial of anger, denial of self-validation, and emotional fatigue. You feel decreasing self-esteem in the uphill fight against subtle everyday messages that tend to invalidate you, and turn your anger inward on yourself. It is an unfortunate downward spiral that does not permit corrective evidence from experience.

130

The first-aid treatment I recommend to clients is to decrease the use of alcohol and drugs, increase physical exercise, and try what I call the N3 Approach. You must force yourself to do things that are 1) novel, 2) nourishing, and/or 3) that express anger as a "no." It can help to make a list of things you have been wanting to do and have not done. Friends can add suggestions to your list. Then force yourself to do one of those things each day. It may be a simple novelty like wearing unusual clothing to the office, an easy nourishment like calling a friend long-distance and luxuriating in the renewed contact, or as complex as refusing to campaign politically when other people are counting on you to do so "because you always do it so well," since you know you don't want to. Very often you can do one thing that combines novelty, nourishment, and the angry "no" in one action, such as taking your telephone off the hook for the day or canceling a day's work to go to the beach or country. If you persevere in using less alcohol and drugs, increasing physical exercise, and doing the three N's each day, you give the world a chance to offer you some positive reinforcement and your own efforts bring you additional self respect. If it does not have too strong a foothold, the depression soon begins to lift. If the first aid does not work, it is time to ask for help from a professional.

Feelings do come and go. When we are not holding on to feelings they come and go with remarkable speed. Most of us have been taught to stay mad or stay happy all day. The Gay person who learns to relocate, appreciate, and stay tuned-in to feelings often is surprised at first to find that he/she is angry one moment and happy the next. The feelings are playing their counterpart to cognitive thought process (thoughts being the other half of the team that is the inner you). And your thoughts move along just as rapidly as your feelings. If you are sensitive and "listen" well to both your thoughts and your feelings, the resulting self-awareness is the vital ingredient in developing self-respect. It is a reclamation of self-awareness that leads to choice. I can choose how and when to express my thoughts and feelings in behavior (be they angry, erotic, or less exotic) only if I am aware of them; otherwise they slip out in confusion and only lead to embarrassment and disguise.

Gay Disclosure

Who should I tell and when should I tell? Letting people know you are Gay takes practice. In the beginning it is likely to be frightening or embarrassing. You are opening up in a way that seems to make you vulnerable to hurt. People you care about can laugh at you or disown you. You can lose your job, marriage, children, or even your Gay lover, who might not be able to afford the exposure and "guilt" by association. Yet the guarding of feelings and hiding of identity is emotionally draining and self-destructive. What to do? As a friend of mine once said, "I think I'll put an announcement in the paper and leave town for a month." Another friend took to wearing a button that is one of my all-time favorites. It has tiny print so the other person must come very close to read the words saying "How dare you presume I'm straight?"

In deciding who and when to tell, you must sort out reality factors from fantasized fears. If you work for a company that openly states it will not employ known Gay people, telling anyone who might possibly leak the information to your employer directly or via gossip is truly a risk to your employment.

A friend of mine who is a college professor has tenure and has attained the rank of associate professor. He has learned during the past few years that he pays too heavy an emotional price in self-respect by hiding his Gay feelings and his Gay identity, though it would be easy to hide with "lies of omission" since colleagues take his wife and two children as visible proof of heterosexual identity. He feels the need to be more open in his Gayness, but is up for promotion to full professor this year. Since he could easily be passed over without any direct reference to his Gay identity and is aware of the prejudice that abounds, he has decided to keep his Gayness a secret on campus for one more year, hoping the promotion will come through and that he then can offer himself as a visible model for Gay students. If the promotion does not come through, he will disclose his identity anyway and face the possibility that the promotion may never come. He has made a decision about how long he can afford to remain emotionally limited.

132

In the overall balance of your life it might be best to leave a job where you would be punished if openly Gay and work in a place where you are free to be yourself, but you still may decide you need a few months to save money for the change and that means not telling anyone for another few months.

On the other hand, if keeping the secret may cause you to lose self-respect, or a lover, or it is taking a serious toll in emotional discomfort or physical health, it might be better to take the risk of telling the boss now and collecting unemployment insurance while you look for more suitable employment. (Some cities and states now have legislation, by the way, that will permit you to sue if you are fired on the grounds of discrimination because of sexual orientation. But the lawsuits are long, expensive, and tedious.)

If your chosen work invariably calls for a security clearance no matter who the employer, you may choose to be openly Gay and fight it out in court (the usual excuse of being susceptible to blackmail does not make any sense for an already openly Gay person) or to retrain for a similar sort of work that can be done without a government security clearance. With most kinds of work, it is a matter of finding a non-discriminatory employer—a task that may prove difficult and time-consuming but not impossible. It does require planning for a possible long dry spell financially.

It is best to work on the assumption that you cannot hold the secret of your Gay identity forever. Each time you pretend to be non-Gay when you are Gay, you give yourself a silent, irrational message that it is wrong or bad to be the person you are. Your intellect may know better and you may have ready rationalizations handy but the primitive emotions inside you accept each act of hiding as additional proof that the Gay feelings are wrong or bad and that you are therefore a wrong or bad person. Also notice that a lie of omission, such as not correcting someone's presumption that you are non-Gay, weighs every bit as heavily within your feelings as a lie of commission, such as stating you are a heterosexual.

Accumulating this emotional evidence (that you are a bad person) over the years leads to serious trouble. It leads to self-destructive behavior. As a matter of habit, you may choose the wrong partners who will treat you badly (as you secretly believe you deserve to be treated). You may abuse your body in ways that help you to become a regular customer of the internist or the surgeon. Many serious physical problems are the result of muscle tension inside the body which was induced by wariness and lack of ease associated with distrust of self. You may misuse alcohol or drugs as a means of momentarily killing emotional pain and at the same time punishing yourself. Or you may simply drift through life, never reaching your goals because you secretly believe you do not deserve them. If you are not thoroughly proud of yourself it will show in your body and your behavior. If you feel like a bad person you will relentlessly punish yourself. Eventually you must be ready to discard the secret that causes you this trouble. You cannot afford to hide being Gay for too many years. It is too costly.

But beware, failure to prepare for disclosure experiences can be a mistake. Several years ago, in a wave of open, honest, good feeling I invited a long time, much valued friend to lunch in an Italian restaurant in Greenwich Village. We had been through the army together, had seen one another through graduate school and the early years of training as psychologists, and had leaned on one another as confidants during the first decade of marriage and child rearing. I disclosed my secret with some anxiety and held tight to my glass of Chianti while my friend reassured me that he had half guessed it long ago, he admired the courage of my choice to be honest, and that it would make no difference in our friendship. He even leaned back in his chair and mused aloud about how it had crossed his mind at times, during army days, when we were off on weekend pass together that we might try to express our feelings for one another sexually. After a walk through Washington Square and more trading of memories and mutual admiration, we parted. The air was cold and the trees without leaves but I felt warmer inside myself and more free. I have not seen or heard from him since. It took time for me to realize that I was not going to hear from him again. It took more time to realize how hurt and abandoned I feel.

But you can prepare yourself for the disclosure. It need not be so painful or frightening. It helps to sit down with yourself or a trusted Gay friend and think through who you need to tell, why you want that person to know, what you want that person to know, how you hope the person will respond, how you fear the person will respond, and what you will do and feel after either a positive or negative response from the other person.

A good example is parents. How often have you heard a Gay friend say, "I cannot tell my parents because it would break their hearts. Let them grow old and die in peace. They've had enough troubles. My father has a bad heart and it would kill him. My mother has no way of understanding it and it would only destroy the picture she has built up of me as someone she feels proud of. I could never go home again."

Why do you want them to know? There is, of course, the mystical parent-child bond. Parents know so much about you during the important years of childhood. If you knew something about yourself that they did not know during those years, you were sure to lie withholding the information because you thought it was bad. Withholding this information about being Gay now is sure to set off those childhood feelings of being bad and contribute to feeling like a bad person today. Perhaps you want them to know because you love them and have shared everything else with them, and feel guilty about holding back this important information about your identity. Perhaps you want them to know so they will stop badgering you about getting married. Perhaps you want them to know because you fear they will find out from another source and you would rather tell them first yourself. Perhaps you want them to know so they can change their will and leave the money to you instead of to your non-existent children. Perhaps you want them to know so that you can be free to be more of a Gay activist and not have to worry about the publicity. Perhaps you want them to know because you are angry at them and hope the information will hurt. All but the last reason are positive. All but the last are signals to go ahead with the disclosure, because you are trying to accomplish something that will make you feel less hampered and better about yourself as a person.

What do you want them to know? Do you want them to know the details of what you do in bed? Unlikely. People do not usually entertain parents with details of heterosexual sex, either. You might have the kind of relationship with your parents that does include such open exploration of information of interest to any of you and they may have had little experience with Gay sex and want details to satisfy their curiosity. If so, prepare yourself to deliver the information gradually. But if you do not usually have that kind of arrangement with your parents, there is no reason why you should feel pressure to respond to a request for homosexual information any more than a brother or sister would feel called upon to respond to a request for detailed heterosexual information.

Probably what you want your parents to know is that you are Gay (and how you define that), that you have been for years, that you are responsible for your *self* and intend to feel good about being Gay and it is not something they are entitled to feel guilt or responsibility for, that you want to be able to present a lover to them as someone deserving the same respect as a wife or husband, that you have Gay friends whom you respect and are proud of, whom you would like them to meet, and that you love them no less because you are Gay even though they are not. Take care to make sure that such a revelation is made when you have gotten to feel good about being Gay yourself. Parents are sensitive to hidden feelings and if you announce you are Gay with the same emotional tone you might have if telling them the doctors have just discovered you have a terminal illness, you can hardly expect them to rejoice with you.

How do you hope they will respond? You probably hope they will be pleased and honored that you have shared this difficult and important information about yourself. Perhaps you hope they will be eager to meet Gay friends and welcome them into the family home. Perhaps you hope they will be interested to learn more about what it is like to be a Gay person and will want to know what they can read or where they can go for more information. Perhaps you even hope that they will join an organization of parents of Gay people and help to fight for their own understanding and for Gay civil rights.

How do you fear that they might respond? You may fear that they will literally or figuratively throw you out of the house and family and tell you not to return until you have changed. You may fear they will cut you out of the will or ask you not to tell your brothers, sisters, aunts, uncles, and cousins, or insist you enter a mental hospital, or pray for your release from sin, or that they will simply say they do not want to know about it and to please keep such information to yourself.

What will you do and feel? Sort it through ahead of time and try to sense how it will be. If their response is positive you do not have to do much more than feel good and celebrate. (Though an initial positive response is often followed by a later shock wave of caution, question, and homophobic doubt. They have lived a long time in this society, too!) Another weight has been lifted from your back if the response is generally positive. If they respond negatively, hopefully you will find your own anger, hurt, sadness, and loneliness. These feelings were there all the time hiding behind the invisible catastrophic fantasy of how your parents might respond.

You have not lost your parents at this moment of disclosure. You lost them long before. They did not love you, they loved a two-dimensional image of you that they and you invented together. Confronted with the real you, they admitted their unavailability as parents to the person you are by nature. All of your feelings are part of mourning the loss of your parents who were lost long before you confronted them with the truth. Loss is difficult. Pretending to have parents when they were lost long ago is an energy drain that ties you down and does not permit you to move along with the flow of life. Hopefully you will admit the feelings of loss, including the anger, get on with the mourning and permit yourself to grow.

The disclosure need not be made in one grand announcement. Often the best strategy is to simply be Gay and let people draw their own conclusions or ask questions if they must. You can act as if everyone already knows. That means not making any effort in the presence of a particular person to cover your tracks, disguise your feelings and attitudes or otherwise misrepresent your true identity. During a social evening at the theater recently a woman leaned forward and whispered conspiratorily in the direction of her husband and me, "Those women up there are really something in their tight pants, aren't they?" I leaned forward with a joyous smile and whispered in response, "So are the men!" The darkness of the theater swallowed the reaction of this woman and her husband but I felt fine. I had simply been my Gay self with no tense announcements.

The timing with which you give pieces of disclosure information is especially important if the person to whom you are disclosing is likely to be threatened by the revelation. This is very likely with husbands and wives. If you let go the floodgates and deluge a spouse with everything you have always wanted to tell someone about your Gay identity, do not be surprised if that person reacts as if he or she is being drowned and thrashes about fighting to stay afloat.

If it is going to be a big surprise, let it come more slowly so that the person can begin to prepare herself or himself to hear it. Letting it be known that you enjoyed a book or a film with a Gay love theme is one good beginning. Letting it be known that you notice the attractiveness of some people of the same gender at the beach or on television is another step. (Note that these are general attractions rather than the person next door who might set off the alarm system in your spouse.) Talking about deep and real feelings of affection for same gender friends of the past and the frustration of never having fully revealed those feelings can be another large step. By now your spouse is alerted that you are not conforming to cultural code and is alerted to the possibility that you are an individual who is different. Your spouse may also begin to appreciate your willingness to share intimate feelings. If you continue to be open in confiding these day-to-day feelings, your spouse is likely to become more direct in asking questions and you can be truthful in answering them. The rule of thumb is to answer only the question asked and not give more information than requested. If a husband asks, "Do you mean that you feel as if you want to be sexual with another woman sometimes?" the truthful answer probably is, "It depends upon the woman, but I do feel that way sometimes." He can take that information and digest it more easily than if you respond to his question with, "Yes, I am a lesbian and have been for years and I'm glad it's out in the open. Not only did I feel that way about the heroine in the movie, but I also feel that way about Gladys and I can't bear to hide it any longer!"

The slow disclosure with someone like a spouse who might be threatened does require effort. It would perhaps be eas-

138

ier to spill it all at once. The slow disclosure is an act of love. You know your spouse has been trained to react to confrontation with wounded pride and passionate, even savage, hostility at you and the "invisible enemy" in an attempt to "save the marriage." The training is so thorough that it seems like second nature. The act of love is to present the information slowly as a sharing of yourself and your secret feelings rather than a sudden confrontation that can easily be experienced as an attack.

Your spouse may react totally negatively no matter how slowly the revelation is made, but you will know that you did all that you could to make a less negative reaction possible. The usual course of events is for the spouse to respond with rhythmic waves of anger and increased intimacy. The disclosure promotes more intimate sharing but presents the dilemma of making the spouse feel that he or she may not be able to trust or rely on you as much as before to care and receive such intimacy. And so the waves of anger, closeness, anger, closeness. Riding those waves will often bring the couple safely to shore with an expanded relationship and ability to communicate. If the rhythm becomes a habit, however, it may be time to seek help from a Gay-oriented counselor.

A rule of thumb for selecting the people you need to tell is whether you are spending emotional energy in not telling that person. If you find you spend time in fantasy repeatedly telling a particular person and/or that you go to some effort to cover your tracks in order to not have the person discover you are Gay, the secret is costing you too much emotional energy with that person. You must, for your own survival, tell him or her sooner or later.

A Gay woman friend of mine has been living with another woman as lovers for six years. They have one bed and have not hidden this from visiting friends and family. They vacation together and each took a turn working to pay tuition while the other completed schooling.

My friend realized she was putting energy into not telling her parents, however, wondering what their reaction would be, even though she knew she had clearly presented them with plenty of evidence of a lesbian relationship over the years. She prepared herself for the disclosure and made it gently over the breakfast table while she and her lover were visiting the parents on the first leg of a two-week vacation. ("I think by now you know Jean and I are a couple and not just roommates.") The parents had guessed, but hoped not to be confronted with the fact. The mother cried and the father was quiet. They tried to induce shame, guilt, and worries about the future ("What will you do when she leaves you?"). They tried to drive a wedge ("You are welcome at home any time without her!"). My friend and her lover tried to show that they were the same lovable people they had been five minutes before the disclosure but the parents were too distraught. Because she had prepared, my friend was able to tell her parents that she hoped time would help them overcome their fright and that she would not ever again present herself to them as anyone less than the Gay woman she is. She dropped them a letter a few weeks later sharing her anger, hurt, and understanding and offered to start anew with them at any time if they would offer her the same respect she offered them. The loss is out in the open now and she feels better than when she was loved as a fantasy person.

It is difficult to lose a parent early in life whether because of death or alienation. But sooner or later each of us must take over the job of our own parenting, realizing there is still a little girl or a little boy inside us whom the adult part of us must take by the hand and help. You can be a loving parent to yourself.

But sometimes the disclosure story has a happier ending, as with the client who told his beloved old aunt. Her response:

"You, too? No wonder you've always been my favorite. Now we have something else in common!"

A last word about disclosure. It is best to disclose your identity to someone close and then have years to explore one another in the light of this information so that an increasingly loving relationship can be built. But there are times when this is not possible. Unexpected accidents and disease may suddenly threaten the life of someone important to you whom you had been preparing to tell. People are sometimes reluctant to tell an important person who is seriously ill or near death. It is your last chance. If you wait too long you may find yourself talking to the dead person for years, trying irrationally to get the emotional bond completed over the impossible abyss. Even if the person is in a coma, you can lean close and talk softly near the ear. Some-

140

where inside, the exquisite human mind that records everything is hearing you.

Why trouble the dying person with it? It is a gift, a sharing, an offering of yourself. You are demonstrating that you care enough for this person to invest something of yourself right up to the last moment. And if you were the dying person, would you want to leave someone you love sensing a secret had been left, wanting to be said, but hiding? Or would you rather hear it?

The person near death may have sufficient perspective on the human drama or be busy enough with his or her own death and not bother to offer much response. But you will know you did not withhold. If the dying person should have a negative response, you will know that you did what you could to permit the bond between you to be strengthened and that it was the other person's choice, even at the time near death, to withhold love.

Gay, Straight, or Bi?

A friend of hearty intellect and insightful humor had one of those experiences in which he was speaking with sufficient volume to be heard by the person next to him above the din of surrounding party noise when the noise level dropped without warning, permitting his last few words to carry clearly to all ears in the room. "I was saying 'sometimes I love a man and sometimes a woman.' Those last words had carried clear and all eyes turned in my direction for just a moment. Then I thought, 'Oh, what the hell,' so I spoke up a little louder and said, 'I seem to be caught on the closet door. Is this what they mean by swinging?' It was amazing how much elbow room I had at that crowded party for the rest of the evening. I could eat canapés *and* sip my drink from the other hand and no one jostled me once. Do you suppose that's how Queen Elizabeth feels at a party?"

Labels that are descriptive and help you to think of yourself as someone with wider horizons or more competence can be helpful. But most labels are limiting. So think twice before hanging a sign around your neck and be prepared to define any label you do assign yourself in ways that will facilitate your own growth.

In our part of the world, people who insist on retaining awareness of their attraction to people of the same gender are labeled homosexuals. The word homosexual is more accurately used as an adjective than a noun. It can be used to described a sex act or a feeling, but it should not be used as a representation of a person. By referring to us as homosexuals, our society is able to create social distance and lessen anxiety for the non-Gays who do not honor feelings of attraction for people of the same gender. If we are placed "over there" in a category with a label that has anxiety-provoking, hence, unattractive connotations, non-Gays can feel more safe and secure in not wearing such a label, therefore logically not belonging to the same category. But the label must be used regularly to keep us "over there," lest we get socially close and stir the conformist's anxiety.

The entire population has ignored the data painstakingly presented in the Kinsey* studies almost thirty years ago. The data clearly supported the observation that humans are like the rest of nature. Human attributes are not a matter of categories but of continua. Categories are manufactured by people. The data clearly demonstrated that it was not possible to separate homosexuals from heterosexuals. While some people are able to restrict their sexual behavior to only homosexuality or only heterosexuality throughout their lifetime, many (perhaps most) change the balance of their interest from time to time during life—at one point being mostly interested in heterosexuality, at another perhaps most interested in homosexuality, at other times being quite interested in both or neither. When these uncomfortable data were first published, people made charges of sloppy research and manipulation of statistics. When the careful scientific workmanship was ably defended, the data were subsequently overlooked and have largely sunk into oblivion. People (even social scientists) have ways of avoiding that which makes them uncomfortable.

But to return to the concept of labels and categories, homosexual is a label that was applied to Gay people as a device for separating us from the rest of the population. Since most of us are invisible, it provides enough social distance and mystery to

---

*Kinsey, A.C., Pomeroy, W.B., and Martin, C.C. *Sexual Behavior in the Human Male*. Philadelphia, Saunders, 1948.

facilitate the growth of negative myths about us. We Gay people have been taught the myths ourselves and now have trouble ridding ourselves of them.

Just last week an intelligent and well-educated man sat in my office and said, "I hardly know what's happening to me. I've been in psychotherapy six months and I am aware that I feel good about being Gay for the first time in my life. That I was prepared for! But I'm beginning to turn on to women, not just one or two special ones, I'm even looking at them on the street! Me cruising women on the street—that I was not prepared for!" It is not unusual that when you begin to appreciate and welcome your sexual feelings, more of them float to the surface.

But the myth is that one does not step out of the sexual category easily. Since the end of the nineteenth century, mental health professionals have lured us with the "promise of cure." With our effort and their help we were told there was some hope that we could change from the homosexual category to the heterosexual category. Repeatedly the professionals were confronted with evidence of people moving back and forth from one category to another. A heterosexual who indulged in a period of homosexuality was said to have experienced a short period of emotional disturbance, dissociation or regression. A homosexual who indulged in a period of heterosexuality was experiencing spontaneous remission, miraculous recovery, or may have been misplaced in the wrong category in the first place.

Religious leaders also offered redemption if the sin of being a homosexual was confessed with true remorse and the sinner prayed and worked for the miracle of salvation by becoming a heterosexual. Heterosexuals who temporarily became homosexuals had yielded to the devil, while homosexuals who temporarily became heterosexuals were nearly saved before backsliding.

In the past couple of decades people in Western society have been more and more open about moving from one category to another (in some other parts of the world, good citizens have been seen doing it for centuries). Our faithful keepers of the categories, rather than consider decategorization, however, created a third category called bisexual. If the homosexual is a freak the bisexual is a super-freak. He or she is said by mental health professionals to have "confused sexual identity," which means behaviorally that the person will not stay still in one of the two categories. What it means in mental health jargon is that the person has not developed normally—has not grown up to a heterosexual or a homosexual but is emotionally somewhere back in very early childhood, sitting on the fence, unable to make the choice that permits maturation or to admit to the alternate preference. Even with today's official enlightened view by the American Psychiatric Association and the American Psychological Association, declaring homosexuals to be not emotionally disturbed, per se, there is professional concern about the person of "confused sexual identity." Most religions are a decade behind the mental health organizations and consider anything less than 100 per cent heterosexuality to be unacceptable. But at least the homosexual can be pitied. The bisexual is willfully unrepentant, sinful and disobedient. The non-conformist is unpopular in our society.

Periodically there is a popularization of bisexuality. The media turn on the spotlights and see the people moving between the two categories and declare it a fad. Then they turn out the lights and report, with relief, that the fad is fading.

So there are three manufactured categorical labels that attempt to describe human sexuality (though it continues to defy categorization). Unfortunately, it is not simply a harmless amusement. It is a destructive process. People are taught, and believe, that they should choose one of the two original categories and remain in it, or be classified in the third and consider themselves emotionally unstable. For those of us who have remained aware of our attraction to people of the same gender there is pressure to call yourself a homosexual (with all the stigma attached to that label) and believe that you are not capable of any satisfying emotional and sexual involvement with a person of other gender. It defines you as deficient, unable to do something. If you are aware of heterosexual attraction you are cruelly teased with the "hope" that you may make it and be honored as a heterosexual if only you can and will forsake the forbidden homosexual interest.

Gay is a descriptive label we have assigned to ourselves as a way of reminding ourselves and others that awareness of our sexuality facilitates a capability rather than creating a restriction. It means that we are capable of fully loving a person of same gender by involving ourselves emotionally, sexually, spiritually and intellectually. It may even imply a frequent or nearly constant preference or attraction for people of the same gender, meaning I (as a Gay man) might notice more men than women on the street or might notice the men before the women. But the label does not limit us. We who are Gay can still love someone of other gender. Homosexual and heterosexual when used as nouns are naive and destructive nonsense in the form of labels that limit.

Our society has developed a complex-menu sort of defense in coping with the foolishly anxiety-provoking phenomenon of human sexuality. We are taught that we must choose from column A or column B. The truth, as any connoisseur of fine restaurants will tell you, is that the adventurous and selective diner orders á la carte and dines to his or her own personal satisfaction.

You would do well not to permit other people to assign you to a category. It is you who must decide when to drink red wine and when white. It is you who must decide the relative strength of each speaker in your stereo system. It is you who must pick your descriptive label, if any, and who must decide which individuals you will love.

Reclaiming Your Body

Three people appeared in my office within a ten-day period. Different as they seemed, they had something in common in addition to being Gay. The first was a man in his late thirties who was a successful business executive. His company had transferred him to San Francisco after a lifetime in a small city in the Midwest. "I cannot believe this city," he said. "Not only is it more beautiful than I imagined but there are so many fantastic Gay people! It takes me a half an hour to walk a block in this city."

His joy about his transfer was not what brought him to see me, however, he told me. "This cast on my arm is the result of tripping over my own foot at home while stone cold sober when the phone rang and I jumped to answer it. And a week before that, I slipped and fell face first getting off a cable car.

And the day before that I shut my thumb in the car door. I had a couple of years of therapy in college and learned enough to know that so many accidents means something is wrong and that's why I'm here."

The second person was an attractive, charming, intelligent woman of forty who was costumed in offbeat "hip" clothing and jewelry. She was a children's book writer and artist who had gained thirty-four pounds in less than three months and had been sent by her physician to investigate psychotherapy. "My doctor says it's from eating, and no diet seems to work. If it's psychological, I can't understand it. I have never been more happy. After a lifetime as a lonely loner I met another woman earlier this year and she is everything I ever wanted in a lifetime companion. We call each other three times a day and I'm even going out to parties for the first time since college."

The third person was a twenty-one-year-old lineman for the telephone company. He looked as if he could pose for ads for toothpaste, shampoo, underarm deodorant or most anything else with his sparkling white smile, shiny blonde hair, clear healthy skin, and bulging muscles covered by a tight, shortsleeve pullover. He had been born and raised in Utah in a very sedate and religious family. He had been having some trouble at work but he knew that was due to late nights and too many pick-ups before his early rising for work in the morning. That problem he intended to fix soon with self-discipline on weekday nights. His problem was chronic tension in the abdominal area. I asked him to lie down and put his hand on the tense spot as I guided him into a fantasy exploration of the tension. Soon he was in tears, pulling up the shirt and clutching at the rippled, hard muscle of his abdomen saying, "It's me in there and I'm crying because I can't get out!"

What these three people had in common was that they were being suddenly bombarded by their own "unacceptable" body-associated erotic impulses. All three were expressing their apparent need to disrespect and disown their bodies, forgetting the simple axiom "You are your body."

Some years ago you sensed that the unorthodox feelings that had been causing you trouble by making you feel different from other people had something to do with your body and the bodies of other people of the same gender to whom you were attracted. Our society is already constructed in such a way as to make us suspicious of anything having to do with self or others from the neck down. We grew up distrusting our body impulses and thinking of some parts of the body as downright unclean (and therefore bad). So, added to the already established alienation from body, the troublesome Gay feelings seemed to you to have to do with the body and increased the need to disown your body.

Disowning your body can be accomplished in many ways. You can simply tune out and ignore it as a vague nuisance used to transport mind and spirit. You can take revenge on it for causing you trouble by causing it to have repeated accidents and illnesses, or simply by overfeeding or underfeeding it. Or you can decide to reconstruct and redecorate it to obscure and hide it in a plastic facade that looks just like the people in the advertisements. Whichever the path chosen, your body is rejected and disowned. It becomes it and not me. That is one way to get rid of the responsibility for those unacceptable body feelings.

Gay people who are rediscovering the richness of their Gay identity and feelings are also discovering the accompanying need to reclaim their bodies. The first impulse is to make themselves look more attractive. (This is a much less heroic effort than the effort required to reject the natural body by hiding it in a perfect plastic model's body as the telephone lineman did.) These attempts to look more attractive often involve visits—rather than residence—at the gym or spa, possibly a sunlamp, curling or uncurling the hair, and some shopping for new clothing, jewelry or cosmetics. These seemingly unnatural first steps at reclamation can be helpful (if they do not become an end in themselves) because they permit perspective, a chance to look at your body differently. It actually can help you to begin to see the natural body beneath the new hair style and jewelry.

Then it is time to get down to the business of reclamation. Basically you must learn to listen to your body and treat it with loving care, respect and appreciation. You must learn to listen well enough to eat only as much of each food as your body really wants no matter how well your memory had recorded the message that you always like to eat a lot of a certain food. Begin to experiment with eating new foods. See what tastes good, and do not assume that your body will always find a food attractive just because it tasted good once. Experiment with eating at different times rather than set mealtimes and snack times. All of the experimentation is meant to defeat old habits and programs and permit you to listen to your body's food needs day by day. You may turn out to be slim or plump, but it is unlikely that your body will choose to be seriously overweight or underweight.

Next comes exercise. Begin to pay attention to how and when and how much your body wants to move at different times. Some days it will need more rest and some days it will feel good to have more exercise. Sometimes strenuous effort will feel good and sometimes gentle movement. Your body is not a machine to be run a certain amount each day. It is your temple, the essence of your being, and will be ever-changing in its needs as the hours, days, years go by. For fun, try putting on different kinds of music when you are alone and pay attention to how your body wants to move. Never mind the style of dance, no one is watching. Enjoy, and learn to continue to enjoy, knowing when movement feels good to your body.

Next comes the unthinkable. Make friends with your body. Take your clothes off and examine yourself carefully. Use small mirrors to help. Make sure you look at and explore each millimeter of your body by touch. This can and should include the easy exploration of body openings such as mouth, nostrils, ears, vagina, and anus. Do not do anything that causes pain. Examine slowly, carefully, and lovingly—looking and touching. You are getting to know yourself and making friends with yourself. If you find that you do not know about a part of your body or how it works, consult some books, ask friends, or see a sympathetic and competent medical doctor or anatomy teacher. It is your body. It is you. And you are learning to know and claim yourself.

Because of years of training in body alienation you will probably need to give yourself some special help in appreciating your body. You will need to repeat the looking and touching exploration many times before you stop finding some part of your body distasteful, unattractive or repulsive. You will need much practice to get over the shame training that taught you to cover or hide your body modestly. Modesty is usually a false cover word for shame.

Another way to make friends with your body is to buy some massage lotion (hand lotion or cooking oil will do) and learn to give yourself a loving massage. This is not the kind of massage they give athletes after the game—that is more like the kind given a horse after the race. A loving massage is done simply by applying oil by hand to every part of the body and stroking with care as you rub it in. Any kind of stroke that feels good is the right one to use. Take care not to omit any part of your body or it will feel neglected and unworthy. Yes, that means the genital area gets its share of stroking. Parents too often neglect this part of baby's anatomy and give the message that that part of you is untouchable and unloveable. If you become sexually aroused and wish to masturbate during your massage, that is fine as long as it is done with the same gentle loving respect given the whole body and the massage is completed after the masturbation.

When you have begun to feel comfortable with your own body as it naturally is, you can help the appreciation of your own body by being appreciative of the natural bodies of friends. Instead of complimenting them on artificial alterations of natural body (clothes, hairdo, muscle-building, or fasting), try appreciating how they look naturally and how they feel. Try reaching out to touch your friends more often. It is a primitive message that you appreciate the beauty of the body-person.

You can try giving a friend a head-rub, a foot-rub, a back-rub or a whole-body massage. You need not be trained in massage techniques. The same thing that feels good to your body probably feels good to your friend. If you give a full body massage, do not neglect any part of the body, including genitals. You want all parts to feel equally valued. If the person becomes sexually aroused during the massage, that is the body's simple way of announcing it is turning on or opening to the affection you offer. You need only give respectful recognition to the signs of arousal by making sure the erect penis or nipple is touched. Should you and your friend decide to engage in a friendly sexual exchange, make sure it is done in the same style of caring, affection and appreciation and that you take care to finish the massage after the sexual exchange. If we touched our human friends as freely as we touch our pets and as often as we polish our cars, there would be many happier people in our world.

In reclaiming your body (and therefore the you that is your body), remember that if you find yourself trying to force it to look like some image you have learned to call handsome or pretty, you are not honoring your natural body. Your hair can be styled, but the style of your hair can reflect its natural state. Your face can be shaved or lotioned but honor the lines or wrinkles as proud badges denoting the accumulation of depth and wisdom that can come only with having had experiences. No body has the muscle tone at sixty it had at forty. Some abdomens will be more round than others. Look to having a beautiful healthy body that radiates your loving care and self respect. Rest assured, that will be attractive to others. Plastic people that look as if they stepped out of magazine ads may be pleasing to look at because of our programming. They are seldom pleasing to be with because they do too much violence to their bodies in order to look that way. They respect their image, but not themselves. People are easily tempted to use them for visual and tactile pleasure and then want to be rid of them like an appliance that answers a temporary need.

Reclaiming body and body feelings is a growthful experience for anyone. For Gay people, it is a must. Gay feelings are connected with bodies and we need to learn the truth that these feelings are naturally beautiful just as our bodies are naturally beautiful.

A Support System

Some years ago, when I was first starting to experiment with Gay groups, a strange event occurred. We were a group of ten Gay men of varying backgrounds, physical types, and ages, gathered in a studio in New York City. We had experimented with sitting together in silence for half an hour. When the time had just about run out, a quiet businessman in his mid-thirties burst into tears. In another moment he was laughing hard, then back to tears, then back to laughter. I had been working with groups for many years already but there was something different in his release of feeling. It was as if a finely tamed horse had broken loose and begun to run free, a sight at once frightening and exhilarating. Several members of the group sat transfixed, some smiled nervously, and others looked worried.

I asked if he could use some words to describe what he was feeling. He wiped his nose and eyes with the sleeve of his sweater, uncaring, and did not bother to open his eyes as he spoke. "It just struck me how alone I've been all my life. I always wanted to have a gang. There were always other gangs I was running away from or gangs I secretly wanted to join but I knew they wouldn't let me. And now in this room I've got one. I found a gang. I'm not lonely any more. I never knew how much I needed my own gang to make me feel safe and wanted. This may not be my gang for life but I see I can get one. Several others now joined in his fitful laughter and tears, an old want and need breaking loose in each of them.

The scene was to be repeated many times before I began to hear the message clearly. We Gay people spent the early years of our lives more alone than most people. We have no reference group, no Gay family to look to for guidance, reassurance, love, and support. Facing a world that says "Vanish," "Die," we need our gang to say "You're fine," "Live!" We need feedback that we can trust from our own Gay family.

When attempting to break free of the non-Gay programming which has conditioned you since birth, you are apt to experience guilt and anxiety so strong that your progress will be slowed or stopped. A personal Gay support system can reduce the guilt and anxiety to manageable levels. As a Gay person, you are trying to grow and develop in an anti-Gay environment. Non-Gay people have their own troubles growing through the years, but there is plenty of support from the community and an available supply of models who have traveled the growth path in individually satisfying styles. The non-Gay can select bits and pieces from many models of growth and fashion a growth journey that seems to suit his or her individual needs. The Gay person can find models in a self-created support system, though not as many, compared to his or her non-Gay counterpart. The Gay person is still a pioneer, cutting a new trail, but it is less frightening if you have the comfort of a few models and trusted friends.

A Gay discussion group or Gay support group can serve as a temporary support system, but the membership of such groups tends to be transient and the members have not been picked by you, so it is best to think of beginning your own permanent support system. You can begin by simply listing all the Gay people you know. If you know only one or two Gay people, ask that each introduce you to one or two additional Gay people and then ask that they each introduce you to one or two more Gay people until you have a pool on which to draw. Having made a listing of the Gay people you know, underline the name of each person on the list whom you like and respect. Draw a second line under the name of any person on the list whom you admire. Anyone whose name is underlined should be considered a candidate for your support system. Anyone with two lines should be a great asset if he or she wants to be in your "gang."

If you have more than five or six candidates for your support system, try selecting the ones you feel most strongly about. Ask yourself who are the ones you would be glad to help even if it seems unlikely the person would ever ask for or need much help. Think of which ones are good listeners and which ones might offer good advice. Make sure the final half-dozen candidates are people who have shown themselves capable of caring and helping and that they have given indication of caring about you as an individual.

When you have six or fewer candidates (even one or two is a good beginning), talk to them about the idea. It need not be a heavy discussion. You can tell why you like and respect the person and how it would be helpful to check things out now and again with such a trusted person. It is a sort of adopted family. Tell the person all the reasons you know for wanting her or him in your support system and explore whatever limitations of time, energy and interest they have in being available to you for support. One person may be available for a letter now and then while another would gladly offer warm arms and a soft shoulder any time.

You need people whom you like, respect and admire, who are glad to be available to you for a phone call, a chat or for physical holding when you are feeling unsure and alone. As you grow, non-Gays who are unfamiliar with the path you are following may tell you that you are wrong or bad. Sometimes it is implied so subtly you wonder why you feel anxious. These may be family or friends who love you but who simply do not under-stand the experience of being Gay in a non-Gay world, trying to free yourself of destructive programming. It is at these unsure times that you need to check in with your personal Gay support system and ask their opinion.

And there will be other times when you feel uneasy or depressed, when it feels good to be held in the arms of someone who understands or cry on the shoulder of someone who has shed similar tears. It is no disgrace to weep or rest or seek com-fort. Fortunately, few Gays have bought the "strength through independence and insensitivity" image promoted in Western and detective films, but in the past all too few of us have known where to seek understanding and comfort.

As you look over feelings and decisions, yours and theirs, from present and past, you will begin to see how to use these people in your support system as models. You may make deci-sions or behave in ways similar to what they tell you they have done in the past, because it makes sense for you. Or you may see clearly a mistake one of them made, and save yourself the same mistake. It still takes a lot of thinking and sorting on your part but it is easier to make a cake from six different recipes than with no recipe at all.

Once every few months or at least once a year (New Year's or your birthday are good times for review), you can go through your support system in your mind and see how helpful each person has been to you. You may decide to make less fre-quent use of one or two people. And you may decide to add one or two people whom you have thought of as possible candidates during past months or years. It is a conscious recognition of the shifting relative importance of the important people in your life.

As the months and years go by, your support system will grow larger and larger, though at any given time, you will make most active use of only a few. If you find that you are not asking for support at all, something is wrong. No one becomes so strong or so sure that he or she does not need at least a sounding board or a reassuring hug. And if you go a year without shedding tears, you are holding back on awareness of feelings. The more you are willing to be honest in your need for support, the more these other people can be honest in their need also. Remember that you are much more certain to survive and grow with a little help from your friends.

Youth, Beauty, and Aging

Thanks to the work of anthropologists and historians we know there is no standard of beauty that holds true in all parts of the world, nor is there one for any given part of the world that would hold true through recorded history. The most constant, perhaps, is a kind of radiance that seems to come from within and communicates to other people (sometimes it is called charisma) that is noted as a variety of beauty in all cultures and times. But shape of various parts of anatomy, height, weight and body proportion are seen as beautiful, passable, boring or ugly, according to the styles and taste of the time and place. The same holds true for age. Though youth is more often seen as pretty to look at and touch, age is often seen as accumulated beauty, and the balance of values assigned the two at any given time and place will determine the local opinion of attractiveness. Today's centerfold woman or man would look peculiar and unappetizing to a cave-dweller of yore or to the tribesman of today who has not been indoctrinated with our culture.

Gay people, particularly Gay men, are caught in a tragedy. We have been programmed to be attracted to a limited variety of body types and to place the standard of body beauty above all others in importance. By following the programming, we hurt other Gay people and, ultimately, ourselves.

Consider the male programming. We are taught to look for pretty girls, pursue them, seduce them with charm or deception, and then display the conquest as a trophy that testifies to our own manly worth. Pretty is defined according to the current styles in bodies used in films and advertising. We are taught to be wary of marrying and settling down with such creatures, however. The plain, good-hearted, loving, practical girl who will slavishly care for our personal needs, home and children is the person to marry. But one need not pursue her. If you are manly enough (as proven by a history of manly exploitation), she will shyly stand nearby admiring. We need merely give the nod and she will fall into our arms, ready for wifely bliss. And the marriage will take care of itself according to the programming, while we continue to scan the horizon for new pretties. Being fearless hunters we must never give up the opportunity to pursue a pretty girl because her conquest will add to our manly worth, another feather in our war bonnet, a reassurance. This program destroys many heterosexual relationships.

For Gay men this program has had its effect also. For Gay men the gender of attraction has been changed but we have been taught the lesson of manly sexuality and its associated self-worth daily since birth. So we are apt to repeatedly pursue any male who looks as if he has stepped out of an advertisement, because we have been taught to respond with desire to such a symbol of sexual attractiveness. He, of course, being trained by the same program, is looking for a male even more beautiful whom he can conquer as a trophy. If, through charm, deceit, aggression, or persuasion we should be so lucky as to seduce someone of superior beauty, we will be happy to show him off to admiring friends and keep the seduction going as long as possible. But we have not been trained to value him as a human being or taught to look for a basis of relationship with such a person, much less have we learned any way to build such a relationship. The "right," less beautiful partner hopefully will appear later.

Later is apt to come much later for the Gay male because the other Gay males have received the same incompatible male programming. It is the women who were programmed to settle down and build the nest. The other Gay males are mostly off competing in the pursuit of male trophy beauties. So the pursuit goes on, each year making us look less and less like the pretty man in the advertising so that we are able to collect fewer and fewer trophies and are pursued less and less often by others. But we try. Small wonder that anti-Gays are able to point to sexual promiscuity among Gay males and pontificate about the shallowness of relationships. We are males competing against males for males. Superficial beauty is the prize we have been taught to pursue (like our non-Gay male brothers). Having been trained as men to value sexual activity, when there are men pursuing men, there is bound to be a great deal of sexual activity. We are following the dictates of our culture's male programming.

Not only is the program ultimately lonely and unsatisfying, we have battered and abandoned fellow Gays strewn in our wake on the battlefield. And each of us feels less good about himself for having done the destructive competing. Each of us feels less good about himself for having been battered by others. Once again it becomes clear that it is urgent to undo the programming and begin to relate to one another as three dimensional humans rather than as sexual objects who may be useful for a short period of time. We must learn to enhance one another rather than destroy one another. The pursuit game has few trophy winners. And ultimately, as the advertisement beauty and charm fades, everyone loses.

For Gay women the program script is different, but equally unsatisfactory. According to the woman program Gay women (like their non-Gay sisters) have been trained to be covertly competitive or alluring. This means, of course, that it is necessary to look as much like the beautiful woman in the advertisements as possible.

Since they are trained to be the desired and pursued (rather than the overt hunter), the accomplishment of this image is imperative (which accounts for the multi-million-dollar beauty industry originally aimed solely at women and now extended to men, and for the phenomenon of fifty-year old women suffering hours of discomfort in a beauty salon in brave attempts to look twenty-nine years old.) The program calls for a two-part lifetime, first as the irresistible temptress and later as faithful keeper of the home. In addition, the programming teaches women to look not for physical beauty primarily in a mate (though that is nice if you can have it also) but to look for reliability, strength, aggression, and other traits that indicate someone who will offer security.

Consequently many Gay women spend a lot of lonely hours being attractive and waiting to be discovered or standing by looking faithful and wholesome. Others spend lonely hours in pursuit, feigning the image of the dashing, aggressive, carefree playboy experiencing the sexual conquests and ultimate loneliness of Don Juan. When two Gay women find one another, there has been a tendency to put a death grip on the relationship that does not permit sufficient individual growth. This is the result of the woman programming of the past. With women today discovering the futility of past role training the picture is changing and providing more flexibility in the lover relationships of thoughtful Gay women. The programmed role training has not been notoriously successful in keeping men and women together in heterosexual marriages, and it is even less successful in keeping two women or two men together.

Many Gay couples are trying hard to find new styles of relating that permit more individual freedom for both partners and do not draw on the role teaching of the past. The incentive is strong. We are beginning to see that there must be a tailor-made relationship that combines individual freedom with commitment and responsibility, that permits shifting shares of assertiveness, patience, protectiveness and vulnerability for each partner. The incentive is strong because Gay couples cannot rely on church, state or family to keep their union together in tough times. As old-fashioned heterosexual marriages fail to give lasting satisfaction with increasing frequency, Gay people can help to lead non-Gays in the search for satisfactory life style.

The programming for mate seeking is heavily reinforced sexually. And the orgasm is a mighty reinforcement. Gays who seek individually satisfying roles instead of following traditional and troublesome male and female mate-seeking roles must invest their energy in avoiding orgasmic reinforcement in situations that tend to follow the traditional script. That means that two men or two women who meet and are attracted to one another would do well to get to know one another in a series of dates before hopping into bed and reinforcing the instant physical attraction with an orgasm, for instance. One's support system can be very helpful in offering congratulations and reassurance for anxiety provoking risks taken in seeking new modes of relating with a wider variety of people too. Ultimately each of us must find a personally satisfying mode of getting together with personally satisfying individuals.

Much of the traditional training for males depended upon visual cues. This is becoming increasingly true for women, as cosmetics and clothing industries have learned how lucrative it can be to have both women and men primping to compete for the few available award-winning "pretties" in the world. A first step

157

in fighting to get free of the programming is to fight the visual cues. You can try asking yourself if you would respond as positively or negatively to a new person you met if he or she looked different. You can train yourself to have visual fantasies of sex and other pleasures with people you like but whom you would not ordinarily find attractive.

A game you can use to break your training is to sit from the very beginning of a TV show with eyes closed until more than halfway through the program. Imagine what the people look like and which ones you find attractive. Since the producers cast the heroes and heroines as pretty people, you will not be in for too many surprises. But once in a while you will find a character very attractive and then open your eyes halfway through the program to find he or she does not look at all attractive to you. When that happens, watch the person through the rest of the program and concentrate on your original feelings of attraction.

Another game that can be played on buses, trains, and in waiting rooms is to locate visually all the people who are unattractive to you and then make up fantasies about what personal qualities might make them so compelling that you'd find yourself quite attracted.

And last, but not least, put lots of effort into touching, holding, and generally making pleasurable body contact with people whom you like a lot but whom you have not found visually attractive in the past.

As I mentioned earlier, you can retrain behavior patterns that are based on what you see. If you meet someone who looks attractive and are tempted by training to get to bed together as swiftly as possible, you can make a decision to behave differently. Arrange a future date for lunch, then another date for a movie, then a dinner date to discuss mutual likes and dislikes, and perhaps even a drop-in visit at work. If all is still well and the other person still stirs sexual desire, it is less likely that you are being motivated by what you can see and less likely, therefore, that you are chancing orgasmic reinforcement of a traditional role pattern.

If the attraction wears thin before bed, it was truly only skin deep and would not have made either of you feel better about yourselves to have had sex. If the attraction stays and grows, with the addition of information about the person, there may be a basis for a relationship.

158

If you are accustomed to giving little attention to friendly but unattractive people who try to pick you up, try engaging each person in conversation for at least a few minutes, giving yourself an opportunity to know about the person, rather than discarding a possibly rewarding lifetime friendship because of the shape of someone's face.

And appreciating the aging process is most important of all. Each of us is growing older. The programming has taught us to worship youth. That means that, with luck, you will be experienced by yourself and others as most worthwhile and desirable for a fifth of your lifetime. What a sad waste! If you have lived your life with care you should gain in wisdom, depth, and even sexual know-how as the years accumulate. You bring much more than your body to any human intercourse (and that includes sexual intercourse.) To permit yourself to be discarded or devalued or to treat other people this way because they are halfway through their lifetimes is as sensible as throwing away the candy and eating the wrapper.

If you are able to fantasize a breathtakingly attractive (not just visually or bodily) lover who is ten, twenty or even thirty years older than you, you are headed toward a secure future because you can imagine yourself being valued ten, twenty or thirty years from now. If you can imagine only younger people as attractive, you are giving yourself a daily message that you are worthless. With the rest of your life ahead of you, this is a facet of your programming you would do well to work on changing. The quality of the rest of your life depends on it.

Youth does have its beauty. The bud is so lovely because of the promise of the unspoiled flower. And youth deserves respect and admiration for its potential. Just as age should be held responsible for the accumulation of wisdom and beauty, youth can be held responsible for its newness and promise.

A much younger person who seems relatively jaded, opinionated, and set in his or her ways has little to offer you except a youthful body, which means a reinforcement of the old program that worships youthful bodies. What the growth-oriented younger person often has to offer that is unique is a fresh perspective, new questions and new ideas. It is the young people who have furnished the fuel for the current emancipation of Gay people. Some of the elders of the tribe used their wisdom to point the way but it took the freedom of a new generation to begin to practice what the few wise elders preached.

So let us learn to appreciate the stimulating promise of youth and the stimulating richness of age and remember which way we are all headed. Both young and old can be appreciated as friends and lovers, but we must remember the direction in which we are moving. Everyone is growing older. Valuing older people helps with the direction of your own life. Driving down the highway looking in the rear-view mirror can be hazardous to your health.

Sex and Nonsex

Some years ago I was in an experimental encounter group in which the leader was trying out some new techniques. The lights were out and we were crawling about in the dark pretending to be some sort of new hatched beings, perhaps part animal and part vegetable. We rubbed, poked, explored and stretched. I remember that it was hard to keep my mind from working but that I did enjoy the various sensations of texture, odor and kinesthetic response. At one point a hand or foot of an other creature came out of nowhere it seemed and touched my genitals directly. It was a gentle touch and there was no cause for alarm but it pulled me immediately out of the wonderful spirit of play and I thought to myself, "Now, this is serious—that was sexual!" No matter that one minute before someone had placed an elbow tip in my nostril and I did little more than smile and stretch.

Later in the same game of maneuvers, the leader was telling us that there was a terrible storm that was shaking the whole world and that we were to seek comfort. I managed to be in a standing position intertwined warmly and comfortingly with at least two other bodies in what may have been a visually grotesque sculpture, while yet another body curled around the shoulders of all of us, perhaps being a python in our tree. As the world continued to rumble and threaten to end according to the leader's instructions, we squirmed and contorted more, writhing in a frantic effort to give and receive comfort. Quite suddenly I realized that we were all sexually aroused which was confirmed when the lights came on a moment later and the leader asked us to freeze in our positions but to open our eyes and then begin to discuss how we had felt. The other two parts of my tree were male and having trouble with bulging trousers while the python was a woman having trouble with her blush.

As has been stated earlier, there is more to your Gay identity than simple sex. But both the sexual and the non-sexual aspects of Gay relationships may be difficult for you to bring into awareness and enjoyment, especially if you have been hiding Gay feelings for a long time.

In the great heterosexual game for which we were all trained, women learned to view other women as competitors while men learned to view other men as competitors. It takes a while to get the hang of treating someone of same gender as a respectable recipient of affection. Women have to learn to trust and respect one another's strength and honesty while men have to learn how to express affection beyond a handshake or backslap and to respect one another's vulnerability. This is just a beginning.

The learning is vast and takes a long time. As a key to what needs fixing, look for modes of relating that seem acceptable and comfortable with people of the other gender yet feel odd or strangely uncomfortable with someone of the same gender. As soon as you locate one of these trouble spots (like two men kissing hello or two women taking a few minutes to talk shop in the social presence of men), start practicing doing that which is uncomfortable if it holds any promise of future satisfaction. After the scare is taken out of it with experience, you can evaluate it and decide how often or under what circumstances you want it in your behavioral repertoire.

Learning to relate sexually is somewhat the same. You are off to a head start because someone of the same gender is put together bodily the same way you are and you know exactly what feels good, what responds to pressure and what responds to a feathery gentle touch. The best way to learn is to explore with no demand that you do more than you want to at any given moment. Sex should be pleasurable, not a contest or an evaluated performance.

As in social behavior, there are a lot of taboos with sex. Use of the mouth may seem appealing but you have been taught that it is appalling. Experiment a little at a time and see if you cannot let yourself have more and more pleasure in using your mouth. There are some particular learnings that take time for most people. The hurdles may be stronger for men than for women. Men have been trained in all sorts of ways to resist being the recipient of another man's penis, probably because of the symbolic conquest or giving up of power involved, so that it may take patient learning to relax sphincter muscles in the anus or calm the gag reflex in the throat. Women may also have trouble being assertive and insertive. Working at releasing such inhibitions will not work. Acceptance of your own natural desires in increasingly small steps will permit the relaxation of body and inhibition so that you can get on with the pleasures of sexual or social relating.

Learning to play with Gay friends can help. You can use a costume party or a romp on the beach as an excuse if you need one. Gay play is important. When we were children we played in order to grow and learn. We watched our playmates in order to study their behavior during play so that we could expand our own behavior-vocabulary. We also watched their reactions to us as we expressed feeling in the safe guise of play. We pushed them and learned how far we could push and which forms of expression were safe and tolerated. The learning from the play formed the foundation of our individual unique expression of self or personality in relation to others.

Recently I was in a swimming pool at night with two Gay women and two other Gay men. We played together as five, daring to break some assumed Gay taboo prohibiting Gay men and Gay women from being sensuous together. Reassured by that play behavior we settled down to more specifically Gay (male/male and woman/woman) play, the water seeming to steer our play in an erotic direction. During all of this we laughed with true pleasure at the abandon, and laughed reassurance to one another as we played out our questions about exploring someone of the same gender. We were asking nonverbal questions about social limits in a situation that did not have punitive consequences.

I was aware that if a non-Gay person had happened upon us there might have been disapproval—almost certainly there would have been discomfort—but a Gay person stumbling upon the scene would be likely to understand and perhaps shed tears of celebration. We were having some beautiful and quiet remedial play, catching up on something long overdue. We missed something in our heterosexual-dominated play world of childhood and we need the chance to catch up. Play can help us to expand both our sexual and non-sexual "vocabulary" with our Gay peers.

Sexual Friends and Lovers

In the Broadway musical *Call Me Madam* there was a comical production number in which people were trying to learn a new dance which involved much switching of partners. In a calculated split second of silence following a switching of partners for a sensuous part of the dance, one hears a tenor say, "My God, it's Mother!"

I have heard a few variations on that theme in my office and from friends. Leaving the dark orgy rooms or other places designed for anonymous sex, people have discovered that they have just had sex with an old friend, a cousin, a sibling—and at least once that I know about, with a parent! The re-telling of the story at a Gay party is always good for a laugh, but the laugh is a nervous one. However, even a taboo must be questioned if you want to grow and become yourself.

The anti-Gay myths tell us that we are freaks whose lives are ruled by unnatural sexual desires. It is all too easy for a Gay person to believe such myths, since we know our sexual feelings are strong and important (as they are for all people) and we have few role models to study. By definition we are breaking the established rules of our culture by honoring our Gay feelings and that appears to support the idea that sexual feelings rule our lives. If we begin to behave as if that assumption were true it soon becomes depressingly close to truth. We must put the necessary effort into establishing self-respecting patterns of Gay sexuality. Other Gay people before you have done it, but the communication media have not permitted them to pass along their wisdom to us. So you are once again a pioneer, cutting your own trail through the jungle. Try to remember that the destination is self-respect.

First, there is the matter of defining for yourself what kind of sex you are seeking at any given moment. Is it sex for recreation or affirmation? Recreational sex is available with strangers to be found at Gay bars, baths, street cruising, in parks or even in line at the employment office. In order to keep self-respect intact, however, it is important to make sure that both you and your found partner are looking for simple fun and body pleasure and are not engaging with one another because of loneliness, need for comforting, respect, or any other unstated need that is not likely to be satisfied.

There are some hazards involved in sex with strangers in public places. In some towns and cities there may seem to be no alternative. It may seem that parks and restrooms, or the one local Gay bar on the edge of town, are the only places where you can meet people who are interested in a homosexual interchange. Often that is not as true as it seems, but we will get to that a little later in talking about sexual friends. If you do indulge in sexual activities in parks and restrooms, be aware that you are increasing the chances of contracting a sexually transmitted disease or having an unpleasant experience with the police. This can start with a vice officer who talks, dresses and acts as if he or she is ready for sexual adventure but who is really ready for a game of torture with you as the victim. It begins as friendly cruising and ends with an ugly scene in the police station, possible loss of employment (because the police may feel it their "duty" to inform your employer), and very often unwelcome publicity when your name and the unflattering circumstances are printed in the newspaper.

Gay bars are socially safer because someone you meet there is less likely to turn out to be a vice officer, but there are still plenty of towns where taxpayers' money pays the salaries of good-looking police officers whose beat is the barstool. With strangers, in general, there is a higher risk of getting involved with someone whose motives are less than loving. Hustlers, rapists, and other people whose emotional conflicts are so complex as to make positive human relationships impossible also work this beat and you may find yourself badly bruised emotionally, physically or financially by someone who seemed an attractive, lonely stranger. Plenty of nice people meet in these places also, and I do

164

not wish to increase homophobia by making it all seem scary and disgusting, but you should be aware of increased risk with strangers meeting in public places for sex. Towns and cities that have Gay baths offer the safest setting for anonymous sex, though these places have been raided by the police from time to time.

Sexually transmitted disease is a big problem for straight and Gay people alike if they are sexually active in any way beyond a monogamous relationship. There are plenty of books and pamphlets that describe the symptoms of various venereal diseases. The advice is always the same: Get it treated as quickly as possible. The second standard piece of advice is harder to follow when you involve yourself sexually with strangers, because it is to inform everyone with whom you have been in recent sexual contact so that they can also be checked and treated. Were our society not so hypocritically righteous, we undoubtedly would have developed vaccines long ago to slow or stop the awesome spread of venereal diseases, but we still seem to be working with the Victorian assumption that a venereal disease is proper punishment for sexual pleasure.

Second, take care not to lessen the self-esteem of another Gay person you meet in a public setting. If you are approached by someone who does not immediately interest you, take a minute to learn something about the other person, exchange pleasantries, and communicate that you are willing to value him or her. If you do not make this effort, you run the risk of implying to yourself that Gay people are as disposable as paper cups if they do not suit your need of the moment. It's a bad thing to tell yourself, because you may one day believe that it is what you deserve.

Another way of having self-respecting recreational sex is with a friend. It lacks the excitement and mystery of a new person, but offers the comfort of someone you already know and trust. Part of the old Gay mystique contained the taboo that you must never have sex with a friend because it will spoil the friendship. That was based on the questionable assumption that sex is bad and you do not do something shameful with someone you value. If you have grown to view sex as a friendly interaction there is no reason not to offer it to friends. If it still feels bad or dirty, it's not good to share it with anyone. And remember that sex is as broadly defined as you choose to make it; it need not be the "performing of sexual acts." You can rub one another, sleep together, cuddle up, or stroke, taking responsibility for doing only things that feel right and good. Try to stay in tune with your friend so that each of you is doing only what both of you want to do together. An excellent way to have it turn out exactly as sexual as both of you want is to take turns giving one another a massage. If the recipient is aroused, a little more stroking will usually bring on orgasm. Whatever is done is bound to feel friendly and each can let it feel as sexual as you wish. The mystique of the orgasm can be demystified. Through friendly exchanges of massage, there can be friendly exchanges of orgasm with no one having been misused in the process. It does involve being sensitive to one another's feelings and frank in your verbal sharing of those feelings.

Don't waste energy on feeling guilty if you and a friend are simply not sexually interested in one another. It is worth the effort to check your feelings and make sure that it is a matter of taste and that the disinterest in sex is that simple, rather than a disguise covering the "no sex with friends because it's dirty" taboo. But if you are both not interested, you are not interested. Mutuality is important in friendship. If one of you is interested and one of you is not interested, there is going to have to be some give on both sides until you get the level of broadly defined sexual interaction set just where you both want it. Without this balancing—if one of you is in constant pursuit of the other—there is usually a silent volcano of resentment that is apt to erupt unexpectedly and damage or end the friendship.

Affirmational sex is hard to find with strangers. It makes beautiful fiction, but it rarely occurs in real life. It takes time for you and the stranger to get to know one another well enough to know what there is to affirm. Affirmational sex is the kind sought when your resources are low and you are feeling unsure and lonely. It is a primitive, non-verbal communication telling you that you are appreciated. The better the person knows you when offering this sexual affirmation, the more you are able to believe it. If your partner knows only the look and feel of your body it is his or her lust that is being affirmed, not your worth. So it is best to seek affirmational sex with lovers or friends of long standing.

Looking for affirmational sexual experiences with people you already know may be easier said than done. They are so close to you that you may not see them as sexual partners. To view them anew, you might try the following exercise: shift your focus from who is attractive to you to who is attracted to you.

To help you get some perspective, make a list of all the Gay people you know whom you like, respect, and enjoy socially. Then on a separate sheet of paper, draw lines to make five columns. At the top of the first column, write yes; over the second, probably; over the third put a question mark; over the fourth, no; and over the fifth, no-no.

Now take from your master list the names of the people who already have made it clear to you they are sexually attracted and available to you and put them in the yes column. In the probably column, place the names of those you know are generally attracted to you and probably willing to experience sex with you. In the question-mark column place the names of people you are unsure are sexually attracted to you. In the no column go the names of those who have made it quite clear that you are not on their sexual horizon at this time. And in the no-no column place the names of people who were not on your master list but whom you find sexually attractive. Now review all the names and put a star next to the name of anyone in whose presence you always feel good about yourself. Your map is taking shape.

The people to pay attention to are those in the first two columns—especially those whose names are starred. If they do not stir you sexually, see what you can do about reprogramming your attractions. You might try some erotic daydreams about these people and you might try touching them more often to get the feel of their body-selves. You might want to try switching to an image of one of these people when masturbating and near orgasm. The latter technique is one too often used to reinforce sexual interest in the wrong people, those in column five, who are of value to you only as sexual objects. That is why that column is headed with a no-no. The less time and energy wasted on those people the better for your mind, soul and sex life.

As with any such list, you would do well to review it now and then to see if any changes have come about. Using the question-mark column as an anxiety-provoking cure for boredom can be very rewarding. Try asking the people listed in this column whether or not they find you sexually attractive. There may be one or two people you will skip rather than risk hysteria or a coronary, but there are surely some with whom the information-gathering could be fun. Of course, you can anticipate the person's asking you the same question in return.

You may find that one or more of your friends, or perhaps you yourself, have a simple, primitive, unusually strong skin hunger. There is no knowing where this skin hunger originates; it may have been in infancy and early childhood when you were not touched enough, or perhaps it originates from some lonely period in later life. The symptoms are clear—the person truly needs to be touched a lot directly on bare skin. Friends can enjoyably help to meet this need, since it also feels good to touch people for whom you have fond feelings unless some inhibition gets in the way.

If friends do not provide the food for skin hunger, it can easily turn into what I call the hustler syndrome. The person may literally or figuratively become a prostitute. It begins with needing the skin contact terribly. It is easy to fall into a pattern of putting yourself in the path of strangers to be touched. If you are an attractive person, you may find some strangers are all too willing to get their hands on you; some, indeed, are willing to pay money. Not surprisingly, after this kind of encounter you feel less good about yourself. You have been used and your skin has been touched but you have not received the message of caring that you sought. So it is off to another stranger with the same probable result. Each time the need for that caring touch grows stronger, and each time you are less trusting that you will receive it. Once in a great while you get a little of it from a sensitive stranger. It is like playing the one-armed bandits at Las Vegas. You find yourself in contact with stranger after stranger, cued by the look of desire in their eyes. Your hunger grows stronger and stronger and along with it grows your distrust of people who want to touch you. Soon you lessen your receptive sensitivity and you cannot feel the caring when it is there.

I have worked with many such people in Gay groups and it is extremely difficult to help the person to open the sensitivity once more. The "prettier" the person by current standards, the greater the likelihood he or she has had lots of experience in being used and discarded, and the more difficult it is to redevelop the trust. The usual first step is absolute assurance that the person reaching out to touch you will do nothing sexual, and while admitting to the pleasure of touching because they care, will touch only as much as you want to be touched. The increments in amount of touching must be small. It is like dealing with a child who has burned his or her hand in the fire. It is a sexual area in which caring, sensitive friends can help a lot if you can share with them the roots of your empty sexual feelings and the kind of help you need.

So there is recreational sex and affirmational sex, with strangers and friends, all of it complicated enough. But what about lovers and spouses? A heterosexual marriage or otherwise recognized heterosexual union has a lot of community support behind it. It does not take care of the big question of jealousy but it provides an amount of security to soften the fright of jealousy. Gay lovers or spouses have much less of this support. Settled Gay couples are not very visible because they are not often invited as a couple to general community gatherings and, like heterosexually married couples, they tend to spend a large portion of their leisure time alone together or within a small circle of chosen friends. But settled, long-term Gay couples do exist in large numbers and they must deal with the question of sexual jealousy just as sexually active heterosexual couples must, unless a path of permanent monogamy has been chosen.

What to do when one person in a committed relationship wants some variety in his or her sex life? Hopefully, you and your partner will re-evaluate your sexual agreement. Monogamy need not be viewed as an identity. It is merely a technique that couples choose to use because they believe its explicit declaration of priorities strengthens the relationship and adds needed cement. But the technique, if used without heeding its suitability at any given period of the relationship, can do more harm than good. Monogamy works only if both partners feel they are gaining because of it. If one or both partners are becoming restless and wanting other sexual experiences, new arrangements must be worked out quickly that still recognize the primacy of the relationship, but permit some amount of sexual involvement elsewhere. If monogamy becomes a prison, people will find a way to break out and keep traveling.

Jealousy is not to be underestimated in its power. It is supported by the culture's programming of both men and women and reinforced by the power of orgasm. The catastrophic fantasy behind it is the spectre of rejection, abandonment and abject loneliness. We do not become jealous or panic if a spouse shares himself or herself in other ways, but we have been trained to respond with alarm if sex is shared elsewhere. Sex, we have been taught, is the expression of (or synonymous with) "love." In fact this is sometimes true, but it can also be the expression of many other feelings including simple sexual lust. Love is expressed by the quality of hundreds of daily interactions, not just in sexual intercourse. But programming does not yield to mere factual truth. We are apt to cling to the belief that love and sex are synonymous, and that if one's lover or spouse is sharing sex with someone else, presumably they are sharing love. The enormity of the fear and hurt makes it necessary to find step-by-step answers that maximize the momentary comfort of both partners. The special danger for Gay couples is that you will yield in hurt and confusion to the millions of subtle messages telling you that it is wrong to be in this kind of relationship. There is always the temptation to give up, but that temptation is especially dangerous for Gay couples because there is generally too little support for staying together. The exception is the Gay couple who have surrounded themselves socially with a group of other stable long-term Gay couples.

It is possible that brief loving-sexual excursions with other people can enrich you in ways that can deepen your relationship with your partner, though, because of societal warnings against it, there is the element of playing with fire. Again, sex and love are easily equated, consciously or not. We have been taught that love is like a loaf of bread in that if someone takes a bite out of the loaf, there will be that much less bread there for me. If love were truly that consumable it would soon vanish and we would all be very unhappy. Love might instead be compared to a muscle: the more you use it the more it grows. If my loved one practices love with someone else, he or she could learn more about loving, and I may have more love available to me. But having acknowledged this, jealousy may still require much time and discussion before it fades. Your partner needs verbal and physical reassurance that he or she is not being devalued in your esteem by your investment of love elsewhere.

When committed partners who live together are trying to find non-threatening ways to open their relationship, locating a calendar near the phone can be very helpful. Avoiding undesired confrontations or accidental requests for permission, the person who wants to go out with someone else, whether it be for sex or a card game, simply records the upcoming date on the calendar. Noticing that your partner already has something planned, you can make a date for the same evening, or look forward to a long-desired evening at home alone. In the beginning it usually helps to declare your home off-limits to amorous activity with other people, since that is apt to stir some primitive jealousy process.

If you are in a fairly settled relationship with a lover (having already gone through a trial courtship of whatever duration), you are receiving a precious gift from life and the relationship is a living thing that takes as much care as a garden or a growing child. As with gardening or parenting, it can involve tedious effort at times but it helps to be aware, while doing the weeding, of the flowers that are already blooming and those that are yet to come. There is something especially sweet and satisfying when a Gay person finds a Gay life partner, a special understanding between them and, hopefully, a special appreciation for a reward earned against great odds.

Copying a heterosexual marriage role model does not work for most Gay couples. Once again, the lack of models forces you to fashion a relationship that uniquely meets your own needs. A friend of mine who is half of a very happy Gay couple said, "I wish that in your book you would say that when you meet your ultimate lover, keep in mind how valuable he is. Express your displeasure about his leaving the cap off the toothpaste but never say or do anything that will make him feel less good about himself. It takes a little discipline, but it is the gift of love." It sounded to me like fine advice. Step by step, one day at a time, if the relationship works for both people, each will be willing to be alert to ways of changing so that both partners find ever-increasing satisfaction.

The search for a lover seems to be a near obsession in some segments of Gay society. Small wonder, since we have been led to believe that a (heterosexual) marriage will yield security and lifetime happiness. In the shaky world provided for Gay people it would be nice if one person could provide all of that. Even the chance that it might be true is sufficient reason for everyone to try to win the lover contest. How do I find her? How do I find him? There is a Zen wisdom to the effect that when the student is ready, the master will appear. I think that is true for lovers, too. If you would find a lover, first make yourself into the kind of person you want your lover to be.

Developing nourishing friendships that can include sexuality is important. Too many people rush about looking for a lover as if such a person were the grand prize of an Easter egg hunt. The lover is not the hidden Easter egg, however, but one of the many flowers in the meadow. One must learn the flowers in his or her meadow well and let them take their individual places in natural order of emotional importance. If one of them becomes most important, that one is the lover. But all of that takes care. It takes care in developing friendships. And in order to develop the friendships, one must reach out.

Reaching Out

For some people, the act of reaching out to strangers ranges from uncomfortable to terrifying. Often the awareness of a sexual motivation adds shame and embarrassment. This derives from the hidden assumption that sex is a shameful thing people do to one another rather than an emotionally powerful and positive exchange. It also betrays the nearly universal fear of rejection. The lurking fantasy is that your open interest in the other person will be greeted by disinterest or distaste. This points up the necessity of constructing a strongly valued self concept—a task made more difficult for a Gay person but all the more necessary.

Once a truly positive self-evaluation is under way, it is not too difficult to meet new people unless you live in an underpopulated part of the world. Grocery stores, banks, dry cleaners, lunch counters, beaches, classrooms, or pedestrians stopped at signals all offer opportunity to turn to someone, smile, and make a friendly remark. Gay people often say they do not know where to go to meet potential sexual friends and lovers. In our age of efficiency we are impatient with the notion of sorting the people met at the pedestrian stop signal. People do not want to go to bars or baths because they have had the experience of being used badly in such settings or simply do not care for the aesthetics of such places. Or they may live in a part of the world where there are no Gay bars or baths.

The safest, most efficient and most self-respecting way of meeting other Gay people who are potential sexual friends and lovers is to ask any Gay people you already know to introduce you to others. Dinner parties are pleasant and can be fun in themselves, even if you do not meet anyone you find particularly attractive in a given evening. If you continue to meet new people who are Gay, you are bound to make friends with some of them, and sure to want to have sexual exchanges with a few. If you meet enough people you are sure to find some candidates for lovers.

It is easier in cities than in small towns and rural areas. If you live in a part of the world where there are few other visible Gay people you may have to consider relocating, taking frequent vacations to a Gay city or settling into a life of abstinence.

One reason for difficulty in finding sexual friends and lovers even where there are plenty of Gay people is the restrictive programming that has taught us to be attracted to a small range of people. If you are only attracted to people who resemble a particular movie star, you are going to have a long wait. If you can expand the range of your attraction by purposely pushing its limits (having body contact with someone who is "too fat," "too old," "too young," or "too dark"—but whom you like a lot), you may end up with someone who fits your original specifications.

If you meet someone who is your specialty number when you have a limited range of attraction, you victimize yourself and him/her by pursuing desperately (ignoring what the person is like), because you have no idea when another one of those specialty types may come along. If the other person has any sensitivity, he/she knows the sudden hot pursuit has little to do with anything other than body appearance and will get away from you as swiftly as possible. But if he/she sees that you have a wide range of attraction and are not desperate, that makes you some-one interested in him/her as a person and therefore someone safe to know.

If dinner parties and expanded range of attraction do not produce candidates, you might try working for some Gay orga-nizations. Working together on a committee will bring out facets of humor, intelligence, and caring not evident at a party.

It is possible to attack your fear of rejection directly. The more experience you have in not being rejected, the more sure of yourself you become, but getting acceptance experiences can be terrifying precisely because they are bound to contain some mix of rejection.

There is a technique called a rejection game which has helped some people. You actually set out to see how many social rejections you can accumulate in one day. You may be up to only one rejection on the first day, and that is fine. Approach someone you are fairly sure will want to have little or nothing to do with you and try to strike up a conversation. (It helps the gain from the game if you follow a second rule of being absolutely honest in everything you say and do with someone whom you expect to reject you.) If the person rejects you by paying little or no atten-tion, you have earned your score for the day. If the person is not rejecting, you must wait until the interaction comes to some sort of natural end (so that you do not reject him/her) and then go on to another person whom you suspect will reject you.

The second day you try for two rejections, the third day three rejections and so forth. This does two things. It slowly de-sensitizes you to rejection (it will always hurt but it will hurt less and less) and it gets you a lot of surprising positive attention from people you thought surely would reject you. It is a guaranteed way to meet people and do some important relearning that can help build self-esteem.

You might also try finding some suitable people through an ad in a Gay newspaper or magazine. You can meet the first time for a cup of coffee and the second time for lunch. Take time to get to know one another as more than bodies who met through an advertisement. If you find someone you like who lives too far away for coffee, letters will help, and you can always arrange a short vacation together.

And if all that fails, you might consider getting help from a Gay-oriented counselor. It is possible that you are defeating yourself in ways you cannot see alone. Whatever you do in your reaching out, make sure you pause at each step and ask yourself if the next step will increase your self-respect.

The most important facet of relearning in this area is the reaching out. As you learn to be comfortable and self-respecting while reaching out to a wider variety of fellow humans, you can also be more selective in the ways you share yourself with different individuals. You will increase your reservoir of friends and find sexual friends and potential lovers who do not fit your original, limited, programmed idea of who is attractive. In learning to reach out, you enrich your personal life and enrich the world you inhabit.

You may worry that in reaching out you will meet people who have a sexual interest in you and that you will have to "give in" lest you hurt them. But other people can get used to the rejection of sexual overtures just as you can. Sometimes you are offered food when you are not hungry. Becoming socially adult involves learning to say "No, thank you" while expressing sincere gratitude for the offer.

Being alone and lonely is unnecessary. Reaching out is simply a matter of practice. You will find other worthwhile individuals who have built walls around themselves. All are people. Many you will care for. Some will become friends.

Pride

Living things grow and change or they die; it is a law of nature. By now it should be clear that my clinical and personal experience has led me to believe there are several ingredients required in the growth and change of Gay people if we are to survive. First we must deprogram by raising consciousness, questioning basic assumptions, and finding support for change. Second, we must reprogram, building a set of guidelines that we consider ethically sound and personally satisfying. Third, we must treat every Gay person with respect even if she/he is a person whom we do not much like, because it is our treatment of the other Gay person that will ultimately assure each of us of our own personal worth and dignity. It is the path to self-respect.

We must learn not to let an insult or stereotypic remark pass unchallenged or we will never be free of the restrictive prison we are helping to support. When you laugh at another person, you laugh at yourself, no matter how different your lifestyle. To-day's new macho fag or ultra-fem lesbian may be tempted to laugh with non-Gay friends at the drag queen or bull-dyke, but they would do well to respect them and see how brave a part such people have played through the years in asserting our right to be. In the years ahead, as we become sufficiently liberated to be the individuals we are without playing roles or wearing masks, the patrons of the leather and western bars or the mod lesbians in double-knit pants suits may look just as dated, yet they will de-serve just as much respect for having helped us all along the road.

But while derogatory remarks and behavior must not go unchallenged, we need not imitate our oppressors. We can do better. We live in an age of simple-minded violence in which chil-dren are taught by TV that the way to settle differences is with gun, knife or fist. The insane assumption is that might equals right. Superior strength equals superiority. Gay people have been beaten or killed for centuries just because they were Gay. And violence begets violence. We have turned ours inward.

If we resort to the same behavior in disagreeing with our oppressors, we are no better than they are and deserve the treat-ment they are giving us. In the past decade, many brave Gay women and men have dared speak our truth aloud, challenging insults and refusing to use violence. Their very style of confron-tation is an act of bravery that belies the anti-Gay myths that portray us as inferior weaklings. They are demonstrating that, unlike our oppressors, we know our truth will be heard. We do not have to club people into seeming agreement. We will not spark yet another spiral of violence. We know where it leads.

We may be near the day when Gay people no longer will make one another feel bad. The sad Cinderella scene of some of today's Gay bars may end. One sees bodies packed into such a bar. Only a few are the correct age range and body arrangement to meet the beauty criteria of our contemporary culture. They are the aristocracy who bear the responsibility of nobility. They have diplomatic relations only with one another, attempting to score a trophy. They are the seeming Cinderellas, transformed from the life of oppression in the daytime world by the soft lighting and loud music of the bar. They are surrounded by Cinderella's sisters who have primped and squeezed and tried to fit the beautiful image, but have not quite made it, yet hope that the prince may be near-sighted. They have eyes only for the aristocracy. And surrounding them are the far larger numbers of peasants who have no hope of passing for aristocratic beauties but who hope for a lucky windfall in the form of a leftover drunken beauty whom no one took home. It is a sad scene that has been constructed by the anti-Gay, pro-youth, superficial beauty programming. But it could not continue if we did not provide the cast of characters and pay the bill at the cash register.

Gay bar owners are people who are in a position to help or hurt other Gay people and ultimately, therefore, damage or save their own self-worth. They can reconstruct the physical plan of the bars and even introduce activities that assure people the chance to meet other people rather than view other bodies. Gay bar owners can guarantee an atmosphere of dignity and respect and feel better about their own Gay identity—or continue the circus, watch the cash register, promote alcoholism, and lose self-respect.

Each and every one of us who is Gay must find ways to reach out and help other Gay people. You cannot help everyone who needs help, but you can help some. And every time you help someone because that person is Gay and you are Gay, you will learn something about the value of life and about your own worth. The more we help one another, the more we will have reason for pride. We will be able to say, "I am Gay" and mean "I am one of those fortunate people who is cared for by others like me as I care for them."

Much attention has been paid to sexuality in this section of the book. It comes into focus frequently because it is the facet of our difference as Gay people that is noticed most by the world in general. But we need not fall into the trap of believing that sex is the most important factor of our lives. We also have hearts and brains, and we have a culture that is uniquely ours, forged in pain

177

from private truth. It is a rich culture. We can share it and help the rest of the world learn.

We are citizens of the wider world that includes non-Gays. As the Blacks learned before us, integration is not possible until you cease to conform to stereotype and recognize your strength and the goodness of your identity. Once you have developed your own self-esteem and found your strength, you are ready not only to help other Gay people but also to help non-Gays who share the social order of this planet. Sooner or later we must help them to appreciate differences. We must help them to see how they cheat themselves when they devalue someone for being different.

Why integrate? Why not just form Gay communities and live there separately? First, because such separatism leads to the we vs. they that too easily grows to war and deprivation of life itself. Second, because the world is too precious not to share.

A Jewish friend told me about a wonderful winter vacation he and his family had taken at a posh desert dude ranch. "But by the second day, we were uncomfortable," she said, "because we realized everyone else at the ranch was a white Anglo-Saxon Protestant. We stuck it out anyway for the whole week because the place was so wonderful, the scenery gorgeous, the sun hot, and the service superior. We decided that we would look for a new place next year and then it dawned on us! If it's so beautiful and wonderful, why should we let them have it exclusively? And guess what? The next year when we went back we found another Jewish family and a Black family! If we hadn't gone back they might have deserted too. So now we figure anybody can go there and enjoy. Why not?"

Most of us are not yet ready for full integration. We must build more strength in our Gay identity first. Legal battles for full civil rights must be fought and won. We must learn to enjoy and be proud of some of the differences we have been told are shameful—like our ability to love when others compete, or our incisive camp humor. We must build our own ceremonies; weddings may be on their way out of style, but we need some sort of ceremony to give public dignity and support to our loving relationships and we need to be able to mourn openly as Gay people when someone Gay dies. We need to develop our own psychology, sociology, and anthropology—our study of ourselves and our culture—and then present it proudly to the rest of the world so that they can join us in celebration. We are Gay. We are growing. And we are learning how to be glad.

3
Loving Someone Gay

I had the honor, if not the pleasure, of being at a friend's coming-out party with his parents a couple of years ago. It had not been planned that way, but his parents were visiting California from the other end of the country and since he was wearing his hair long, living collectively, and eating with the help of food stamps, we thought a traditional dinner party in a suburban home would be reassuring for his parents and show them that he could still live in their world.

But as the evening wore on he drank far more than usual and made veiled allusions to "telling them"—the allusions being followed by a draining of color from his face and a temporary inability to speak. I collared my friend in the kitchen and said, "For God's sake, either tell them or don't tell them before we all die of tension." "I want to, but I can't," was his response. So I had another sip of wine and said, "OK, you tell them or I will."

We sauntered back into the dining room, he pale and I developing a headache, and listened politely to the conversation for ten seconds before he interrupted and said, "Listen, there's something I have to tell you and I want to tell you tonite. I'm Gay."

Due to the preceding hours of tension, what followed was more like a Marx Brothers adventure than any high drama either of us had foreseen. "I knew that long ago. Could I have another cup of coffee?" was his father's response. His mother placed a fixed smile on her face as the silent tears began to flow onto her blouse. Things livened up within the next few moments when the first notes of anger surfaced. His father, in a tense attempt to remain calm, accidentally addressed me as "Honey" and followed it with "I'm sorry, Doctor," when we had been on a first-name basis all evening. His mother said repeatedly, "I just want you to be happy," as her tears filled her napkin. Someone made the mistake of suggesting an after dinner drink and the father, focusing on the mother's damp napkin, said, "Look, dear, it's a *Vera*!" By this time my friend was in tears, half from relief and half feeling sorry for himself in the midst of the farce, and said, "You don't understand how much I've needed both of you all these years!" His mother put down the Vera napkin and raised her voice for the only time during the evening as she said, "Listen, parents are only people!"

A good reminder. Parents, husbands, wives, daughters, sons, sisters, brothers, friends and other relations are only people—each no better than another, each different, each an individual with his or her own quirks, weaknesses, moments of pride, doubts, and dreams. Each person is a different person, and the role of parent or sibling assures only a very minimal sharing of experience with all other parents or all other siblings in the world.

That is true of Gay people too. Each of us is different. Each of us has our individual strengths and weaknesses, individual quirks that would endear us to you or perhaps cause you to react with distaste or distrust. I cannot generalize about the Gay person you love. He or she is different. I can only offer general thoughts and probabilities that may help you to clarify the unique relationship that the two of you have.

Three years ago, something very nice happened to me. A mother called me and asked if she and her husband might come in to see me for a consultation with their sixteen-year-old son. Their son had told them that he was Gay and they wanted some help.

My fantasy was that I would have to help the parents see that their son had a right to be himself. I could help him sort out whether his presumed Gay identity was a whim or an inner truth;

182

that would be easy. The part I braced myself for was helping the parents to see that a Gay identity did not mean there was anything necessarily wrong with their son or that they had failed in some way as parents. I was prepared for plenty of tears.

As it turned out, the only tears shed were by me. When they arrived, the three of them told their story together. The son had made his disclosure to them about a year earlier. They had talked about his feelings through many long hours. In the process they had learned to love and appreciate him more. They were proud of his honesty and courage. The reason for the consultation was to help the three of them think through possible future pitfalls. They knew the world was not kindly disposed toward Gay people. The parents did not want their son unnecessarily hurt but they knew they could not shield him. The three of them wanted to do whatever they could to make the future good. We had a very good talk, I referred them to some Gay organizations, gave them a reading list and we parted, all four of us enriched by the experience.

But that is an unusual story. I could match it with a hundred stories of how love became twisted in storms of irrational pressure to conform to some ideal of normal existence. It is possible for people who love someone Gay to see that person more clearly if they are willing to try.

I presume that you are reading this book because you want to know more about what the subjective experience of being Gay is like for the person you love. The earlier sections of the book have given some of that flavor. Perhaps the one possible generalization is that it has been difficult. It has been difficult not for any reason that need be true in the infinite scheme of things but because our contemporary culture does not value diversity. Lack of conformity makes us uneasy, and uneasy people too easily strike out to hurt someone who seems different. That phenomenon has made necessary some hiding of true identity for the Gay person you love. And when you have to hide part of your true self it is very easy to begin to feel like an unworthy person no matter how convincing the covering facade of achievement and seeming self-confidence. You can express your love for someone Gay by taking the responsibility for learning more about what it is like to be Gay and offering the unconditional caring that facilitates the growth of self respect.

The Gay person you love, no matter what he or she is like as an individual, has held tight to an inner truth and identity in the face of formidable opposition. Most Gay people do not consider this fight for integrity as a mark of bravery. Most do not even consider it a fight. People who grow up in the Arctic expect lots of cold weather. Most Gay people are used to the world the way it is. Each has found a way to survive day by day. But there is, for me, something touching about it. It brings to memory the childhood story of The Emperor's New Clothes. Everyone agreed to agree that the emperor was wearing fine new clothes lest the neighbors think poorly of them. Only a child who had not yet mastered the art of self-deception spoke the truth about the emperor's clothes and saw the deception. Each Gay person grows up like that child, seeing a personal truth, threatened by an angry crowd, yet somehow needing to hold on to that truth and to share it with others. In a world so full of deception, I hope that this book helps you find pride in sharing love with someone Gay.

Receiving The Disclosure

Like the dinner party described earlier, the only thing predictable about the disclosure experience is its unpredictability. A fellow psychologist in his mid-forties recently became convinced that it was time to tell his eighty-year-old mother, lest he wrestle with her ghost for the rest of his life. He planned the event with great care, first going over all possibilities with friends. His greatest fear was that she would die on the spot. She had been talking about her weak heart for as long as he could remember. He wanted to let her know that he really did care about her and reasoned that actions would speak louder than words. So he planned a special winter vacation in Miami for just the two of them. They stayed at a hotel she had always wanted to visit and took two of her friends out to dinner the first night they were there. The next day they went out together on a brief shopping jaunt, during which he bought her a colorful silk scarf he could tell she wanted—though she kept protesting it was foolishness to spend so much money for something that would one day be a rag. She napped after lunch and joined him on the beach for an hour before they went to their rooms to dress for dinner. That evening he took her to a sedate but "in" restaurant away from the center of the city. Near the end of the meal he reached across the table and took her hand. "Mother, I want to tell you something about me that I have never told you. First I want you to know that I love and respect you. Second I want you to know that I have held off telling you for years because I was afraid it might hurt you. Now I know that it is good news and that I am cheating both of us by not sharing it."

"So what is it, already?" she asked. "You've got a secret wife, or maybe two of them?"

"No, Mom, it's that I'm Gay. It means that I'm more attracted to men than to women."

His mother's brow wrinkled as she thought it over. "That's how come you been living with Tommy all these years? That's how come you bought the building together?"

"Yes, Mom, Tommy is my lover and it is like we are married." My psychologist friend was now in a sweat.

More wrinkled brow. "So how come all these years I never met his parents?"

"Because, like I said, I was afraid to tell you, and Tommy was afraid to tell his parents."

Her brow arched. "Funny world, different than when I was young. Tommy's nice. You could have done worse."

There was a long silence now. His mother seemed lost in thought. She looked around the restaurant at the other diners. "Is there anything else you want to ask me, Mom?"

"About that? No. Tommy's nice, but I think I should meet his parents."

"But you were so quiet, Mom. You must have been thinking about something."

"I was thinking how nice Miami is. Just like I expected. And I was wondering what kind of a restaurant we're going to eat in tomorrow night."

Telling someone that you are Gay is an important event. The Gay person is apt to have spent many hours in thoughtful preparation and shares the information with keen awareness of the possible risk. The first thing you can do to take more respon-

185

sibility in improving your relationship with a Gay person is to pay appreciative attention when the disclosure is made.

There is no way for the Gay person to predict your reaction accurately. You have spent your entire life in a society that teaches you to despise Gay people. Though this particular Gay person is someone important in your life, there is no way to know in advance how able you will feel to throw off those years of training and respond spontaneously and gratefully to such an intimate offering of self.

It is a moment like no other. There is no parallel to the situation in which two people who have known one another very well—perhaps for a lifetime—face one another as one of them risks abandonment by revealing a pervasive fact of identity that may have been invisible to the other. Appreciate how deeply you are valued by this Gay person to justify his or her taking such a risk.

Both of you are changed by the moment of disclosure. The Gay person has gained more freedom and the strength of integrity. There is no longer any need to hide this fact of self in your presence. And you are changed because you are no longer asked to, or permitted to, ignore an important part of this person you love. The situation demands that each of you relate more completely to one another from this moment forward.

Yet the Gay person standing before you is still the same person. It is important to understand that he or she has not changed. You may be shocked by the revelation but this is still the person you have loved. Do not let the shock lead you to view her or him as suddenly different, or bad. Because a label has been assigned, do not permit the years of negative conditioning to transform your perception of the Gay person you love into a monster who fits the stereotypes. What has been kept from you is a truth about loving and identity. You now know that this person can love someone of the same gender completely. You have no reason (except for the hate message of our society) to believe suddenly that this person is morally depraved or emotionally unbalanced.

If you are religiously inclined, you might consider a prayer of thanks that the person has risked all in order to share and move into a closer relationship with you. Whether or not you are religious, you might consider thanks directly to the Gay person.

Religion does present a conflict for many of the recipients of Gay disclosure, just as it has presented conflict for many Gay people who were working their way toward integrating their Gay identity with other facets of their lives. The conflict runs just as deep whether the church is fundamentalist or liberal, highly intellectual or salt of the earth. A woman friend from the Ozarks told me about a conversation she had when making the disclosure to her older sister back home. "It says in the Bible it's wrong and that's that," her sister said. "It says you shouldn't do it. Especially men shouldn't do it but that don't excuse you. Remember Sodom and Gomorrah! I want to be able to love you just the same as always but I don't see how I can do it and hold my head up in church. I know all you homosexuals are headed straight to Hell. All the boys mincin' around and the women pushy and uppity. I'm surprised you dare wear a dress."

My friend had expected some such reception and was prepared. "All of that stuff in the Bible has to be taken with a grain of salt, Sis. You know it says in there that women shouldn't wear red dresses either but plenty of women we know do wear red without worrying about going to Hell. And all those ideas about hard, pushy women and limp-wristed young men are just stereotyping."

"Hey, I don't know what kind of typing it is," her sister interrupted. "I do know you'd have been better off if you had stuck to typing and maybe got a job at the courthouse instead of getting a swelled head and going off to college to be a lawyer. If they find out you're that way they ain't going to let you be a lawyer, are they? I sure do want to love you like a sister but I just don't see how I can."

A client who is planning to leave the priesthood this year and take up residence with his newfound lover also recently had a heart-to-heart talk with his brother who is devoutly religious and teaches in a Catholic university. They both cried when my client revealed that he was leaving the priesthood after twenty years of service and added that he felt it was urgent for him to be open and honest about himself and that he had come to the de-

187

cision after years of internal struggle and counsel with trusted superiors.

His brother's response was, "Johnny, you've always been a good person and I know that. Everyone in the family has always respected you and I'm sure we will continue to do so. But you know that the Church says it's wrong. You know we are taught that it is sinful. I respect your decision and I admire your courage, as always, but things will not be the same for you with anyone in the family. We cannot see you fly in the face of the teachings of the Church and accept it. You've turned into a renegade, Johnny. Perhaps God is trying to lead you somewhere. Perhaps He is punishing us for our sins. It is not for me to question, but I do feel the loss."

The religious conflict may not be resolvable. Hopefully the Gay person has prepared herself or himself for that possibility. Churches change their dogma or their interpretation of it and some are starting to relate more directly to Gay people today. There has even been a start at the open ordination of Gay ministers in a couple of denominations.

When the Gay person you love makes the disclosure to you, search your thoughts and feelings for the information you need and then ask. Don't ask questions that would have been considered rude within the relationship you had before the disclosure. This person has the same sensibilities as before. But you may well need to do some catching up. So "push" yourself to ask questions. Some common questions are: How long have you known or suspected you were Gay? Will you introduce me to your Gay friends? Why do you say "Gay" instead of "homosexual?" Is there someone special? Has it been hard for you carrying this secret? Is there some way I can help you? Have I ever offended you unknowingly?

Be honest and open about your feelings. It makes the sharing more complete and makes change possible. If you find it hard to believe, say so. If you find you are reacting with emotional repugnance but want to learn more so you can throw off your prejudice, say so. If your feelings are totally negative, you can say that, too. It is a possibility the Gay person has certainly considered and risked. But in fairness to yourself admit aloud that negative feelings may change, so the Gay person will leave the door open for you to return if you are able to get past your training. We Gay people are accustomed to hurt, but with someone close the rejection may hurt too much and we may have to get away.

Beware of trying to induce shame or guilt. Usually, by the time the Gay person has developed the strength to make the disclosure, he or she is also sufficiently in touch with feelings to respond to such attempts with understandable anger. Even such mild attempts at guilt or shame induction as "Why did you keep me in the dark so long? Why didn't you tell me long ago?" can get you into trouble. Use your head and realize there were many pressures operating on this Gay person and be glad you were told now. You have been trained to believe that Gay people are bad and will be irrationally tempted to elicit proof in the form of shame or guilt. Resist meeting your irrational needs and give yourself time to get rid of such poison in your thinking.

What do you value about this person? Receiving the disclosure of Gay identity does not happen in a moment—it goes on for weeks or years. During this period of readjustment, try to remain aware of what it is about the person you value, and share that information aloud. It may be sense of humor, intelligence, fairness or even small things like remembering your birthday or a reliable smile in the morning. Sharing your appreciation aloud is reassuring to this person who has just risked all with you, and helps you to stay focused on the individual and not get swept away by generalizations about people "like that."

You may well be tempted to break the bond you have with this Gay person. Though he or she has not changed, the information now confronts you and your homophobic training. A conflict may be inevitable. Just as some people develop specific phobias (heights, snakes, deep water, etc.) many people take in the anti-Gay messages of the culture and develop homophobia It is a disability like any other phobia and you can get help with it through psychotherapy, provided the therapist does not share your phobia. But just as the person who is phobic about deep water may be unaware of anything more than a discomfort with and avoidance of oceans, lakes and rivers, the homophobe may be aware only of discomfort in the presence of Gay people and the desire to avoid them. If you are prone to homophobia, you will be strongly tempted to rid yourself of this previously valued relationship by quick rupture or (if that induces too much guilt in you) by a slow undermining of the relationship. If you see the symptoms and want help, try to find a Gay-oriented psychotherapist. Don't risk unknowingly working with a counselor who shares your homophobia. If you destroy the relationship, chances are the Gay person will be hurt but survive, having been prepared through life for such a reaction on your part.

If your homophobia is of the very mild variety (like the person who can take the elevator up twenty stories but does not want to visit the tallest building in the city) you can get help from reading and from making social contacts with more Gay people. Prejudice thrives on the lack of contradictory information. Integration destroys stereotypes. The more Gay people you meet, the better your chances of ridding yourself of mild homophobia.

A client who is a physician in his fifties recently told his son, a college freshmen, about his Gay identity. The father reported that the son "played it cool— almost no reaction." That was at first. On a visit together some six months later, his son said, "I have to tell you, Dad, that you're being Gay is far out. It's made me think about a lot of things differently. I'm taking this philosophy course and we are supposed to write about our own lives and the lives of people we know and think about what's good and bad, and since you told me about being Gay I've started to look at everyone differently. I used to think a person was good if he did what he was told to do—you know, what we think we're supposed to do. Now I'm beginning to see how complicated it is. For one thing, you can't possibly be good if you aren't honest with yourself and try to be the person you really are." My client unashamedly shed tears in the restaurant and that was a "first," too. Even his son's eyes got moist, as he quietly said, "That's the first time in all my life I ever saw you cry, Dad. I think you're getting better all the time."

The gift of disclosure provides the opportunity and perhaps the incentive for you to begin questioning many of your assumptions about the rights and wrongs of our world. Gay people must question the given morality and build a personally satisfying code of ethics as a matter of survival. Friends and relatives may get some of this as a fringe benefit. As a result, you may find the scope and quality of your own life improving.

Not a few recipients of the gift of disclosure also have found it a stimulus to taking on more civic responsibility. We live in the society we create. The inequalities and injustice can be changed. The place to start, if you love someone Gay, is in working for needed law reforms and against the massive discrimination that exists today. This is done, not as a charitable gift to the Gay person you love, but as a result of the gift that person has given you. The disclosure can be an eye opener, showing you more clearly the kind of world you tacitly support by lack of protest.

Sometimes it seems to me that Gayness is being talked about everywhere all the time, though I know it is because my ear is finely tuned to catch it. I was eating dinner alone in a restaurant last evening, near the borrowed house where I have gone to finish this book, and I heard a man seated at the table behind me say, "I wonder sometimes whatever happened to her after we had that scene when she told me she was Gay. It must be ten years ago and I feel bad about it every now and then. I just didn't know how to handle it, but I don't feel like I came through as much of a friend."

If you received the disclosure some years ago and now feel that you handled it badly, it is a waste to blame yourself. Like the rest of us, you only do as well as you can at any given moment. If the Gay person is still living, it might do you both good if you wrote a note from the vantage point of your feelings and awareness today. The relationship may have been irreparably ruptured and you may not get a reply, but it can only help both of you to show that you know better today. Perhaps the Gay person feels that he or she did not handle the revelation well either, but has learned a thing or two since then.

If the Gay person is no longer living and you feel the pressure of unfinished business, search for a positive experience that can help you feel finished. A letter to an editor, a contribution to a Gay organization, or a chat with a friend or relative of another Gay person could help take care of the unfinished business and leave you feeling better about yourself.

If you know or suspect that someone you know is Gay and have not yet been told, appreciate the fear and anxiety that inhibits the disclosure. All you can do, usually, is to make it openly known that you appreciate Gay people. Actions speak louder than words, however. Gay friends and Gay-oriented reading material in your home do more than announcements of pro-Gay feelings, which can sound phony. In some relationships the silence goes on too long and is too costly. If you feel oppressed by the secret, you may need to say so and precipitate the disclosure. In weighing your decision, however, bear in mind that the Gay person may be building strength, getting ready for the possibility that you will react badly. He or she also may be battling internal anti-Gay feelings. But approach with care. The person who is still doing battle within would sometimes literally rather die than have anyone he or she values guess at the Gay identity. Truly that person has not yet become Gay. He or she is not ready to "come out." Discussions based on your own pro-Gay reading can help to sound the person out and, if needed, may help him or her to move along the path to celebration of Gay identity. One sign of readiness for the confrontation is when you notice that the person about whom you are concerned no longer denigrates anyone else for being Gay. An even better sign is if he or she has one or more Gay friends who are admired and respected. From there on it is a matter of using your sensitivity. If you know the person well, you can tell if you are being frightening when the topic is brought up. If so, back off and wait a while longer, still letting it be known now and then that you are learning more good things about Gay people day by day.

Parents

It's a secondhand story but I believe it. A friend of mine who rides a commuter train to work every day swears she overheard the following conversation between two men early one morning. They had no sooner fallen into their seats and opened their morning newspapers than one said, "Today I made the discovery that I'm middle-aged." His companion continued to look intently at the front page and said, "You shouldn't use that electric blower, it only makes more hair come out."

"That's not how come I'm middle-aged."

"So what then?"

"It's when you realize you're stuck."

"How come it took you until today to realize you're stuck?"

"Well, you know, when I wanted to be a college student, I went to college. I decided I didn't like it so I dropped out. Later I decided I needed the piece of paper so I went to another college. I wanted to try drugs so I tried drugs. I felt like I was getting hooked so I stopped using them. I didn't like my first job so I quit. I didn't like living alone so I got married. I didn't like the marriage so I got a divorce. But this weekend my kid was visiting me, four years old and cute as can be. I sat looking at her yesterday morning and I thought to myself, 'This is it.' I'm stuck. You can get out of most things but you can never, never, get out of being a parent until the day you die. We may love or hate each other but I'm always going to be her parent. She may decide she doesn't want me for a father and split but I'll still be her father. I mean it never ends until I die. That's stuck. And when you're stuck, you're middle-aged."

Parenthood is a responsibility. If you are reading this book because a son or daughter is Gay, you are undoubtedly trying to live up to your responsibility. If you have chosen to read it on your own, it indicates that you are the kind of parent who will go out of your way to understand and help facilitate the growth and well-being of your offspring. If you are reading it because your daughter or son has asked you to try it, they are trying to tell you that they value you as a parent and want to use the book as a means of strengthening the bond between you. They may hope that the book will speak to you in ways that are difficult for them.

Parents are likely to have strong emotional reactions to learning that a daughter or son is Gay. You are apt to feel frightened. New information is often frightening, and it is not the first time you have experienced fright during your career as a parent. As in the past, you take it as it comes, one step at a time, learning more, helping to reassure your youngster, and staying alert to ways to make the situation better. It is the same with a skinned knee or a first date. As you learn more you will feel more comfortable and be better able to help your son or daughter.

193

Part of your fear when suddenly confronted with a part of the world so unknown to you is for the well-being of your offspring. You may also experience guilt because of the false but prevalent belief that it is bad to be Gay and that parents are responsible for it. It is the unusual parent who is so familiar with Gayness and has such a good communicative relationship with his or her offspring that sincere appreciation for the information can be expressed immediately.

The most frequent first question asked is, "What did we do wrong?" Well-educated parents who have read the wrong books or columnists may be all too prepared to answer their own question. "It was because we didn't pay enough attention to you; smothered you in love; favored your sister; let you get too close to Uncle Al; lived in the wrong neighborhood; sent you to the wrong school; burdened you with our drinking problem; didn't talk to you enough; frightened you with the example of our bad marriage; were too close to one another and shut you out; let you play with the wrong kids; kept you home too much; didn't make you go to church; let you get too close to the pastor; forced you to be too good; etc."

All parents have done some things "wrong" in the rearing of children. But the fact is that we do not know why some people retain awareness of attraction to people of the same gender and others follow the dictates of our culture and lose the awareness. Nor does it much matter, unless we accept the destructive assumption that Gay people are bad and innately unhappy (or unless we want to rear all children to retain Gay awareness). Gay people are Gay, and non-Gays are non-Gay, as the result of millions of factors that include: some present at birth, usually described as *temperament* (how active or passive one is and whether visual, auditory or tactile stimuli are most likely to cause a reaction); early and later learning experiences and child-rearing practices that together build the core of the person, sometimes called *character*; and the millions of experiences inherent in living in an unpredictable world that build on temperament and character and create the unique personality. The reason the causative factors are not important is that Gay people can be every bit as happy, satisfied, and productive as non-Gay people and perhaps live in a wider, richer world than most people. Their problem comes from a punitive society, not from their own identity, desires or behavior. Besides, any one factor could as easily contribute to a heterosexual as a homosexual preference.

So parents are not entitled to the credit or blame for a Gay son or daughter. They can be held responsible for how they behave after learning this information, however. Granted, you have your own years of prejudicial training to overcome, but love has been known to help parents fight greater odds. Experienced parents know that children grow best when given daily doses of love, respect, understanding and support. Grown children continue to develop best as adults when parents continue to offer these important emotional vitamins. And your Gay offspring, denied the love, respect, understanding, and support of the larger community is especially in need of yours.

"How can I rejoice when I know my daughter will feel pain?" a distraught father asked me some months ago. The answer is that you are not expected to rejoice in anticipation of the pain. You are asked to face the pain as an adult parent, help your daughter or son to get through it and grow from it, and do what you can to fight the malaise of community ignorance and prejudice that inflicts the pain. You are asked to rejoice in having a son or daughter who fights to preserve integrity and truth and who cares enough about you to risk your withdrawal of love in order to share and come closer.

Once upon a time, people selected the most beautiful and talented youths of the community and ceremoniously threw them into boiling volcanoes as an offering to appease the angry gods who might otherwise destroy crops and homes. Some parents are still willing to sacrifice their beautiful Gay offspring to appease the god of conformity. Parents are no better than other people. They have their own pitiable anxieties and weaknesses. I feel anger but I also feel compassion for the parent who breaks the sacred bond and turns away from the outstretched arms of a son or daughter because he/she has been taught that it is "the right thing to do" if they are Gay. Somewhere within the parent lives a deeper level of truth that has been violated, and that is an uncomfortable burden to carry to the grave.

For most parents of Gays, the disclosure of Gay identity does not come as a complete surprise. Usually you know your offspring fairly well and there have been clues. After the initial confrontation, however, your job as a parent is to encourage your offspring to become a self-respecting person who need hide nothing. To do this, you must quickly learn what it means to be Gay. Your son or daughter is one expert, but only one, and may still be inexperienced and misinformed. You need to turn to all available sources of information, including books and people.

But a word of warning. There are some psychiatrists and psychologists who have built their professional reputations and their livelihoods on the assumption that Gay people are "sick," emotionally disturbed or emotionally underdeveloped. There is plenty of evidence to the contrary* and the supposed evidence of these anti-Gay experts rests on their own prejudiced experience with patients who have sought help from them because they had already accepted the "sickness" assumption. Their point of view was the only one permitted in print for decades and it has the air of absolute authority. Do not let it intimidate you.

The so-called experts neatly subvert parental support by pointing an accusing finger and saying it is your fault that your offspring turned out so badly. In my more forgiving moments I try to remember that these professional people-helpers began with misleading information and then understandably developed blind spots, and eventually their professional reputations and livelihood depended on proving themselves right. But there are times, when confronted with the dead and the wounded who have been subjected to the unnecessary pain fostered by such professionals, that I am not so forgiving. Well-intentioned or not, they have Gay blood on their hands, and some of them are not yet rehabilitated.

Some parents have united in their support of Gay sons and daughters. There are organizations of parents with gay daughters and sons that actively fight community attempts to harm Gay people by depriving them of civil rights. There are national and local Gay organizations supported in part by parents and friends of Gays who sponsor sane research and fight to protect our civil rights.

---

*An early watershed study was: Hooker, Evelyn. "The adjustment of the male overt homosexual." Journal of Projective Techniques, Vol. 21, 1957, 1831. Also reprinted in Ruitenbeek, Hendrik M., (ed). *The Problem of Homosexuality in Modern Society*. Dutton, 1963.

Sometimes there is a culture gap as well as a generation gap. It may be hard to understand the Gay culture of your son or daughter, just as the culture of a different generation can be mystifying. You can ask questions, read, and honestly communicate your incomprehension and differences of values. You need not suddenly become Gay any more than you need become a generation younger to span the gap. All that is required is good will, support and effort. It is the trying to understand that communicates your caring and that is the most important parental gift.

Husbands and Wives

I have seen quite a few Gay men or women in my office who are paired in heterosexual marriage with a non-Gay partner. It is a fact of life that runs contrary to myth. According to anti-Gay myth, Gay people do not enter into heterosexual marriages because they are carrying too much "hatred of the opposite sex" and are unable to perform the necessary sexual acts. Further, according to the myth, when a Gay person does enter a heterosexual marriage, it is a "cover" or marriage of convenience that is sexless. Stories abound of Gay men married to lesbian women for the conventional convenience of both, perhaps because they are movie stars with heterosexual box office appeal. Interestingly, I have yet to meet anyone in such a marriage though I am sure that the combination, like all others, does exist. The Gay married people I meet are usually serious about their marriage and usually there are children involved.

Most often they appear in my office because disclosure day has come and there is some heavy fallout. Within recent months, for instance, I can think of the woman who consulted me because she had joined a women's group, become more honest and aware of her feelings for other women, met another woman on a camping trip, and fallen in love. The other woman was divorced but dating men and living with her single child. My client was living with her husband and two children. She had told her husband of her feelings and experiences and his reactions were generally liberal and considerate. That is, up to the point where she used the word love. Then he got worried. He felt threatened that the two women were growing so close and more threatened that they seemed so content with their sexual relationship. He asked that they try to have sexual relations as a threesome, but it was a disaster because he assumed he would be the focal point and he was more of a third wheel.

The two women came to see me, but we could never get the husband to join us. His tolerance faded rather quickly and he started issuing ultimatums. He wanted this childish nonsense to stop. A fling or an affair was permissible but this close love between his wife and another woman was out of the question. The women tried separating for a time but, having once experienced their truth, they found it impossible not to see one another and even more impossible to hurt one another. My client also did not want to hurt her husband. And everyone was concerned for the welfare of the children.

Matters resolved themselves as they often do. The husband entered into an affair with another woman, moved out of the house, officially separated, and then filed for dissolution of the marriage. The women are going to live together with the children, though there was a threat by the husband for a time of custody battle based on his wife being an unfit mother because of her lesbian relationship.

Then there was the strapping six-feet-four garage mechanic who worked out in the gym every other day and dressed up in women's clothes when his wife was out of the house. Cross gender dressing is called transvestism and probably about half the transvestites are heterosexual. This man's pattern was to dress like a woman and then pick up a man for homosexual sex. He eventually tried homosexual sex without cross dressing and the cross dressing without homosexual sex and found that it was the contact with other men that he was after. Curiously, he was able to tell his wife about the transvestism but not about his interest in men. He promised to give up the dressing and declared himself cured, intending to remain chaste with men.

More usual is the early-thirties professional man who presented himself in my office because he knew he was Gay, having half suspected it all his life. He had married his college sweetheart (he from the best fraternity and she from the best sorority, both active campus leaders and both terribly good looking) and promptly had one child in graduate school and another on completion of his professional training. As he said during the first interview, "I'm not certain what I want to get from this. Mostly I'm yelling, 'Help!' I don't want to stop being Gay and I don't want to stop being married to my wife or being a father to my children. I like my work a lot and I don't want to stop that. I guess I want to continue everything but with no secrets and without the worry about losing it all if someone finds out."

In the short time I have been working with him, he is already doing fine. He has told his wife and they are making adjustments to their newly discovered relationship. They both hope they will remain married, but are not sure it will work. He has begun to reveal himself to trusted people at work and has pretty much abandoned anonymous sex in favor of sharing sexuality with people who are willing to share themselves in other ways too. He has been slightly surprised to find that his alcohol consumption dropped, and amazed to find how frequently he carries suppressed anger. He is not surprised to find that some nasty pains in his stomach are going away. His big fright currently is what will happen if he meets the right man. Can he manage a lover and a wife in the same lifetime? His wife is worried about that, too. The word divorce hangs in the air unspoken. Each of them already sense that he has a need for the right man rather than a collection or series of men and both are unsure where that would lead.

Some husbands and wives know their prospective spouse is Gay before marriage, but more learn the fact later and there are reasons for that. Most of us who are Gay and heterosexually married entered the marriage in good faith, having been led to believe that our heterosexual feelings and love for the woman or man we were about to marry were proof that the Gay feelings should be discounted as not very important. Most of us were taught by books, therapists, counselors, and cultural myth that if one has both heterosexual and homosexual feelings and there is love in the heterosexual feelings that the homosexuality is just a phase. It is the "fooling around" proudly reported in English novels and biographies detailing boarding school days. It is the harmless childhood infatuation with friend or older idol that helps one learn one's proper sex role through identification. At worst, we were told, we were delayed in growing up or a bit confused, but a good heterosexual marriage should take care of all of that.

After the marriage vows, many of us realized that the feelings were not going to go away and some of us began to suspect that they might even be respectable and worthy facets of self. At that point, the married Gay faces a decision of whether to disclose the information and, if so, how much and how soon. The risks are even greater than usual. There is the fear of greatly hurting the spouse because of his or her own sexual identity training ("Why am I not man/woman enough to satisfy you entirely?"), possibly losing the important loving relationship altogether, and—if there are children—the possible loss of love, custody, or even contact with one's children. This is a heavy decision, and it is small wonder that most Gay husbands and wives choose the lonely pain of the secret rather than risk the possible seemingly catastrophic consequences.

If your husband or wife has taken the risk and has shared through disclosure, it may seem at first that the world has turned upside-down. Nothing in your training for marriage has prepared you for this. You have ahead of you the monumental task of ridding yourself of anti-Gay misconceptions and prejudices while somehow keeping your marriage and self-esteem afloat.

There is no reason for self-esteem to be damaged, but it is almost always threatened. During the initial period of reorientation, try to hold onto the fact that you are not worth less because your husband or wife happens to be Gay. You did not make your spouse Gay any more than parents do. You will hear echoes of anti-Gay myths telling you that it is because you did not provide enough sex, demanded too much sex, drove your spouse away, held too tight, etc. Forget the guilt. It is not your blame or credit. The fact is that this person of greater than average respect for inner truth and integrity chose you for marriage. From there you go on, armed with the additional information that your spouse is Gay.

Step two is the decision about whether to stay married. Even though the marriage license makes it more difficult to dissolve a relationship, it is a decision faced frequently, privately, by most married individuals even when neither are Gay. Each of the partners continues to change after the original commitment and the changes may lessen the compatibility or the satisfactions of being together. The Gay person must now consider Gay needs in the ongoing weighing of whether to continue the marriage. The husband or wife of the Gay person must decide if the revealed Gay identity reduces the desirability of the partner for whatever reasons or takes too much away from the union in any way.

Sometimes a spouse's anti-Gay training or homophobia surfaces immediately and the suitcase is packed soon after the disclosure is made. Usually, because it involves two people who love one another, the sorting takes much longer. The Gay identity of one partner becomes one more ingredient in the constant weighing of satisfaction in the relationship. Sometimes it is decided to stay together because of the children. If this is the only factor keeping the marriage going, it is almost always a bad idea and creates enough tension to make life worse for the children than divorce or separation would.

Remember there is no need for the marriage to be less sexual or less sharing. The announcement of Gay identity does not reveal a totally new person, it simply adds a new dimension. Sexuality and sharing change throughout the years of marriage anyway. The changes are not likely to be the sole result of this now-shared information.

For a few Gay people, the disclosure is about as far as it goes. They abide by vows of monogamy and behaviorally there is no change in the marriage. More often, there is some amount of change. The Gay spouse is likely to insist on exercising some personal freedom, on establishing some social-emotional-sexual involvement with one or more other Gay people. The non-Gay spouse may claim the same freedom at this point, find the Gay spouse's freedom intolerable, or hardly ruffle a feather. The only certain prediction is that the status quo will change and there will be discussion. The evolving formula for balancing the needs of the two people depends on the needs and temperament of the individuals.

If the two of you decide to preserve your relationship, more questions will come up. How much sharing does the non-Gay spouse want? Should details of Gay activities be shared or kept separate? Which friends, neighbors, or relatives are to be told, and how much are they to be told? When and how much are the children to be told? How are separate times to be arranged—prior announcement on the kitchen calendar, the spontaneous phone call, or simple absence?

The more both people are willing to share feelings (including the non-Gay spouse's hostility and anti-Gay feelings and the Gay person's feelings of deprivation and anger), the greater the basis for discussion and a satisfying marital arrangement. It is important to remember to respect feelings of love and mutual support during this sorting and to permit quiet periods of appreciation during which you enjoy your relationship rather than examine it. If it all seems too taxing and complex at moments, think whether you would change places with the silent bored couples one sees in restaurants.

There are fewer problems if each of you remember that the other person is his or her own person and does not belong to you like a possession. Your sense of well-being need not depend upon the other person's being in attendance at all times. Sharing the other person is easier if you remember that the more one loves the more capable of loving one becomes, so there is no need to worry about less love for you unless you actually feel the love for you being withdrawn.

Primacy of relationship can be very important as a reassurance. After much sorting, the couple often decide that the crucial factor is declaring the primacy of the relationship to one another. "There may be other people involved in my life but I am first and foremost devoted to you. Not every minute, but most of my caring energy goes to you and you come first. We will grow old together."

Sometimes a husband or a wife of a Gay person seems so well-prepared by experience or disposition as to make the disclosure a matter of only minor surprise or appreciation. I am thinking of a wife whose Gay husband prepared his disclosure for half a year. Within an hour she learned that her husband was Gay, had been all his remembered life, had had numerous brief amorous adventures over the years, and had for the past year been settled down with a lover who had been presented to her and others as his best friend.

Her response was, "I can't say that I care much for the deception, though after some explanation I see how he felt it was

202

necessary. I'm envious of all those secret adventures but don't feel cheated. He's been a terrific husband and father. Now I understand better some of his good qualities like his sensitivity with me and the kids and his willingness to stick his neck out and to stand up and be counted on civil rights issues. There is no big deal about having a lover except a change of name. My father had a best friend with whom he went on hunting vacations and for all I know they had sex, though I certainly never thought about it. So he has sex with his best friend and calls him a lover. I don't see what all the fuss is about. But I'm beginning to see how Gay people have been mistreated. I don't see any real change in my feelings for him except that maybe I appreciate him more and love him more now that I know him more completely."

Sex outside the marriage is usually the big issue. The gender is less important. You may have feelings about the kind of people your Gay spouse picks for partners; if they have a lot in common it may be threatening; if they have too little in common it can be seen as demeaning, since sex is the sole apparent basis for the relationship. You may be worried about contracting a venereal disease if your spouse indulges in casual sex with strangers. You may worry about blackmail if your spouse is not open about being Gay and becomes sexually involved with strangers. But in the long run it is these considerations rather than gender that cause concern and must be discussed and worked out to mutual satisfaction. It is very difficult to be Gay and remain monogamous in a heterosexual marriage.

The disclosure forces you to re-evaluate what you want from marriage. You may be glad you were stimulated to reconsider this question now, rather than permit your life to be guided by outmoded values formed in youth, before you decided to marry. You may find you have a better chance of getting what you want with this partner than with any other you have met. You may also find that you love your spouse as a person and truly want him or her to discover self and claim potential even if that means that your paths may one day separate. That is a truly unselfish love. You may have the kind of love that rejoices in the loved one's pleasures and victories rather than the kind that holds tight and kills growth. You may discover that you are in love with the person rather than in love with the marriage.

At best, the disclosure will open each of you to changes and growth and stimulate your sharing and mutual respect for differences. At worst it will mean a parting of ways—and if that is needed it can be done with love and respect.

I know of one such couple who are dissolving their marriage now. They are being subjected to terrible pressures from both sets of parents and some friends. She (non-Gay) is being told that he is a despicable person to have passed himself off as an eligible husband when he was nothing but a homosexual and that she should get every penny she can from him by way of compensation. He is being told that if he had married a truly feminine and caring woman, the homosexuality would never have become an issue and he could be a happily married man with children today. Because they do care for one another, they are trying to stay focused on the positive experiences they had together, the rich pool of memories they will have to share always, and their genuine good wishes for one another's future.

As they end their marriage, they seem to me to be more truly devoted and caring for one another than the average couple I see plodding their way through what they understand to be normal married life.

Daughters and Sons

I believe that it is important to be open and honest about your Gay identity with your children starting at the earliest age possible. There are, admittedly, occasional embarrassing consequences. When my daughter was about six years old, I was sitting outside reading *The Advocate,* which is a national Gay newspaper. Reading some of the words over my shoulder, my daughter asked, "What does 'Gay' mean again, Daddy?" I explained for the hundredth time that it means a man knowing that he could love another man and have sex with him or a woman knowing she could love another woman and have sex with her. My daughter went on about her play and I continued my reading.

A few minutes later the babysitter arrived and my daughter said she had to ask me something before I left. She wanted to know if I knew if the babysitter were Gay. I said I didn't know. Unperturbed, she said, "I'll ask her." Not yet as liberated as I would like to be, I said, "Maybe you ought not to do that, Honey. Some people are embarrassed by that question because they think it's too personal." My daughter said, "It's OK, we're good friends. She won't mind if I ask." I was left with my mouth open while she went off to ask. I would love to have heard the conversation between the two of them but the babysitter did not offer a report, my daughter forgot, and I am still wondering. I suppose that one of the advantages of having an openly Gay parent is that you get used to taking the world as you find it and letting the shock fall where it may.

Generally speaking, it is important for the Gay person not to hide Gay identity from offspring, because they are too close to keep in ignorance. To hide it is to give yourself the message that you are ashamed and that there is some cause for shame. To hide it is likely to give them the same message. And it is not such a good feeling to have a parent who is ashamed.

The longer you wait to tell the harder it is. The inevitable questions, whether spoken aloud or not, are "Why did you wait so long to tell me? Why did you let other people know and not let me know? Is it really bad? Didn't you trust me? Is it fair that you expected me to share my innermost secrets with you when you were not willing to share with me?"

With infants it is no problem. If you simply talk freely about being Gay and have Gay friends in the house and Gay reading material around the house, they will take it all as a natural part of life as they grow up. With older children it is more difficult—especially if they are teenagers or pre-teenagers, when anything having to do with sex is overloaded with importance and apt to produce blushes and giggles. But the rule of thumb still holds. If they are teenagers, it is still better now than later. Some Gay parents hold off telling for fear of influencing the sexual development of their offspring. That is just old anti-Gay cultural poison floating around again. No one minds trying to influence them to become heterosexual every day of their lives. If you take away the hidden assumption that heterosexual interests are superior, it no longer makes any sense to fear influencing their development. Also, heterosexual parents have been producing homosexual offspring for centuries and there is no reason to believe that the reverse is not true.

If telling is difficult and getting ready to tell is taking a large energy toll, perhaps it is best to simply plunge as you would into a cold pool. A friend of mine had been getting ready to tell his two pre-teen sons for six months. Last week he set aside the whole evening and worked up his courage. Over dinner he set the stage in a manner worthy of a well-trained college lecturer. He went through the history of the world, including slavery, and the varying customs of different cultures. Then he covered the civil rights movements in this country, the women's movement now in progress and led tactfully up to his question. "How come you guys never ask anything about the Gay struggle? You know we have Gay friends and you see books and articles about it around the house but you never mention it. I want to get into a serious discussion of it with you because I know it will make me feel better." One said, "Could we do it tomorrow night, because I have bowling tonight." And the other one said, "And Joe's Mom promised to take him and me to a movie that's in fifteen minutes." So much for preparation. He now swears that next week he will plunge. His wife was much amused by the whole drama. She has been rooting to get it all out in the open for months.

Many children do have Gay parents. Contrary to anti-Gay myth, Gay parents too often keep the children in ignorance for fear that the children will tell their peers and heavy repercussions will follow. Given the vigor with which children mirror our society's punitive enforcement of conformity codes, there is some genuine cause for concern. Their peers may give them trouble for having a non-conforming parent, but they can learn how to handle that kind of trouble and grow stronger as other oppressed minority children have done.

It is easier to have your Gay mother or father disclose their identity to you than for you to discover it. Anti-Gay feelings being what they are, too many children have been traumatized by making the discovery in a newspaper account describing their father's arrest. Others have learned by overhearing neighborhood gossip about their mother. If you learn about a parent's being Gay from someone other than the parent, the first thing to do is to ask your parent about it. It may be true and it may not. If it is true, it may take parents weeks or years to find the right words to explain their feelings, why you were not told sooner, and what it all means.

It means that your father or mother is different than other people, different from the way our television programs say a parent should be. Your parent is different because he or she is able to love another man or woman fully, body and soul. Is that so bad? In a world where grown-ups compete, cheat, steal from one another, and even kill one another for what they believe are good reasons, it is not so bad to have a parent whose "crime" is the ability to love.

There is another advantage too. Having a parent who is different makes it easier for you to be different. Certainly it makes it easier to explore your own Gay feelings, but that is only part of it. It also makes it easier for you to dare to be different in other ways. You will not be as tempted to take other people's word for what is right or wrong. You are much more likely to think for yourself at an earlier age than your friends who have no Gay parent, and that means you are much more likely to build a life that is personally satisfying.

There are possible disadvantages, too. If no one helps you or your Gay parent to get free of the prejudices against Gay people, you may think that your Gay parent is bad. You may resent him or her for having kept the secret from you too—not understanding the self-hatred that had been learned or your parent's fear of losing your respect and love. Once you know you have a Gay parent, you can begin to think those things through for yourself and consider the possibility that your parent is a better person than most for having remained true to his or her feelings in a world where people try to be like everyone else at any cost.

Your Gay parent may turn out to be a person with whom you can share your most intimate thoughts and feelings. Other people may be more tempted to tell you to feel ashamed or guilty. Your Gay parent has already had too much of that medicine and may be more likely to help you sort your own feelings and beliefs no matter what the rest of the world says.

If you are teased about it by other children, remember it is the same as other teasing. The children who tease are trying to express their own unhappiness and are looking for diversion by trying to make you feel bad, pointing out some way that you are different. They know they can hurt you most by attacking a parent you love. Deal with them as you would with anyone who is unhappy and mean. Stay out of their way until they are more calm and have more control. At that time, tell them you are proud of your mother or father because they have the courage to be different.

But if the teasing person threatens you with real harm and you cannot avoid that person, do not permit yourself to be harmed. Find a responsible adult or hit back if necessary. These unhappy people seem strong because they are not admitting how frightened they feel. If you hit them with your awareness of how unhappy and unsure they are, it is hard for them to maintain their balance. You have nothing to be ashamed of and no need for fear. You have a parent who is different but not bad. It is the people who tease who are bad and who are building more unhappy lives for themselves.

Sometimes sons and daughters must help parents. If you learn about your parent's being Gay when you are no longer a child yourself, and if your parent has not learned self-respect, you can help. From a newer, less prejudiced generation, you can introduce your Gay parent to today's thoughts about how diversity equals richness, and how people are more free to grow and develop if they are not busy trying to conform. You can even do some research and help your parent find some help, some healing reading and contact with other self-respecting Gay people and Gay organizations.

If you have sad or bad feelings about your Gay parent, try to get them said out loud. You can talk them out with a trusted friend, with the other parent, or with another trusted adult who does not mind your parent's being Gay. But if they even hint to you that it is wrong to be Gay, beware. They have been infected with anti-Gay prejudice.

When you are ready and not so afraid of hurting your Gay parent, talk to him or her about your feelings and see what you can work out together. By letting your parent help you with your bad feeling, he or she may clear some things up, too. Many parents throughout the centuries have hidden their Gayness and turned into bitter, lonely people because they were afraid of rejection by their children.

Whatever your age, you can help yourself and your Gay parent by learning from sorting your feelings. If you are honest you will come to feel proud of your parent eventually. Sharing and showing that pride can help.

Sometimes a parental marriage ends and it seems to be because one parent is Gay. In other circumstances, when a marriage ends, the children sometimes feel relieved because the parents did not get along well and did not seem to like one another very much, thereby creating a constant tension in the household. When the marriage ends because one parent is Gay, the children may be more mystified and hurt. There may have been little tension and little, if any, indication that the parents did not like one another or were not getting along.

It is a kind of divorce that we are seeing more of these days. It is not the result of hatred or cruelty. It is the result of two people having lived together as partners for some years and then finding that each has grown in different ways that makes them no longer suitable as partners. Each realizes that she or he must go off on a different path to continue the process of self-development and growth. A possible contributing factor to that sort of marital dissolution is the growing awareness of one parent's Gay identity.

The younger the offspring when such a marriage dissolves, the more difficult it is to understand, though, ironically, sometimes it makes simple acceptance of the situation easier. The important thing for you to find out from your parents is that each still loves you and that they are not parting because of you. The parents may be so preoccupied with the emotional and practical complexities of disengaging that they forget to let you know and you may have to ask. Sometimes you will feel better if you ask several times in different ways.

If your father is Gay and happens to go off and live with another man whom he loves, or your mother is Gay and happens to go live with a woman whom she loves, it may be difficult for you to accept this other almost-parent into your life (but not much more difficult than when the mother or father go off to another heterosexual union). Try to be patient. Time is a great teacher. Try to trust that your parents have done what they needed to do, sit back and let them love you while each of them tries to get their individual lives straightened out. You can learn a lot from watching them. There will be times in your own life when you must make difficult decisions and have the courage to change the status quo.

Our world is changing its social fabric slowly but surely and we are making progress in questioning old assumptions, such as the ones that have until recently kept adoption agencies from considering Gay parents for legal adoption. First has come the willingness of some agencies to place children with single parents and more recently we have seen the beginning of agencies placing adoptive children with Gay parents. But it is just a beginning.

Several months back I appeared on a panel in Reno, Nevada for a national meeting of child welfare agencies. The panel was made up of four admittedly Gay parents who were also professionals with something to say to this sort of audience. Our discussant was a judge from Arizona who was charming and intelligent and went out of his way to be friendly to the panelists. After our presentation, however, he announced that he was a prototypical judge and felt it his duty to reflect the mores of the community and that if those mores were to change, we Gays would have to shoulder the burden of education and furnish our visible martyrs.

He discussed how, in the cases that came before him for custody or adoption, it was rarely a "clean" case because the Gay parent was often unfit for parenting for some reason other than Gay identity. He said he was about to face the problem of the first "clean" case (which he had in his briefcase). He said he had never met the two Gay men who were trying to adopt but that, by all reports, they had everything to offer as parents. They had a stable relationship, good education, money, and status in the community—but they were Gay. In response to a question from the audience as to how he might rule in the case, he said he would rule against the adoption because the community was still not ready for it. At that point, a handsome, well-dressed, soft-spoken and articulate pediatrician arose from the audience and announced to the judge that he was the clean case and had travelled from Arizona to Nevada that day to see the face of the man who was to judge his fitness to be a parent without ever having met

210

him. A stirring moment! I think it was clear to everyone in the room which man would be a better parent.

There is one last myth to be exploded. I know a lot of Gay people who are parents, and I do not know one Gay woman who loves a son less because he is male or one Gay man who loves a daughter less because she is female. Openly Gay people have given up the pretense that they can love only people of the opposite sex and know that they can love anyone regardless of gender. A Gay person may generally be more sexually attracted to people of the same gender, but has learned through hard-earned freedom that it is only possible to love a person because of the way the whole person is. Your Gay parent loves you because you are you, and not because of your gender. But if you are not sure, ask him or her.

Sisters and Brothers

I have a dear friend who teaches in the school where my children are students. We always hug and express our mutual affection for one another when we meet and it is quite genuine. But every now and again she makes some negative remark about her brother whom she has made sure I know is Gay. Once I asked her if she disliked him because he is Gay and she said that she did. It does not fit with her generally enlightened outlook on life and I told her that. She has swallowed a lot of the Freudian psychoanalytic jargon about infantile homosexuals and every time he does something to irritate her, she reviews her psychoanalytic learning and finds the proper explanation for the irritating behavior in terms of his Gay identity. I continue to tell her that it does not fit with the rest of her. She would not resort to such useless dogma in explaining any other experience in life, yet she returns to it again and again when she is feeling bothered by her brother. Perhaps I will never understand her reasons fully.

It is easy for me to understand how a sister can be irritated by a brother even when they are grown up and live thousands of miles apart. It is easy for me to imagine how a sister might have been told that she had to love her brother during defenseless years when she was experiencing him as anything but lovable. But I would be unfair to theorize about my friend's relationship with her brother. I can only say that it smacks of putting too many eggs in one basket to ascribe all his negative qualities and behavior to his Gay identity. I can also say that it insults me as a Gay person. And I have said so.

Refreshingly, in today's crop of young people I have found sisters and brothers who are loving and supportive of siblings when they discover their Gay identity. At a recent mostly Gay party, I heard someone ask a young man if he were Gay. "No, I'm not, but my sister is," he said. "She's the blonde over there—the good looking one. She is also smarter than me. Guess she got all the good genes." He was partly joking, of course, and handled the friendly banter about "why don't you try it, you might like it" smoothly. What struck me most was the look of pride and caring that came into his face when he looked at his sister. If that is the new generation, maybe there is hope for us all.

Of course, when you first learn that a brother or sister is Gay, you may feel frightened. You may fear for his or her present safety or future well-being since you have heard stories of how tough the world can be with admittedly Gay people. You may also fear that you are Gay. Your fears are probably based on the misconception that there is something wrong with being Gay; otherwise the prospect would not be too alarming even if there is a cruel world out there. You may also have been indoctrinated with some misinformation that can be straightened out first by reading, then talking with a Gay-oriented counselor, or simply sitting down and asking your Gay sibling.

A Gay friend of mine was asked by his brother if being Gay meant he liked dressing in women's clothes. (Answer: No, that's a transvestite, who is just as likely to be a straight heterosexual.) Or if being Gay meant he wanted to have surgery to become a woman. (Answer: No, that is a transsexual.)

If you are afraid that you are Gay because you inherited it or that you may have caught it by growing up in close proximity to it, relax. It is not a disease. It is not inherited or contagious. It is an ability to love and you must develop it on your own. You may be Gay also, but your Gay sibling cannot take the credit for your identity. If you are bothered by an occasional homosexual feeling, you can again relax and congratulate yourself on your honesty. Almost everyone has such thoughts or feelings at some

212

time. The difference is that many people fear to admit them. If you are Gay you will know it because you will find people of the same gender quite attractive. You feel drawn to them emotionally and you feel sexually attracted—just like the ads say you should feel for "someone of the opposite sex." Your Gay brother or sister is someone you can talk to about regular or occasional Gay feelings or attractions because he or she can understand and appreciate them, but you will have to decide for yourself if you, too, are Gay.

If you are heterosexual, you can still do a lot of sharing with your Gay brother or sister and each become enriched in the process. You are of the same generation and speak the same language. You grew up in the same home with the same parents and shared childhood—yet this sibling is someone who has had very different experiences.

It is as if your brother or sister has spent some years in a foreign culture. You are sure to be full of questions about differences of language, values and and how they are explained by the differences in cultural history. Your brother or sister may not have all the answers, but will have many, and together you can explore the possible explanations. Anyone who knows two languages or two cultures is richer than the person who knows one.

Having a Gay brother or sister is bound to stimulate you to search out your own prejudices, not only against Gay people but also against other disadvantaged groups. It is bound to make you more sensitive to the injustices of the world and more likely to make you a socially responsible citizen. It can open up enough questions in your mind to make you more appreciative of people's differences and more personally open to change. All of this may begin to show you that you are actually indebted to your Gay brother or sister for helping you find a richer life.

As is true with parents, your Gay brother or sister needs your open showing of love, respect and support. The Gay person's running path is a lot less lonely if the family is cheering. But do not hold back on negative feelings. Only by getting out your hidden prejudices and bad feelings can they change. Once out, they will not hold up as you get to know your Gay sibling and his or her friends.

You can also help your parents leap the gap since you are distanced only by differences in sub-cultures while they have to contend with generational differences as well. Whatever you do, let it be wholehearted. Your Gay sibling needs your appreciation (or clear rejection), not patronizing acceptance.

Friends and Relations

The wife of a Gay male friend got tipsy at a party recently and made a speech which the next day's hangover made impossible to recall in detail. But she knows it had something to do with looking around the room and realizing that "in the last two years almost all my really good friends are women I've met through my women's group or Gay men. I am simply less and less interested in straight men. I didn't have any trouble getting used to a Gay husband, and I see now that it's some of the same qualities that drew me to him that draw me to other Gay men, like his not being afraid to be gentle and caring.

"But someone at that party had the bad taste to refer to me as a 'fruit fly' or a 'fag hag' and that's what set off the speech. I think by the time I finished I had everyone listening. I'm afraid it was a discourse on how you can be a good fag hag or a bad fag hag. First, I explained to everyone, as if they didn't already know, that a fag hag or a fruit fly is a woman who spends almost all her time with Gay men and finds them the best friends. I explained that you get teased about it because people assume Gay men are not sexually interested in women and that's OK with me because the people doing the teasing deserve their own stupidity and the fun it cheats them of. I also explained that, just as you don't have to be Jewish to be a Jewish mother, you don't have to be a woman to be a fag hag. I know some men who are fag hags because, while they can't locate their own Gayness, they look around one day and find almost all their best friends are Gay.

"Having elegantly laid the groundwork for my lecture while some devil refilled my glass, I then discoursed on how there are good fag hags and bad fag hags. The good ones being the ones that appreciate the laudable qualities of Gay people such as their not being stuck in sexist roles, and being able to relate person to person. The bad fag hags, be they men or women, are the

214

ones who hang around those awful Gay bars that are from the 1940s and reinforce every damned stereotype about Gay people that ever existed—like saying some man is your sister and that's why you like to go shopping with him, ugh!"

It seemed to me that her point was very well made. Whether one is a relative or a friend of a Gay person, you are a good friend if you take the person as an individual and do not try to reinforce those dreary and harmful old stereotypes.

Some friends and relations of Gay people want to relate better but are not sure how to do it, while some react negatively, wishing the Gay person were not Gay. The reason for the latter reaction is usually a fear that close association will reflect badly and make people start wondering about you. And that, of course, is based on the anti-Gay assumptions and myths which decree that it is bad to be Gay.

If you truly care for your friend or relative who is Gay, you will take the trouble to talk with him or her about it, do some reading and thinking and try to educate yourself. In the Dark Ages, Gay people were literally burned at the stake as "faggots"* because they were non-conformists, deviants, and therefore considered dangerous to the establishment. In recent years, the forms of punishment have been more subtle but still inexcusable. Those days are ending and anyone who is interested can learn about Gayness now.

If your reluctance to become more familiar with Gayness and Gay people is based on a general distaste for the subject and the people, you are probably suffering from homophobia. As earlier suggested, you can seek help for this condition; or at least be honest enough to tell your friend or relative that you do not want to be closely associated with someone Gay. The response you get may well be anger, but that is an appropriate response to an honest slap in the face. The two of you are at least being honest about your feelings about one another and less likely to truly hurt one another.

If you are a relative or friend who is not close, but learns of the Gayness and feels supportive, make your support known.

---

*Small sticks of wood used in building the fire.

It may strengthen the relationship, but even if it does not, the voicing of your support is bound to make you both feel better.

If you are a relative or a friend who has hidden your own Gay identity, here is a person with whom it may be safe to open your closet door and share. You may not be ready to disclose yourself to most other people and may need to ask that your wishes be respected. But in the meantime you can share common experiences, concerns, and joys and each feel less lonely.

If you want to relate better but are not sure how, the first step is to say so. The second step is to do some reading and the third step is to start meeting more Gay people. If I want to be closer to you and you come from another country, I will make efforts to learn the language and customs. If I know people from your country are disadvantaged and discriminated against, I will make it my business to fight that discrimination and protest the disadvantages. I will show you with my behavior that I want to be closer to you.

Your Gay friend or relative may not seem appreciative. There are reasons. When Gay people first start to reclaim their feelings, they get in touch with a lot of anger that has been stored up for years. Much of it is anger at the unthinking cruelty of the average non-Gay citizen (family and friends especially included). So, if you begin to become more sensitive to Gay people you may become aware of the anger toward you and other non-Gays from your Gay relative or friend. The anger is legitimate and real, no matter how unfair it may seem to you at first. It is only by being aware of, and expressing, this anger that the Gay person has hope of reclaiming feelings and surviving. When a good amount of the old reservoir has drained off, the Gay person will simmer down to expressing anger to you only when you do something or say something anger-provoking, and then the anger will be more efficiently aimed and quickly over. It is a phenomenon that has puzzled many about other awakening minority groups. The initial rush of anger is unexpected and frightening. It is inexplicable unless you have some sense of how it is to live with that anger dammed up inside you and how liberating it feels when it begins to come out.

You do not have to prostrate yourself in the path of this anger and ask to be whipped for the sins of all non-Gays either.

216

Just understand where it is coming from and try not to get in the way of the anger too often until the first rush is passed. And be honest with your own feelings (including anger) in response.

That is really all that is asked of you as a relative or friend of a Gay person. You are asked to listen and share if you can, to be honest in presenting your feelings, and to show you care, if you do. We Gay people will do the rest. And if anti-Gay bias has not closed your mind, you will find us good neighbors and good friends. We know how to appreciate differences and we know how to find fun, even during periods of painful growth. We know how to laugh and how to cry. Above all, we know how to love and appreciate the love of others.

4

Helping Someone Gay

This final section of the book is intended for professionals who earn their living by helping other people. As a professional you realize that each person with whom you work is an individual, not quite like any other person. No set of generalizations, therefore, applies to that person. But also you probably have learned that a set of generalizations can help you tune in more quickly to the individual by providing a focus that enables you to scan and compare which are and which are not relevant to this person.

If you work with someone who is Gay, or the relative or friend of someone Gay, keep in mind some psychodynamic generalizations about what is happening or has happened to the Gay person.

Psychodynamic Generalization

(1) The Gay person has learned to feel different. In this society, which values conformity, the person feels devalued or worthless even though he or she may be outwardly successful and accomplished.

(2) The Gay person has learned to distrust his or her own feelings. This process began with the dim awareness of attraction to people of the same gender and the environmental message that

such feelings of attraction are wrong or bad. Add to this the fear induced by anti-Gay myths, and the specific myth that it is almost impossible for someone with such "perverted" feelings to control the expression of those feelings into behavior.

(3) The Gay person is likely to have decreased awareness of feelings. The anger generated in a punitive environment and the anger at self for being different seems unjustified and therefore must be sent out of awareness where it continues to accumulate. The other feelings are affected through a process of generalization and are also given less awareness or attention.

(4) The Gay person, being invisible to others, is assaulted daily with attacks on character and ability. These attacks may come in the form of anti-Gay jokes and statements or in the form of omission when heterosexuality is being praised. Awareness of the hurt associated with these assaults (often from friends and family) is kept to a minimum so as to keep anger out of awareness.

(5) The Gay person feels alone, wrong, and fears further lack of support and affection if he or she reveals true thoughts, feelings, and identity.

(6) The Gay person is apt to be the victim of depression that includes some degree of immobility. Much of this stems from the hidden anger, the self-imposed limitation on awareness of feelings and interpersonal interaction, and the lack of emotional nurturance.

(7) The Gay person is likely to be tempted to dull the pain that surfaces now and again through misuse of drugs and alcohol or to end the pain by suicide. The use of alcohol is reinforced since Gay bars are one of the few community-approved meeting places for Gay people and suicide is encouraged by the community's failure to recognize the existence of respectable Gay people.

The professional who would help the Gay person can work toward reversing the psychodynamics presented in the preceding seven points. To illustrate, I shall offer some general suggestions to four different groups of professionals—teachers, clergymen, medical workers, and police—as to how they might work toward helping Gay people. Then I will focus on the work of teachers, providing detailed examples of how they might act in various situations to reverse the psychodynamics listed in the seven generalizations. Finally, I shall list some guidelines for psychotherapists and counselors, suggest techniques that they may find helpful in working with Gay people, address a few words to researchers and talk about my own clinical work and my personal growth as a Gay professional.

Let me begin with some ground rules to be kept in mind by anyone working with Gay people.

Ground Rules

(1) Help can be offered but not forced. Gay people have had too much damage done by would-be helpers who forced us to move in ways that we sensed were wrong or foreign to our nature. We will be rightly suspicious of help offered until we can sense its personal validity. You would do well to describe in advance what sort of help you intend to offer (in detail) and why. The Gay person will not truly accept help until a bond of trust has developed.

(2) Your primary objective should be to help the person to become more truly himself or herself, which means that you want to help the person become more truly Gay, developing conscious self appreciation and integrity that includes the integration of Gay thoughts and feelings. You will not encourage self-destructive behavior and attitudes. You will not encourage conformity, per se. You will encourage integrity by encouraging behavior and attitudes that match inner feelings.

(3) Try to find your own homophobic or anti-Gay feelings and seek whatever help may be necessary to rid yourself of them. If you keep them hidden they will act as blind spots and sabotage the work you are doing to help a Gay person. Having grown up in this culture, no one begins entirely free of these feelings.

(4) Be willing to admit to yourself and others your own homosexual feelings as well as your general feelings of attraction to people of the same gender. If you do not recognize and honor those feelings within yourself there is no basis for trust. You may choose seldom or never to act on those feelings but your reasons for that choice must be clear also.

(5) Do not inform on the Gay person by telling others—especially family. We Gay people are keenly aware of how this information can be used against us and must choose for ourselves who and when to tell. Divulging information about Gay identity is an absolute violation of trust as well as an ethical violation of confidentiality. These five ground rules easily become part of one's natural style in working with Gay people because they facilitate the work. Neglect of the ground rules slows down, disrupts, or terminates the process.

Professional Helpers

TEACHERS. From nursery school through college, the teacher is the one professional person who is sure to have contact with every developing Gay person. Much of the early learning about our society (and consequently much of the early negative learning about Gay self) happens in school.

Gay children—those who already realize their true feelings depart from the supposed norm of attraction between males and females—are entitled to the same education as other children. They are entitled to learn about themselves and to feel good about themselves.

Teachers have thousands of opportunities to teach youngsters to appreciate their unique selves and to appreciate differences among people. It is important to help youngsters learn to devalue conformity and to value integrity—that diversity offers riches while conformity leads to mediocrity. The lesson can be learned again and again in every area of human endeavor from science to art. Creativity makes the unusual possible, and it is the unusual that advances our civilization. We need to be able to evaluate both the unusual and the usual—to be capable of pragmatic and moral judgment—but not to be enslaved and impoverished by the norm. And it is about time children were helped to free themselves from the labeling of behavior as "masculine," "feminine," or "queer," so that each child can simply be the person she or he is. That would help everyone.

Teachers can, with casual remarks, reinforce the idea that Gay, like other natural human differences, is honorable and worthy of respect. You cannot ignore that some of the heroes of past and present are Gay. Gayness was an important factor in the life of Walt Whitman, Sappho, the Emperor Hadrian, Gertrude Stein, Julius Caesar, and Alexander the Great. Such information must not be hidden, because these omissions are dishonest and defeat understanding.

Within your teaching situation, you can raise the consciousness of your colleagues by challenging bigoted jokes even when they are aimed at Gay people and questioning the supposition that heterosexual is better. If you do it with tact and good humor, some of your colleagues are bound to begin to see, sooner or later, just as they did with Blacks and women. Some may even surface as Gay themselves. And respectable everyday models are badly needed.

Much of your service is to invisible students. You do not know as you look over a classroom which students are now Gay or will become Gay as they mature and unfold. Much of your pro-Gay stance is to give messages that will bolster the self-esteem of these developing youngsters. You will protect them from indignities the same way that you would protect any other minority group member in your class. The fact that you do not know which students belong to this minority group makes it more pressing rather than less, though their invisibility makes it necessary for you to remind yourself more often rather than reacting to visual cues.

And keep this in mind. If you do not help the Gay children, who will? They do not know how or where to find validating information. They rarely feel they can turn to family because they fear rejection. Their Gay peers are invisible. They get bad ideas about themselves in libraries that have old books. They cannot even approach known Gay adults in Gay organizations. The legal risks for the Gay adult who reaches out to help a Gay child are extreme; caring can easily be interpreted as "impairing the morals" or "contributing to the delinquency" of a minor, if not distorted hysterically as outright "child molestation." Some of these invisible developing Gay children are quite literally depending on you for their lives.

CLERGY. You are the first person, if you are trusted, to whom the Gay is likely to turn in distress for understanding and advice. In the past, Gays have often been told by the clergy that they are sinful and immoral, that they must repent and mend their ways. This does not help.

Perhaps you could examine your religious beliefs and the teachings of your particular religion. Is there only one interpretation? Would Jesus or Moses or Buddha have found a Gay person distasteful or inferior and demanded change? Are you so sure that Gay is bad?

Even if you are unable to see the beauty and dignity of Gay people, even if you continue to believe that Gay is sinful and immoral, be good enough to tell the trusting Gay person who consults you that it is your opinion and your interpretation of your religion. Say even that others agree with you, but in fairness say that other respected religious experts do not agree with you and tell them where they can find someone who has pro-Gay opinions. They might be interested to know, for instance, that the Rev. Troy Perry has founded a church for Gay people called the Metropolitan Community Church which has spread across the country, that there is a highly respected group called The Council on Religion and the Homosexual, that there is a Roman Catholic Gay group called "Dignity" and a Jewish Gay group called "Achvah"; and that the Rev. William Johnson was the first publicly Gay man to be ordained by an established church. Your congregant might want to read some pro-gay books written by respected theologians, biblical scholars, and people of various religions who are actively involved in ministry.

If you cannot find it in your heart or in your religion to serve the Gay person with respect, give him a chance to find that appreciation elsewhere. He may live to thank you. You may save his body as well as his soul and you may feel truly blessed.

For those of you who do feel good about Gayness, it is important to let the person know that you see it as a viable life style. Do not paint the picture dark because of past oppression. Let the person know that oppression can be fought. Every religion has had to fight its oppressors. You can use religion to show that lack of popularity does not equal lack of worth. As a trusted religious guide, you can show that it is the quality of your life, the way you honor your religious beliefs and serve your fellow man that counts, not the gender of the persons with whom you choose to involve yourself intimately.

PHYSICIANS AND NURSES. Medical people are the group next most likely to be sought out by the developing Gay person who is searching for answers about identity. There are plenty of data to support you in reassuring the Gay person that, while not statistically average, Gay is quite normal. It is not sick. There is no need to seek medical treatment for it. Because of a bigoted society there are problems associated with being Gay, but those are problems that can be solved and there are people who will be glad to help with the solving. And there are books that can be read, books that talk about Gayness with respect.

Be willing to use your authority to reassure families. Most families are not very sophisticated and have been exposed to all of the anti-Gay myths, including the myth that Gayness is the result of, or related to, some sort of medical illness. You can reassure them that it is simply a normal variant, the way some people develop, and they can learn more about it by doing some reading and/or consulting a Gay-oriented counselor. It would help both the Gay person and the families if you had a list of Gay readings and Gay organizations to hand out.

You can also be helpful by not assuming that a patient is exclusively heterosexual. It can be embarrassing for many patients to have to announce to a doctor or nurse that they are Gay. When examining a patient, taking a history, or prescribing treatment keep in mind the possibility that this person, regardless of appearance, may be Gay unless he or she has volunteered the specific information that they are exclusively heterosexual. Your tactful and tacit assumption that a patient may well be Gay will cause you to be experienced as more professional and trustworthy by your Gay patients. It is bound to give support, and may inadvertently save a life.

POLICE. It is a commentary in itself to say that Gay people rarely seek out the police. Jews did not seek out Cossacks during the pogroms, either. Police are often viewed as the visible enforcement of discriminatory written and unwritten laws. Nonetheless, knowingly or unknowingly, a policeman or policewoman will often be in contact with a Gay person. Do not depend upon stereotypes. Assume that anyone may be Gay.

You can help by showing non-phobic, tactful, courteous understanding and approval of Gay people even when you are not sure if there is one present. Gay behavior is now, or one day soon will be, legal behavior. The laws against us are discriminatory and unconstitutional and are rarely enforced by law enforcement agencies except as part of a discriminatory campaign, vendetta, or political attempt to divert public attention. The weight of your authority in supporting us can be very helpful. You can support us individually and you can support us as a group publicly as we lobby to change the antiquated laws. If you are Gay yourself, the day may come soon when you can openly announce yourself and still keep your job.

An unprejudiced policeperson knows a lot about the varieties of people of all backgrounds—their wants, needs, and habits.

Gay people are good citizens. Except for the laws that forbid being Gay, we are less likely than the average citizen to break a law. Most Gay people have been buffeted enough to have developed respect for the rights and property of other people. Police cannot work without the support of the citizens. Gay people are ready to support the police if you demonstrate that you deserve our respect and support by lending us your respect and support.

In most cities and towns, Gays can still be blackmailed, beaten and harassed with impunity. These conditions are intolerable for any group of citizens. Show by your professional behavior that you know that it is our tormentors and not we who are the criminals and that you will use your authority to help us.

You can also help by educating your colleagues. Some of them have been guilty of outrageous atrocities toward Gay people. You have probably witnessed or heard about some of them yourself. You can help by refusing to condone such behavior among your colleagues. You can help by laughing at the code of machismo that has been used to drive some of your colleagues to fear association with us. You can help by not laughing at anti-Gay jokes and gently assisting in the raising of consciousness within your profession.

226

PSYCHOTHERAPISTS AND COUNSELORS. In some ways we are the priests of this new world. People look to us to tell them what is good ("normal") and bad ("sick"). Because of the mistakes of past and present, prejudice and ignorance masked by professional expertise, those of us who have had professional training as psychotherapists and counselors and who offer this service to the public must prove ourselves to prospective Gay clients. They would be more than foolish to believe that we can help them simply because we are licensed as psychiatrist, clinical psychologist, clinical social worker, or marriage and family counselor. As such, we are part of the small army of professionals who have been most destructive to Gay people struggling to understand themselves in a homophobic society.

Just this morning, I had a telephone call from a dear friend. He is himself a well-trained, licensed clinical psychologist. He and his wife have been having some difficulties with their marriage and she has had some unsureness as to how she is being affected by his identity as a Gay man. They decided that they would do a few months's work with a woman whom the wife had been seeing for individual psychotherapy. My friend talked to the therapist and was assured that she sees nothing wrong with Gay identity.

Yesterday, after two months of working with this couple, the therapist told my friend that his homosexuality is indeed pathological. She assured him that it was not genetically inherited, but that it is deeply ingrained as a character disorder. She told him that he must either face up to living with and compensating for the disability, or that he might try to rid himself of it through some strong measure such as Primal Therapy. (As it happens, she has been in training as a Primal therapist.)

My friend was hurt and angry, knowing that he had been badly served. He was calling for some support from me. Even after all the effort he has put into finding his worth as a Gay man, the years of self-doubt and insidious insult from the world around him rushed to the fore in that dreadful confrontation yesterday. The therapist had waited until he had opened, dropped his defenses, trusted her, and was willing to distrust himself in order to learn new behavior. At that moment she delivered herself of her homophobic message. By today he was in touch with his anger and resentment and knew what he must do. He knew he must telephone her and point out her unprofessional deception and do what he could to forewarn other Gay clients from becoming involved with her. But with all his training and stability, he had been knocked off balance. Imagine the average citizen coming in from the cold!

There is no reason for any professional to assume that he or she has the competence to work with Gay people. Gay-oriented retraining programs are becoming available. Even a Gay therapist would do well to experience such a program and check for blind spots built in by years of living in an oppressive society. Certainly no non-Gay therapist or counselor should assume competence in serving Gay clients without retraining and Gay-oriented supervision to unlearn the prejudices and misinformation acquired in life and in professional training programs.

Psychodynamic Reversal

Taking one profession, teaching, as a focal point, here are some detailed examples of how the seven generalizations and five ground rules listed earlier can be used in everyday situations to help reverse the usual destructive psychodynamics surrounding the developing Gay person. (The teacher's style will vary considerably with grade level, background of the child, and personality of teacher.)

(1) Conformity. When the teacher gives an assignment to be written on lined paper, someone is sure to write on unlined paper. Someone else is bound to add some absent-minded doodles. It is an opportunity for the teacher to tell why the original request or demand (to do the assignment on lined paper) was made and to appreciate, nevertheless, the originality that prompted a couple of people to be different. "I love the flower that Gladys drew in the corner of her paper because it is something of Gladys. You see, I never could have assigned each of you to draw a flower because it would not fit all of you, but Gladys' flower will give me a treat while I'm reading her paper." "Mr. Smith did his composition on unlined paper. My reason for asking that it be done on lined paper was to make it easier to read. But your handwriting is clear, neat and attractive, Mr. Smith, so I'll have

228

no trouble reading it and it will provide a break from all that lined paper. I hope it doesn't embarrass you if I use this as an example to point out to people how you can make yourself noticed and valued by other people if you dare to stand out from the crowd by doing something your own way while not disadvantaging anyone else."

(2) Distrust of feelings. In a high school discussion class a student says, "Well, Narcissus fell in love with himself and that's wrong." Teacher interrupts the discussion. "That's an interesting statement I wish everyone would think about. I know that I used to think some of my feelings were wrong and then I began to see that all of my feelings—even the ones other people wouldn't approve of—are right because they are my feelings. But it's my behavior I have to watch out for, because sometimes it can get me into trouble. Fortunately, I've also learned that the more I know all of my feelings are OK, the more I feel able to control my behavior. What about Narcissus? Can you separate his feelings and his behavior?"

In third grade there is a heated discussion about where the group will go on its class trip. The question is finally decided in favor of the suggestion made by Tommy and Joe. In the mild uproar of jubilation when the question is settled, Tommy and Joe spontaneously hug one another. Susan, who is sitting near them, giggles, points, and says, "Look, Tommy and Joe are in love." Everyone laughs. Tommy and Joe are embarrassed. The teacher says, "It takes more than a hug to show someone you're in love. But I'm glad Tommy and Joe are free enough to be able to show it when they feel good about one another. I know a lot of people who are so scared of what other people will think that they hardly dare let anyone know what they're feeling even when they're feeling good. It's a shame to rob yourself of your own feelings. You can always control them but it's nice to be able to show at least some part of every feeling you have."

(3) Decreased awareness of feelings. Anthony swoops across the playground and takes the handle of the wagon just as JoAnn is about to reach for it. JoAnn looks glum and retreats from the group. The teacher has noticed the incident and goes to her. "I can surely understand that you feel bad, JoAnn. If that had happened to me, I'd be really angry."

An eighth-grade class is taking a brief look at English history and has come across a king who is considering executing a man who had been his best friend and trusted advisor. One boy volunteers, "He don't care about nothing, man. That's how kings are." Teacher says, "When somebody says 'I don't care,' that person is trying to tell you that he wants you to believe he has no feeling. I never believe that. I know people always have lots of feelings. I know that when I say I don't care, I'm usually hiding hurt and anger—maybe because I caught myself loving someone and have the silly idea that I shouldn't. Do you see how the king might be feeling that way here?"

(4) Attacks on character and ability. A first grade girl during show-and-tell says, "When my friend Janet and I grow up we're going to live together and not get married and go all over the world together, and maybe we'll be astronauts but we're not sure yet." Another girl laughs and says, "You and Janet gonna be too ugly to get husbands." The class laughs. The teacher says, "Some of the most important and beautiful people in the world don't marry and choose to spend their lives with a friend. When you get older you may read about two women named Gertrude Stein and Alice B. Toklas, who were famous and very important people in the world not too many years ago. People are still writing books about them. And some day you will learn about two men named Hadrian and Antonoüs. Antonoüs was the most handsome man anyone knew and Hadrian was the most powerful king and they were friends who needed to be together. So, even though I know Ruthie may change her mind when she grows up, I don't think it's silly that she wants to spend her life with Janet."

A teacher overhears the end of a joke just before the bell rings to begin class. "So—get this—the guy says, 'Listen, honey, I ain't carrying any heavy rifle, I slept with the General last night.'" Much laughter and knee-slapping. The teacher says, "That joke was funny but it was also sad. You know, once upon a time people used to tell jokes like that about Blacks and Jews. The problem with those jokes is that they get you believing the stereotypes are true—like believing that all Gay men are puny and weak. I've met some Gay men with a lot of muscle and I'll bet no one here would want to get into a fight with one of them." "No, they might lick you," another boy says and there is another uproar of laughter.

The teacher laughs and says, "Are you beginning to get the idea? That one made us laugh because it reinforces the idea that Gay men are so desperate that they would be delighted to have even furtive body contact with each and every one of you gorgeous men in this room. Can you see how that might not be true?"

(5) Alone and unsupported. The third day of kindergarten, George bursts into tears. "I don't care," he says. "I don't want to be a brave boy. I want to go home." The other children do not know but the teacher knows he is the only child in the class from a home where neither parent speaks English. He has a trace of an accent himself. The teacher picks him up and puts him in her lap for comfort and says, "You know, George, everyone in this class feels the way you feel now sometimes. It's especially hard if you think you're all alone and the only person who feels the way you do. It even happens to me sometimes and I'm a grownup. I don't think you have to be brave, but I hope you'll let me hold you a little while because it makes me feel better."

The day following a test, a high-school girl says, "I don't think the test was fair. It wasn't a fair test of what we learned and I think you should not have given it to us." There is a long silence as the other students watch and wait to see what will happen. The teacher says, "Thank you, Susan. Naturally, I don't like being told I'm a poor test maker or an unfair person but I'm certainly glad you spoke up and said what's on your mind. I'll bet some other people here feel the same way but were afraid to own up to their feelings because they were afraid it might get them into trouble."

(6) Depression and immobility. A second grade teacher is worried about Grace. The child is no trouble but she sits by herself most of the time and rarely interacts with the other children. Nor does she seem busy with her own ideas or tasks. But Grace is always willing to do what she is told. The teacher announces that he wants everyone to help him think of something they can all do each day that will be a new way of doing something they are used to doing. "Let's have fun," he says. "For example, we might try changing the hand we write with today and see how it feels and tomorrow we could spend the whole morning making sure that each person is holding hands with another person at all times. But I'd like to have your ideas."

In a senior-high literature class a teacher noticed several students who seem quiet, inactive, and unhappy. "Where do you suppose writers get their ideas for literature?" she asks. "They have to use imagination and very often they start by remaking the world the way they would like it to be. For this week's assignment, I would like each of you to invent three situations you have never been in that are plausible. In each situation I would like you to invent two people whom you have never met. Make one person someone whom you are genuinely surprised to discover you have loving feelings for and the other person someone you are surprised to find makes you angry."

(7) Drugs, alcohol, and suicide. A third grade boy comes to his teacher and says , "I have a funny feeling and I want permission to go to the office and get an aspirin." "What kind of funny feeling," asks the concerned teacher. "It's not really a headache," answers the boy, "but my Mom and Dad left this morning on a trip and I've had this funny feeling ever since I said goodbye." "That funny feeling may be sadness, or loneliness, or missing, or even anger," says the teacher. "I'd really like you to get to know your feelings even when they seem uncomfortable. Would you do me a favor and see if you can think about exactly how you feel so that I can write it down for you during recess? If you still think you need an aspirin after that, I'll send you to the nurse."

An eighth grade teacher starts a general discussion with the class by saying, "I'd like to talk about how people learn to handle painful feelings. You know, on TV you often see someone take a drink when something important happens that hurts his feelings, or you see the heroine reach for pills, pull her hair and scream that she can't go on living. I don't think that drinks and drugs do much to solve problems and jumping off the bridge doesn't give you a chance to change your mind later. What do you think?"

Retraining: Twelve Therapeutic Guidelines

As part of a professional's retraining seminar sponsored by the Association for Humanistic Psychology in 1974, Betty Berzon and I created twelve guidelines which I will state and explain here. Some of the retraining must be experiential, since didactic instructions have little effect upon attitudes. Some of the retraining must also involve supervised therapy with Gay clients, since hidden attitudes, prejudices and blind spots are notorious for their many subtle disguises. The twelve guidelines are explained here, not as a retraining program in themselves, but as a suggested sample of the ingredients that go into such retraining. Those guidelines that cause greatest discomfort are apt to be the areas where self-examination and retraining are most necessary.

(1) It is essential that you have developed a comfortable and appreciative orientation to your own homosexual feelings before you can work successfully with Gay clients. This applies whether you consider yourself Gay or non-Gay. And having accepted the existence of your homosexual feelings is not enough. You must appreciate and value those feelings. Your private truth will out in the intimate counselling relationship no matter what your party line supposedly is. If you believe that homosexual feelings are okay but heterosexual feelings are better, you are going to transmit that destructive message to your Gay client. If you believe that your homosexual feelings are fine but the thought of ever translating them into behavior makes you nauseous, you have homophobia and you will sooner or later communicate your devaluation of Gay sexual behavior. You may choose to restrict your sexual behavior to heterosexuality because you know you have been too damaged to sustain a deep, positive, loving relationship with someone of the same gender. You may choose to restrict your sexual behavior to heterosexuality with one partner because both you and your partner are most satisfied and secure that way. But if you choose not to translate homosexual feelings into behavior because you feel that behavior is bad or distasteful, all the rationalizations in the world will not prevent you from communicating your secret message that you devalue homosexual feelings. As for the professional who says he or she has no homosexual feelings, they are about as well off as the psychotherapist who says he or she never dreams. It indicates that you are out of touch with your inner emotions and would do well to consider another profession.

(2) Consider very carefully before entering into a psychotherapeutic contract to eliminate homosexual feelings and be-

havior in your client. Willingness to enter into such a contract implies that homosexuality is pathological and undesirable. Even though homosexuality has been eliminated, per se, from the "sick list" of the diagnostic nomenclature of the American Psychiatric Association, the memories will linger in the mental health professions for a long time. There are still counselors and therapists who are willing to consider accepting a client with the agreement that they will work together to eliminate undesired homosexual thoughts, feelings and behavior. The professionals take the seemingly broad-minded stance that they are there to serve the public and would not think of trying to eliminate Gay identity, but are willing to work with a client who wants to get away from homosexuality if that is his free decision. Hopefully you can see the foolishness of their reasoning if you change the word homosexual to heterosexual. Would you agree to a contract in which the intention is to help rid a person of heterosexual thoughts, feelings and behavior? Rationalizations again do not help. Even if there is something pathological about this particular person's homosexuality, it is the pathological facet that needs examination and elimination, not the homosexuality itself. Some leaders in the field of behavior modification have taken a public stand against working to eliminate homosexual behavior, and it is about time. Practitioners in this field have committed more atrocities than even the followers of Freud (not Freud himself, I am happy to report) and the Primal Therapy brigade. It was the behavior therapists who thought to attach electrodes to genitalia in order to move people along the path to conformity.

(3) All Gay people have experienced some form of oppression related to their being Gay. The subjective reality of that experience must be brought into consciousness so that it can be worked with. This is an area where a therapist or counselor is at a serious disadvantage if he or she is not Gay or has not worked with a large number of Gay people. The clues to experienced oppression are likely to be quite subtle. A client may laughingly tell a story about how she was sitting at a large family gathering around the Thanksgiving table when her uncle told one of his tired fag jokes. No one laughed much but she was vastly amused to think how surprised they would all be to know there was a lesbian at the table. Behind her laughter is the hurt and

rage, the feelings about being alone within the family once more. In early childhood we all began to learn the myths about homosexuals. We learned that they are defective people who are not able to perform well in many areas valued in our society. Most Gay people have had plenty of times in their lives when (like their non-Gay peers) they felt unsure of ability in some area and then consciously or unconsciously associated the presumed inability with their presumed inferiority. Rather than be found out, they have changed course and tried for success elsewhere. That is oppression, and when the awareness of it begins to hit consciousness, changes can happen. But it takes a sensitized therapist to pick up the cues. More blatant oppression, such as being fired from a job or disowned by a parent, may not be passed over lightly either. It is very likely that the Gay person pushed aside many of the feelings associated with the experience because the feelings were so overwhelming and there was so little available support. He or she needs room in awareness, the liberation of affirming his or her own validity so that it becomes possible to move on.

(4) Help your client to identify incorporated stereotypes of Gay people and begin deprogramming and undoing the negative conditioning associated with these stereotypes. The stereotypes are there. We all grew up with them. Gay people are sexually promiscuous, unreliable, capable of only shallow affection, weak, passive, etc. Gay men are limp-wristed caricatures of female sex goddesses. Lesbians are castrating women who are too full of anger to love anyone. The list could go on and on. You may be able to catch your client making veiled reference to some such trait in himself or herself. More often you will catch a hint of it when your client is talking about another Gay person or voicing some negative feelings about you, if you are Gay. It is always a signal to flush out these stereotypes. Do not push them away with quick intellectual denial of their validity. They feed on emotional fears of the past and present, not on intellectual facts. Better to let the poison out. Better to incite your client to rant and rave and spit out all the bad things he or she has ever heard about Gay people. Better to keep the client aware of how much these old stereotypes are still alive within, waiting to sabotage growth. After some practice doing this a number of times (it is

even more effective in group therapy than in individual sessions), you can begin to laugh together about the bitter foolishness of it all. But do not laugh too soon. Those stereotypes have been killing people for centuries. Each time the poison is out in the open, you must do something to help deprogram. Ask for examples of real-life Gay people who do not fit those stereotypes. Ask for examples of Gay people, including the client, who display behavior and abilities that are the opposite of the stereotypes. And then laugh again, because it is just as sadly funny that some Gay people have run to opposite extremes to elude identification. The ultimate goal of the deprogramming in this area is the emotional message that it is all right to be whoever you are, regardless of gender and sexual orientation.

(5) While working toward expanding the range and depth of awareness of feelings, be particularly alert to facilitate identification and expression of anger, constructively channeled, and affection, openly given. Gay people too often learn early in life to hide feelings from themselves and others. It is a story partly true of any oppressed minority group member. Such a person usually becomes adept at hiding feelings from others, but still has the support of family and friends who share the minority identification and are apt to be relatively safe recipients of expressed feelings, so that it is not necessary to hide feelings from self. But the Gay person usually grows up alone with no one in view who shares his or her feelings and deserves the mutual respect and confidence. The early message is that the erotic and affection feelings are wrong. This alone generates some natural anger since you are being told it is wrong to be you. But the young Gay person is still too defenseless and does not feel entitled to the anger, so it gets buried along with most of the awareness of erotic-affection feelings for people of the same gender. This violation to one's nature, along with the myriad of insults that accumulate during the years of growing up invisibly Gay, create enormous anger which never seems justified. Then there often develops a fear that if the anger begins to leak through the dam, there will be no holding back the flood. Through commentaries on daily events shared in individual therapy sessions and through experience in therapy groups, the Gay person must relearn to express her or his feelings of erotic-affection and anger at every given

opportunity. She/he must experience these feelings as perfectly acceptable. The anger need not be destructive and can be voiced softly. The erotic-affection need not be orgiastic and can be expressed with a few moments of touch and/or voice. Reassurance is gained with each expression. These two hidden areas of feelings are usually so powerful in their presumed need to be hidden that, through a process of generalization, they have invalidated some parts of a wide range of feelings and cheated the Gay person of much of his/her emotional life. The reclamation of the wider range of feelings depends upon the therapist's alert, prompt and relentless assistance in identifying and expressing all feelings, with special attention to anger and erotic-affection.

(6) Actively support appreciation of body-self and body impulses. Don't be afraid to touch your client as a means of demonstrating that you value and trust physical contact. The key word here is appreciation. First you must help your client to question what, if any, harm there is in any body impulse or what, if anything, is unattractive about any part of the client's body-self (remembering and emphasizing that the body is something you are and not something that you have). But this work together will tend to highlight the acceptance rather than the appreciation of the client's body-self. Most Gay people have been taught that it is their bodies and their body impulses that make them different from the "normal" person and therefore subtly defective and subject to so much harassment and difficulty.

It takes willing and active effort on the part of the therapist to counteract the years of training that have taught us Gay people to hate our bodies and distrust our body impulses. Direct references by the therapist to the attractiveness of the client's body can help. This most especially should be done when you catch a hint that your client is discounting the value or beauty of his/her body in some way. That is the moment to reflect what you are hearing, query the client as to higher negative body feelings, and make your own positive body observations about the client.

You can also suggest techniques the client can use to reclaim more positive body feelings. Auto-massage and tender generalized masturbation can be recommended. Anything that helps a person to learn to appreciate the body once more is helpful.

Then there is the matter of touching your client. Some therapist's say all of the right words of appreciation and never touch a client more than to shake hands. No matter how sophisticated your client or how profound the theoretical explanation of this stance, there is a primitive person inside the client who is recording a primitive negative message: "If you really thought I was attractive, instead of just giving me some words to make me feel better you would want to touch me and you would find a way to touch me no matter what your ethics or training." And it is true. A good hug, pat or appreciative touch on the arm now and then give the primitive and powerful message of body appreciation that goes far beyond mere words. And in so doing you give the additional message that one need not fear one's body impulses.

But here is an area where the therapist may need to get his or her own personal feelings and fears straightened out. Therapists, like other people, have grown up in a society that is distrustful of body and sexual impulses. Under no circumstances would I recommend explicit sexual activity between therapist and client. My strong feelings about this are not because I believe that sex is bad or that sex between therapist and client need necessarily be bad. I do believe, however, that sex is as complicated for therapist as for client, and that if the two engage in sexual intercourse, the chances of the therapist maintaining perspective sufficient to do the job for which he/she is being paid drop significantly. When I am asked this question by a client, this is my truthful answer: "My reason for not acting on my sexual attraction to you is that I am afraid it would rob me of the perspective I need to work with you. It would be too easy then for me to see you in terms of my needs rather than yours. It is something that therapists and clients may learn to manage productively someday, but I'm not up to it yet."

It is very important that the appreciative touches of the client's body be sincere—teasing is seldom helpful since it is apt to confuse both therapist and client. I am willing to exchange a backrub or massage with a client in a group setting where there are social controls, but would be unlikely to do so in an individual session because of socially conditioned notions of seduction.

238

To the extent that you can communicate ease of body contact that is appreciative of your client's body, you demonstrate beyond words that there is nothing to fear—that just because you enjoy body impulses to touch, there need be no automatic or compulsive move into sexual activity. There is also the opportunity to demonstrate your respect for the client's right to accept or reject behavioral expression of your body impulses.

In my experience, therapists who have had Gay-oriented training are much more clear in this area of body contact and sexuality because it is covered so directly as part of the training. We must be clear about it, because we are dealing with the anti-Gay myth that Gay people are so enslaved by their sexual desires that they cannot be trusted not to translate sexual desire into instant behavior. It is the traditionally trained heterosexual-oriented therapist whose training was inadequate in this area who is most apt to "slip" into sexual activity with a client.

As a psychotherapist, you are there for reasons other than sex, but when you are sexually appreciative of a client it certainly is helpful to make that known. It may be a minor matter. The client may have little or no sexual interest in you. But it can help the client one more step along the way to considering his/her body positively. Seeing your own relaxed appreciation of your body impulses helps enormously. The client is helped to see that the impulses can be given life in various ways and need not lead to interactions that are, for whatever reasons, undesirably complex.

(7) Encourage your client to establish a Gay support system, a half-dozen Gay people with mutual personal caring and respect for each other. Like everyone else, we Gay people need support from people with whom we can identify and people whom we trust. Most of us grew up feeling alone and lonely, different from other people. And perhaps we are. Certainly our reality is a shade different than the supposed reality of our culture. So each Gay person can create his own "family" by selecting at least a half-dozen people who are Gay and whom he or she likes and trusts. Of course, the client must check with these people to see if the liking and trust are mutual. Respect is important. We have been taught lack of respect for ourselves as Gay people. It is important to have mutual respect with the people in your support system. The client may not need to see these people very

often but needs to be able to check in with them from time to time to hear their gladness and experience their valuing. And these are the people to turn to when the world is telling you that you are crazy, wrong and bad because of something having to do with your Gayness—just as my psychologist friend called me after the unfortunate experience with the therapist he and his wife were seeing. After a lifetime of being told you are wrong, there must be a small circle of trusted supporting people to whom you can turn and check out reality. If they tell you that you ought to think it over again, you do. If they tell you that you are being persecuted by some homophobe you can believe it. They provide the security that a family is supposed to provide, so that you can grow. Each of them offers a hand to hold, warm arms to enfold you until you feel safe, and a soft shoulder to cry on when the need is there. Together they stand ready to celebrate with you anytime. They represent the beginning of the end of loneliness.

(8) Support consciousness-raising efforts such as Gay discussion groups, pro-Gay reading, and involvement in Gay community activities. Raising consciousness means simply becoming more conscious. It is imperative that Gay people (like Blacks, women and other disadvantaged groups) become conscious of the ways in which we are disadvantaged. Meeting with other Gay people in a discussion group or support group is one very helpful way of identifying facets of oppression, but it does more than that. Just to sit in a room full of Gay people is a meaningful experience. Remember that each of us felt pretty much alone at one time. Seeing all the different kinds of people who are Gay reminds you that you are not alone and that you need not follow any stereotypes. There is room for everyone and each of us is uniquely individual. And as people open their hearts and lower their defenses we discover the universality of feelings—some of them are feelings that we thought were ours alone but we find that they are common among other Gay people. We receive immediate consensual validation. Sometimes as you hear people talking about a particular feeling related to some common aspect of Gay oppression, you begin to realize that you too have that feeling within but have kept it so dim that you never admitted it to yourself. Pro-Gay reading and work in the Gay community can have much the same influence on opening and validating feelings.

Ultimately each Gay person must learn to validate his or her own feelings, but this sort of community support gives an enormous boost. In addition, the pro-Gay reading gives the authoritative weight of the printed word to tell you that you are OK being the person you are. That is hard for non-Gay people to understand, but we have been reading about ourselves as second-class citizens all our lives, and we have been brought up in a culture where the printed word has almost sacred authority. Now to see Gay people writing Gay words of wisdom is like a reprieve that gives sudden perspective. You begin to be in a position to evaluate instead of defending yourself against the onslaught of judgment. And working in the community does one more thing. It assures you of your own strength and ability to help other Gay people. It assures you that other Gay people (and therefore you) are worth the help. It is the ultimate statement of self-worth as a Gay person.

(9) Work toward a peer relationship with your client. The message: you are not a second-class or inferior person. It is probably the "Doctor-god, keeper of life and death" medical model that has so infected the mental health professions. We even seem to be stuck with the word "health." Whatever it is, psychotherapists and counselors are terribly prone to come on as omnipotent sages. This is reinforced by the client's need for models. In the usual therapy process a dependency develops and then is worked through, just as one earlier worked through the dependency on parents, only hopefully done more thoroughly and constructively with the paid help of the therapist. Even so, the client usually terminates believing that this wonderful therapist is superior, if not superhuman. Since life's path usually carries the client away from the therapist, there is no great harm done by this lingering mystique and it makes the therapist feel grand. But with Gay clients, this phenomenon is counter-therapeutic, and the therapist must have the courage to prove beyond any doubt that he is no better a human than the client. The reason is that we Gay people have had a whole world telling us that we are inferior all of our lives. If this one person who helps us most is slightly superior then we are still, after all, inferior. It is easier for a therapist to show his vulnerability and unfinished and unpleasant facets in a marathon group than in individual therapy, but whatever the setting it is important to demonstrate that you, the therapist, have

defects and that you share with the Gay client the human dilemma of always being on the road and never reaching the destination, while not being bad or incompetent. Sometimes you can even point to an area in which the client is clearly a better person and, if you care about the Gay client with whom you are working, that should give you a thrill.

(10) Encourage your client to question basic assumptions about being Gay and to develop a personally relevant value system as a basis for self-assessment. Point out the dangers of relying on society's value system for self-validation. It is a long, tedious, terrible job but the Gay client must be helped to go back through his life (a written autobiography is sometimes a good stimulus) and root out nearly every assumption he or she has learned about the goods, bads, rights and wrongs of human feelings, attitudes and behavior. Having identified these learned assumptions, the client must be helped to re-examine them in the light of today's information and adult judgment and decide which assumptions need to be kept, which discarded, and which altered. This provides the foundation for a personally relevant value system that can be used as a rudder for steering through the unpredictable and turbulent waters of life. To survive, a Gay person must see that she or he cannot afford to accept unchallenged any pre-packaged set of assumptions even if they were given by such exalted authorities as parents, church, government, or revolutionary political group. The Gay person has grown up in a world that uses an interlocking set of assumptions surrounding the basic assumption that Gay is bad. Accepting a part of that interlocking package with no questions asked is going to give a feeling of vague discomfort because of logical inconsistencies that develop when new assumptions are squeezed in to replace the few that were deleted. So the new individually tailored set of values must have their own internal logic and must feel right to the individual. For a Gay person to trust any culturally given set of values is suicide—often literally.

(11) Desensitize shame and guilt surrounding homosexual thoughts, feelings and behavior by pleasantly encouraging graphic descriptions of Gay experiences and, when appropriate, sharing your own. One of the things that has helped us to survive is our available "camp" humor. It pokes fun at the ultimate fool-

ishness of everything and provides a broad foundation of acceptance for that which is human. Humor is by far the easiest way to get at the guilt and shame surrounding homosexual thoughts, feelings and behavior. "Had any good fantasies lately?" with raised eyebrow can do a lot to move things along. Sometimes you ask directly that the client be sure to report any thoughts, feelings or behavior that have been homosexual and embarrassing in some way. You need only hear it out and calmly state the usual truth that you do not see anything wrong with the homosexual parts of the report, per se (you might even daringly add with a smile that you found that part interesting and stimulating). You are working to desensitize and quiet the guilt and shame. Sometimes there is a wrongness or badness involved; sometimes the client has violated his or her own standards and values and understandably feels guilt or shame. But never need guilt or shame be related to the homosexuality itself. And the surest way of communicating this, if it is permitted within your style of psychotherapy or counseling, is to mention your own homosexual thoughts, feelings and behavior now and then. Best of all is to use group therapy situations to show that you are having such thoughts, feelings, or behavior on the spot and feel relaxed and self-appreciative about it, or do feel embarrassed but know that it is only a hangover from your own past oppression.

(12) Use the weight of your authority to approve homosexual thoughts, behavior and feelings when reported by your client. This is important to counteract experience with disapproval by authority figures. Like it or not, as a counselor or psychotherapist, you are an authority figure. In the preceding guideline you were instructed to use therapeutic techniques to induce the client to reveal more and more homosexual thoughts, feelings and behavior so that he or she could be desensitized by the lack of negative reinforcement. In this final guideline, you are asked to use your authority flatly to counteract the authority of a lifetime that has said homosexuality is bad. It can be done with a smile, a handshake, a hug, or the use of simple, sincere words like "good" or "God, that must have been fun and felt good." Or, in a group, if you see one client touching another in a manner that has sexual overtones and it looks as if both are enjoying the contact, you need only smile and nod to undo some of the dam-

age of past years. This is the guideline that is most likely to make many counselors and psychotherapists uneasy, and it betrays how deeply ingrained is the cultural instruction that homosexuality is bad.

How to Help

For almost all of us who are in the helping professions, a large part of the motivation for going through all of the training was a real desire to help other people. Each of us had to learn—partly in the course of training, certainly in the early years in the field—that even with good training and good intentions it is impossible to help everyone. Each of us has our individual limitations.

Many individuals who happen to be professional counselors and psychotherapists have spent a lifetime keeping distance from their own homosexual feelings and impulses. For some of these people the effort has been reinforced and the strain compounded by the homophobic teaching of Freud's followers. They have been subjected to the preaching of heterosexual superiority in the guise of objective studies of human behavior. I know a number of psychotherapists personally whose lives are tortured by their attempt to maintain a nearly total heterosexual adjustment when their inner nature yearns for Gay companionship. Two of them have a series of idiopathic grave physical illnesses. One has nearly killed himself "accidentally" several times. One died recently from an unexpected coronary at an early age. My heart goes out to them, but they cannot be helped until they are willing to risk giving up the dogma that has instructed them to follow the heterosexual path at all costs. And the risk is not that bad if you disclose slowly and with the help of pro-Gay friends.

If you know that you are struggling with this sort of conflict, consider psychotherapy with a Gay-oriented therapist or counselor. If you intend to hold tight and continue to try for a thoroughly heterosexual orientation while struggling with your conflict, you must admit to yourself that you are not in a position to help Gay clients. In fact, if you have any reason to believe that you are somewhat conflicted about homosexuality, you must admit the likelihood of blind spots that make you unsuitable to work with Gay people. It is your moral and ethical responsibility to admit this disability to yourself and to any Gay client who may seek your help. Sharing this information with a prospective client and referring him or her to a Gay-oriented professional can be a major contribution. That is a way to help.

If, on the other hand, you know that you are Gay, feel inclined to explore that part of yourself, or are simply attracted to Gay people, why not get some Gay-oriented retraining? Get rid of the destructive prejudices and myths you have collected and prepare yourself to be of help with direct service to Gay people.

We need all the help we can get, provided that help is competent. It is not because Gay people are sick that we need all the help. It is because Gay people are asked to cope with a heavy yoke of oppression without the help of natural family and community.

We must start when young to shoulder the burden and find the strength to seek out friends who can help. Because of the extra burden, we need extra strength, and we can use the help of competent professionals in building that strength. We can also use your help in reducing the burden placed on us by society.

Great help can be offered by pressing community mental health facilities to offer a Gay Services Program staffed by Gay-oriented professionals. There is no reason why the Gay taxpayer should have to find the money to pay a private Gay-oriented therapist when he might prefer to make use of the mental health services supported by his tax dollars. Such programs have surprised and pleased health care administrators with their success, based largely on word of mouth advertising.

A real asset that a Gay-oriented professional has to offer is the ability to assess when a Gay person does and does not need professional help. Too many non-Gay-oriented professionals believe that the person automatically needs help if he or she is Gay. The Gay-oriented professional takes the Gayness as a given, knows the additional stress involved and strength required, and can listen to hear whether the person is managing adequately. Sometimes you need only serve as an information center, telling the inexperienced Gay person where to meet other Gay people and how to get involved in Gay organizations, or what sort of

Gay-oriented reading material is available in the library and book-stores.

Most of all, we need help from professionals in treating the homophobia that is rampant in our society. As more professionals get rid of their own homophobia and learn to appreciate gay as natural and viable, they are in a position to challenge symptoms of homophobia in the Gay person's parent, sibling, colleague, employer or teacher, whom they may be treating. Help us get rid of homophobia and we can live our lives without putting such a large portion of our energy into that struggle each day. But first, of course, you must rid yourself of whatever traces of homophobia linger in you, or at least identify them and point out to others whom you would help how you are struggling to rid yourself of the noxious influence.

Orientation, Style, and Technique

From my personal professional experience and the experience of the professionals whom I have helped to train, it seems to me that any orientation, style or variety of techniques can be adapted to use with Gay people. Bioenergeticists, Primal therapists, post-Freud Freudians, and behavior-modification people have been the most dangerously homophobic, though there is nothing in their theory or techniques that make this necessary. A homophobic tradition has developed in these groups, but within each group I know of more than one person today who is trying to help his and her colleagues break free and see the homophobic tradition for what it is.

My own style in individual psychotherapy tends to be an eclectic conglomerate with telltale traces of heroes past and present, including Freud, Reich, Jung, Sullivan, Rogers, Perls and Maslow. Like most therapists who have been in the field some years, I have had to learn what works well for me as a unique therapist and what techniques apply in particular situations with particular clients. I have added or polished some techniques because they seem to work well with many Gay people. These would include the use of an autobiography to explore not only past history but unquestioned assumptions and value systems; the use of an angry book or feeling book in which the person is asked to

246

write feelings for ten minutes each day; breathing exercises and self-massage as a means of reducing tension and making friends with the body-self; examination of dreams for messages from the inner self about past, present and future; and the assisted search for quiet expressions of anger.

For me, the most effective work with Gay people is to be done in groups. Partly this works for me because I am a group-oriented therapist, but I also believe that Gay persons derive special benefits from a group because of the years of being invisible and alone while building a negative self-image. I conduct one ongoing weekly group myself and supervise others. In addition I lead a weekend group once every six weeks. Typically, I will see someone individually until I feel we have formed a sufficiently strong bond of trust and understanding and then will introduce the person into a weekly group, decreasing the frequency of the individual sessions until the person is seen in group only. The person may attend a weekend anytime we both agree he is ready.

The weekend group is very different from the weekly group and I shall describe it shortly in some detail because it illustrates the use of the twelve therapeutic guidelines given earlier. The weekend group is designed in such a way that an artificial community is purposely created, emotions are deeply stirred, and the person is shown how much he or she could be getting from life. The ongoing weekly group I sometimes call the "struggle group." People are continually frustrated because it is not as pleasing as the weekend group. It is structured to be half way between the artificial, Utopian community of the weekend and the pale everyday world. Each person in the weekly group must struggle to change himself and the group to bring it closer to a satisfying reality in which more needs can be met. It is the "how to" group. The difficult learning acquired in the struggle is directly applicable to the world outside and can be transferred to other relationships the next day.

The format of the weekly group changes from time to time but a typical format as of the time of this writing would be as follows. The group has approximately twelve members. People group in fours in order of arrival and discuss the emotional highs and lows of their week for fifteen minutes. At the end of the fifteen minutes they decide which person of the four should have a massage and that person is massaged for fifteen minutes by the other three. (The massage helps everyone get centered, provides primitive messages of caring, lowers anxiety, builds trust, and facilitates individuals having contact with one another who would ordinarily have little to do with one another in a group of that size.) After the massage the entire group assembles for announcements of anything that any person wants to explore during the remaining two-and-a-half hours of group time. We never have time to get into all agenda items but the whole group is aware of the things that are avowedly on other members' minds and hearts. A wide variety of group techniques is then used to work with items brought up until five or ten minutes before ending time when each person is asked to say briefly whatever is on his mind.

I say "he" because, to date, the weekly groups and most of the weekend groups I have conducted have been composed solely of Gay males. That is because I have been operating on the assumption that Gay women would do better working with a Gay woman therapist. I have done some mixed (Gay and non-Gay as well as men and women) weekends over the years and some Gay-oriented mixed groups in recent years and am currently on the verge of changing my mind, partly because I am now better tuned to the realities of women (particularly Gay women) and partly because the mixture gives an added richness to the group. The description Gay used to screen men for the groups, by the way, is defined broadly. I am willing to consider the man Gay if he is aware of sexual, emotional, spiritual and intellectual attraction to some other men and knows himself to be capable of acting behaviorally on that attraction. He may be monogamously involved with a woman at this point in his life but may still be considered Gay if he knows he could involve himself as fully with a man tomorrow. In years past (starting in 1967) I led all-male mixed groups but found that too much energy was drained from the Gay men in educating and satisfying the curiosity of the non-Gay men in the group, so I switched to leading Gay groups.

The weekend group is special to me. I have been conducting Gay male weekend groups since 1969 and have been following pretty much the same format since 1970 and I have yet to tire of this experience. Twelve men are selected. They may or may not have had previous experience with psychotherapy or with group.

248

Each is screened in a fifteen-minute interview some time before being accepted for the group . We ask name, address, phone number, age, description of previous therapy and group experiences, permission to contact any current therapist, social, sexual and occupational history, experience with drugs, alcohol, and suicide, source of referral, and a positive and negative fantasy about the weekend. People are screened out if it seems likely the weekend will stir too much emotion too quickly to be productively assimilated.

People assemble on Friday evening after dinner, between 7:30 and 8 P.M. We have a home-like, comfortable building all to ourselves and people arrive, as per instructions, with sleeping bag, pillow, toilet articles, a favorite record album, and a picture of themselves as a young child. Candles are lit, music is on the phonograph, coffee, tea, fruit, cookies and other snacks are waiting.

We begin at 8 P.M., seated comfortably on pillows in a large, but not vast, group room. I ask that people take the opportunity, before getting to know one another too well, to fantasize about one another. Each person looks around the room, picks a fantasy cast for a movie he will create in his mind and then shuts his eyes and watches the movie for five minutes. Those who want to share their movie verbally, do. That is the first ground rule of the weekend. No one will force or coax you to do anything. If you want to try something suggested and/or to share your private experience, do so because you want to, not because someone else wants you to.

We then have introductions with each person passing around his picture of himself as a child and truthfully saying as little or as much as he wants to about how he got from that child to this adult, his name, what music he brought and why, and his expectations or fantasies of the weekend. In the course of this I suggest that the music is usually played on break times but that, like everything else for the weekend, each person should attend to his own needs. If he wants to hear music at any time he should put it on the phonograph and if someone else has different needs he will turn down the volume or take the record off and somehow it will all work out. (And it does.)

Next comes some sort of fantasy exercise involving child-hood memories. The one most frequently used culminates in dar-ing to write a poem about a particular childhood memory. The poem is shared with one person and then with another. We then reconvene as a group and listen to anyone who wants to share his poem with everyone. Once again people are reminded not to wait to be urged because no one will urge. Few if any evaluative com-ments are made after the readings. People listen respectfully, there is a brief silence, and then someone else reads his.

The next fantasy exercise is one that spans all the years of one's lifetime and culminates either with the old man (who is you) whispering a truth in your ear the moment before his death or with a fantasized wise old man of the mountain answering your question. Again, people share the experience verbally only if they wish to share.

Now, having some fantasy and reality information about one another and having shared some experiences of childhood and expectations of old age, life and death, we move from the fantasyland of mind without body to the body-person. Each per-son finds a comfortable spot to stretch out on the floor without touching anyone else. Lights are extinguished and people are led through a sensitization exercise that helps them to relax, become more alert, and tunes them in to awareness of their own body. Throughout the exercise each person is reminded to quiet the words in his mind if possible and do without categories, judg-ments and evaluation while experiencing the body-self.

For the second phase, people are invited to try the same exercise again, but the second time without clothing if they wish. Before the third and final phase each person is told that it will involve body contact with other people and invited to find a quiet place at the edge of the room if he wishes to sit it out. Those who wish to participate are asked to find a comfortable standing po-sition with eyes closed and then to begin to move comfortably through the room. They are guided through the same sort of body exploration with others that they had done with themselves and again reminded to stay as free of judgments, categories and words as possible.

This ends with a contemplative resting period during which time anyone without clothing who wishes to dress himself partly or fully may do so before the lights are turned on again. Then there is a sharing verbally of what has been experienced with the reminder that there is no requirement to share, nor need that the person manufacture a reaction to share, but to be alert to energy wasted on wanting to say something and holding it back. Reactions once again underline the uniqueness of each person and the lack of a group "party line" to which one should conform.

Then the "want ads" are introduced. One whole wall of the group room is designated as the community bulletin board for the weekend and people may use it as they see fit. Each person is asked to keep two current wants up on the board at all times. And each person is urged to feel free to experiment with expressing wants as a way of tuning in to his own feelings. People are reminded that there is a difference between feelings and behavior and that they may feel free to express any want even if they would choose not to translate that feeling into behavior. The purpose is to let yourself and the world know about your feelings as a means of reassuring yourself of your right to them.

For years, I then put out a half gallon of wine and asked each person to make sure he drank very little (less than his usual amount) since the purpose of the wine is to facilitate relaxation and talk rather than to create escape in inebriation. Lately, I have stopped offering alcohol since it is so easily abused in the "gay bar" training. Instead I ask that people experiment with finding ways to relax socially without the aid of alcohol. The final ground rules are added: no illegal drugs for the weekend, no other drugs unless prescribed and necessary. People will experience conflict with other men we remind them, and be tempted to resort to societal programming of fight or flight, but are encouraged when that happens to stay and look for alternative means of satisfyingly resolving the conflict. They are asked to let the rest of us know if they want help. People may sleep anywhere in the building that they wish, but there are to be no permanently closed doors or secrets from the rest of the group. Massage oil and sheets are available and all the food is available to be eaten at any time. We set a starting time for the morning and then adjourn for social talk and the writing of want ads. Throughout the evening, I and any co-leader present have participated in every exercise and duly reported our personal experiences truthfully.

On Saturday morning, after a self-help breakfast (sometimes a few people are inspired to prepare a special omelet for others), we assemble as a group and share whatever feelings and thoughts have accrued since the group disbanded the night before. This time each person is asked to say something as we go around the room. If there was any sexual activity, it is treated like any other event—we want to know how the person felt about it and whether it created any particularly positive or negative feelings. (It is made known that group leaders will not involve themselves sexually with group members—not because sex is bad but because it easily clouds one's perspective.) There is a constant subtle reminder to each person to take the responsibility for his own behavior, but know that the rest of us are there to help if needed.

Next we have a full hour during which people are relieved of words and asked to try to pay attention moment by moment to doing exactly what they want to do. They are told they may leave the building but should stay within the context of the "community" (taking someone else for a walk, for instance) and should regard this one hour as a lifetime that may be spent satisfyingly without prejudging how one wishes to live it. At the end of the hour there is almost always a reluctance to use words once again. It is usually a powerful and moving experience to relate without the shield of words while being honest with yourself as to your wants, needs and feelings. The sharing of this experience verbally usually leads us into some natural interactions in the group. People begin to express more feelings about one another, both positive and negative.

The afternoon is difficult to predict. Most commonly we get into finding ways of expressing anger that are not too frightening. Sometimes there are explorations of death, friends who have committed suicide, parents who have died. Sometimes we create funerals so that someone can locate and express feelings about someone important from the past. Invariably a deep closeness and bond develop during the afternoon.

We eat out on Saturday evening in nearby restaurants in a Gay section of the city. We usually go in groups of two, three, four or five, but there have been weekends when the whole group needed to go out together. The dinner is usually a high. People find themselves in public with other Gay people who were strangers twenty-four hours before and about whom they have real and deep feelings now. There is some experimentation with the expression of these feelings in public, usually to the amusement and pleasure of observers, who thereby lend support and positive reinforcement.

After dinner people are tired and not wanting to encounter or get into "heavy" emotions. It is at this time that we do another body exercise for those individuals who want to feel better about their bodies. It involves one person at a time standing in the middle of the room, undressing as others watch quietly, and talking about his entire body from head to toe in terms of what he likes about his body and what he does not like about his body. He is asked to say his most favorite and least favorite part of his body. He then goes around the room maintaining eye contact with each person as that person silently and carefully touches the part of his body he has stated is his least favorite. The person then goes back to the center and listens as people give honest reactions, both positive and negative, to his presentation of himself and their feelings about his body. This is not a beauty contest, and evaluation of each unique, natural body is encouraged. The exercise is uniformly anxiety-provoking for the person in the center, gives him eye-opening, corrective information from others and has a sleeper effect of making him feel much better about his body in the weeks and months that follow. Only those who volunteer go to the center for this exercise.

The other usual after-dinner Saturday evening activity is a "party." We provide costumes, music, soda, juices and food, and sometimes some games such as tag or spin-the-bottle. It is reliving of childhood with the humor, grace and wisdom of adults. It is a celebration of Gay identity. Leader and co-leaders have once again participated truthfully throughout the day and evening. We try to end the evening on a note of fun and thoughtful musing as to one's values.

Sunday morning starts with the sharing around the circle but the rest of the morning (which starts early) is unpredictable, since what happens has to do with the accumulated existing needs in this particular community. Throughout the weekend people have been reminded to stay in touch with their feelings, keep their want ads up to date, and express feelings when possible. Much of Sunday morning is often devoted to working out the feelings about one another and relationships that have begun to develop in the group. The constant question: "What could you do right now in this community that would make you feel better?" Other people may give hints and suggestions but the ultimate responsibility and value-based decision rests with the individual. Sunday morning is almost sure to contain laughter, tears, and an exquisite bond of closeness. Here is a Gay family containing honored positive and negative feelings, with strong bonds created from individuals who could not trust one another a day and a half before.

We end near noon on Sunday with a focus on each person, one at a time, while anyone who wishes says anything that would feel left unsaid if he were never to see that person again. The goodbye is presented as related to death and people are reminded that we must always be ready to let go of another person. So each person is asked to consider that he may well never again see each person in that room and make sure that he is "clean" or "up-to-date" or "not withholding" with each person before they part. And so ends the weekend, almost always with a few lifetime friendships having started and a much better idea in everyone of how to create and nourish your own Gay support system.

Each participant is invited back for an individual half-hour followup interview some weeks or months later as a way of giving us feedback and of sorting and fixing the learning for him individually. I personally leave each of those weekends feeling cleansed, renewed, hopeful, and exhausted.

I have detailed the weekend here not as a cookbook recipe for others to follow but as a portrait of how I have taken the twelve therapeutic guidelines and attempted to weave them into an experience that uses my eclectic approach, my penchant for groups, and meets what I believe to be the needs of my Gay clients. It is cited as an example of the invention of techniques that fit my personal style and my professional orientation and that get the job done.

It has been my privilege to participate in the training of other Gay-oriented professionals and I have watched as each of them fashioned his or her own techniques, drawing on personal style and a particular professional orientation. Psychotherapy is something of an art form anyway. While each of us has a unique approach as an artist, we are duly impressed and appreciative of another artist who works quite differently to achieve the same goal.

A Word to Researchers

Look back through the research abstracts and you will see years of attempts to identify, classify and scrutinize Gay people. Most of the effort went into looking for the causes of homosexuality. It is mostly a foolish occupation. It makes as much sense as looking for the causes of heterosexuality. There are too many causative or antecedent factors and there is no need (other than basic academic research) to identify them anyway. Our "scientific" interest in the causes of homosexuality signals a devaluation of Gayness and a desire to exterminate it. More often than not, we look for causative factors and antecedents when we want to eliminate something or create more of it—rarely is it done in pure scientific pursuit of information that will add to our store of knowledge.

I have steadfastly refused to take part in any study that would locate and identify Gay people, particularly Gay children. When I believe that our world has evolved to the point where Gay people are so highly valued that we want to locate the Gay children early in order to help them develop their Gay identity optimally, or where we want to find causative factors so that we can help everyone become more Gay, then I will be happy to participate in research designed to identify Gay people, particularly the children. Certainly Gay children need all the help we could give them today, but for the time being identification would only increase their persecution.

The place where researchers can help today is in working with publicly Gay people to study what "works" in building a satisfying life and how some Gay people are able to find the extra strength to survive in a toxic environment. That information could be helpful to everyone, but particularly to other Gay people who are struggling to survive.

And the place where the greatest help can and should be given is in identifying the symptoms, causes and antecedents of homophobia and searching for effective means of treatment. If homophobia can be eradicated, Gay people can live with no more difficulty than any other citizen. Homophobia is costing valuable lives. It is a disturbance that needs serious attention from researchers.

My Own Growth as a Gay Professional

I am always curious about the people who write the books I read. I wonder why they felt the need to write the book and what it has to do with their personal lives. Perhaps it is simple voyeurism, or perhaps it has to do with a kind of "positive paranoia" connected with my Gay identity—an unwillingness to trust any evidence at face value without knowing the motivation of the person who produces it.

There is no beginning to this book for me unless it was the day I was born. But I can identify a place in my life where the motivation picked up speed and the focus began to sharpen, even though I still did not know then that this book was in the making.

Having finished graduate school at the end of the fifties, I devoted about ten years of my professional lifetime to the clinical education of teachers who would teach the poor. My motivation seemed fairly clear to me. School had been an unhappy place for me as a child and much of it had to do with my poverty.

In the academic year 1968-69, I took an overdue sabbatical and some offered funds from the Carnegie Corporation of New York and did a year-long study of the human potential movement and its encounter groups, looking for application to education and psychotherapy. It was quite a year. I had been enamored of groups since undergraduate days and had purposely done my clinical internship in California so that I could be where group therapy was flourishing at the time. Instinctively I had steered clear of organizations of group therapists, who always seemed too eager to get it all wrapped up in a neat package instead of exploring truly new horizons. Over the years I had experimented with seemingly daring innovations: first the white coat came off, then people called me by my first name, then I dared speak honestly of my own feelings in groups sometimes, and sometimes I even dared suggest one person touch another. So when I heard about other people doing encounter groups, sensitivity training, sensory awareness, massage, and what have you, my thirst for the new surfaced again. I spent the year speeding around the country on jets, interviewing the stars of the human potential movement, and involving myself in every sort of group that held some promise of being a little different than what I had already experienced.

By the end of the year, I knew I was changing but I did not know how. I spent the summer writing my report and taking time to read all the Black authors I had never had time for while teaching and directing a clinic. I did not know why I had to do that reading but I knew I had to do it.

Toward the end of that summer it started to happen. I would read "Black" and think "Gay." I would read "Negro" and think "homosexual." The year had made me a lot more aware of my emotions and by the end of that summer I was shocked at how much hurt, anger and fright I had been holding in all my life. I grew up knowing I was Gay and then got convinced by education and psychotherapy that I was "normal" with a slight disability in the form of "leanings" in the homosexual direction and that I must keep it under control, like diabetes. I was married to a woman I loved and had two children I adored. I also had this large empty spot inside and a terrible ache that was related to the hurt, fear and anger.

At the end of the summer, the Association for Humanistic Psychology had its yearly meeting in Silver Spring, Maryland. I found myself in a leaderless encounter group with ten hidden leaders. Our second time together, a young man said he needed help from the group. A smartly dressed young woman looked at him sagely and said, "I know what your trouble is. Boys." He said, "You mean I prefer to have sex with men? That's right, but that's not what I want help about. I want help about a job interview I'm going to tomorrow."

Then, to my astonishment, all of the white liberal trashing I had been reading about all summer came up. The color of the victim was lavender rather than Black but the techniques were the same. People actually said things like, "Some of my best friends are homosexual," and "As long as you stay in your part of town I don't care what you do." I am not sure how open or verbal my reaction was but I know it was intense. It seems to me I sat there for an eternity with my mouth and eyes open very wide. I do remember that I announced in a voice trembling with fear and rage that I had had plenty of homosexual feelings in my lifetime and I couldn't believe what I was hearing in that room.

The young man, Chris, wanted experience in leading groups. I had plenty of that experience to share. We both lived in New York. He knew the Gay scene there and I did not. We hatched the idea of trying to do a Gay weekend group together. It was a half-disaster but we both learned a lot from it and no one was emotionally or physically injured. Chris became a friend. Later he produced a first-rate, general-audience, commercial Gay-oriented film. I went on to pursue clinical work with Gay people.

I liked the experience of being with Gay people in a group. It felt good. Now I began to understand those years of trying to help Black people in the ghetto and why they kept patiently telling me that I was white and they needed to help one another. I realized I had found my people at last and that we needed one another. Slowly I resolved to use whatever talent and energy I had in helping Gay people, myself included—though in the beginning I was not sure I was entitled to full inclusion in the community.

During my years of clinic directing, teaching, and research, there had been no time for a real private practice. But now I found Gay people coming to me for talks, asking if I would take them on for psychotherapy. I took on a few and found my taste for the academic world rapidly diminishing. With some trepidation I decided to let go of my academic security blanket, the hard-earned tenure, the rank, and even the carrot of financially comfortable retirement just twelve to fifteen years down the road. I first resigned as Clinic Director, and six months later decided for sure to resign from the university.

Since my internship days in California I had always wanted to return there. It occurred to me that if I was going to shift into private practice and work with Gay people, I could find them in California just as easily as New York. I was frightened by what all of this change might do to my happy, loving family relationships with my wife and children but some sort of momentum was carrying me forward. There were many long talks with my wife, who was willing to risk our marriage and be my companion in exploration and growth.

The day after Christmas, 1970, we climbed onto the plane for San Francisco, all four of us. In addition to the luggage, I carried plenty of anxiety, not much money, and an exciting inner voice that told me this was right.

The years between then and now have been the best years of my life, the real years of learning and growing. Reading related to my work had always been a chore, now it became a joy. Everyday my face-to-face contacts taught me more about Gay people and, subsequently, more about myself.

Soon after I arrived and presented my credentials to the visible members of San Francisco's Gay community, I was asked to fill in for a missing panelist at the Western Psychological Association meetings at the Hilton Hotel in San Francisco. It was a panel of Gay psychologists. "My God," I thought, as I climbed onto the platform, "does that mean everyone will think I'm Gay too?" In those days I had gotten up the courage to talk about my homosexual feelings in public but I had yet to open my mouth on a stage and say, "I'm Gay!" I don't remember what I talked about but I remember looking at a sea of smug faces. They had that "I've been analyzed for twelve years and resolved my homosexual hangups" look on their faces, or so I imagined, and I was swept by one of those moments of inspired and unexpected rage. I told the audience what I imagined I saw in their faces and suggested anyone who felt that complacent ought to put his or her right hand in the crotch of the person of the same gender seated nearest, leave it there for five minutes and see if they still felt complacent. To my amazement, that moment of sudden truth was greeted by the audience with a spontaneous, loud ovation. It was not long before my good friend Betty Berzon and I had found one another. We cautiously expressed our mutual interest in working with Gay people but neither of us were up to any personal announcements on our first meeting. But it did not take long. Betty has been one of life's great gifts. And we have helped one another have courage for each next step.

We soon found ourselves together often on platforms where we more and more directly talked about being Gay. Each such public appearance was a little less frightening and each one made me feel more whole and human. I was standing there telling the truth about myself at last, and the sky did not fall. On the contrary, there was applause and smiles and those touching few people who came forward always at the end because they trusted me enough to say quietly (but aloud) that they, too, were Gay.

One of the funniest and saddest growthful times was when I was the keynote speaker for the annual education conference in South Dakota. They had wanted Carl Rogers, and got me. My speech was entitled, "Humanistic Teaching—A Vote for Deviance" and in it I spoke of my own homosexuality during the growing-up years, the educational drive to conformity that devalued me, and the need to risk personal exposure as a teacher. Well, I certainly exposed myself. I had carefully groomed and dressed myself but I may as well have been a dirty old man flashing his disgusting member in an old raincoat. There was a smattering of polite applause and then enough social space around me to make me feel as if I had a contagious social disease—and I guess they thought I did. But even from that experience I grew. I had said it. I had told my truth. They had punished me with cool distance but I was alive and a better person than I had been before the trip to South Dakota.

My life moves on and I, least of all, seem able to predict its rate of flow or direction. Some years ago I met a colleague who was also becoming aware of his Gay identity. We discovered that we were similar in many ways though different in a few interesting ways too. Like me, he was married to a woman he loved and had two children to whom he was devoted. Our friendship and mutual caring grew until we realized that we had become lovers. That has added a deep and long-needed dimension to my life, a completion that I secretly suspected was not possible for me because too many years had passed with too little self-awareness. It has helped me learn again that all things are possible when the wanting is clear. This, and subsequent major changes in my life have helped me to empathize in joy and sorrow with clients who find surprises as they follow their own unique paths of change.

260

As I have been carried forward on the tide of my own changes, there has been sadness, pain, and loss also—though there is a feeling of rightness to it all. My wife and I separated almost a year ago and are now in the slow process of dissolving marriage and finding new ways to relate to one another as people. It is still too recent and the feelings too raw for me to have perspective on how this major shift in my life is related to my development as a Gay person and as a Gay professional. My increased celebration of Gay identity is an important part of my personal change in recent years but I think it would be naive to believe it is the sole causative factor responsible for the termination of a loving eighteen-year marriage. The children live with my former wife half time and with me half time, and so far seem to understand and accept the changes at least as well as their parents. Perhaps, being from a new generation, they do not perceive change as negative per se, and therefore it is not as frightening or unsettling.

There are no words to portray adequately the learning of these years of group and individual work with Gay people. My Gay community is huge, diverse and strong. I have been cleansed by the tears, the laughter and the simple sharing. I feel more alive than I have ever felt in my life. And at this moment it feels as if it were all leading to this book. Not that this is the final word—it is more of a progress report. But something has been growing in me these years, and now that it is out on paper I feel relieved and joyful.

There is a simple Christian hymn titled "Amazing Grace." I am not much attracted to organized religion but its words could apply to my own evolving Gay identity. It expresses my experience as a Gay person so well. "Amazing grace. . .that saved a wretch like me. I once was lost but now am found—was blind, but now I see." I am grateful for special people in my life—particularly my children, my lover, and my former wife—who helped me see my need to change. I am grateful for my work. And I am grateful that I rediscovered my Gay identity in time. It has been like coming home. Except that there never was any home before. And all of this is why I wrote this book.

261

Index

AIDS: Books that can help

☐ *AIDS Treatment News:* Volume 1 (Issues 1 through 75)

by John S. James

The first 75 issues of the widely respected newsletter which described all manner of standard and experimental treatments for AIDS and related conditions. Completely indexed, this is the only easy-to-use reference suitable for the layperson as well as professionals.

$12.95 paper, 560 pages

☐ *AIDS Treatment News:* Volume 2 (Issues 76 through 125)

by John S. James

Covers the latest research, detailing treatments, symptoms, medications, research topics, and more.

$16.95 paper, 300 pages

☐ *Living in Hope:* A 12-Step Approach

by Cindy Mikluscak-Cooper, R.N. and Emmett E. Miller, M.D.

The first and only 12-step program for people who are HIV-positive, or at risk for infection. Using daily affirmations and guided imagery, this book provides powerful tools for coping, change, and healing.

$12.95 paper, 300 pages

☐ *Serenity* Second Edition by Paul Reed

Emotional support and guidance for people with HIV, and their families, friends, and caregivers. Leads readers from despair to action to hope.

$6.95 paper, 112 pages

☐ *The Q Journal:* A Treatment Diary by Paul Reed

An intimate journal, detailing one author's experimental treatment with the new drug, Compound Q. Probes many issues surrounding AIDS—loss, hope, research, treatment, anger, coping, and the courage to go on living.

$8.95 paper, 176 pages

☐ *Psychoimmunity and the Healing Process*

Third Revised Edition by Jason Serinus, C.H.T.

A compendium of alternative therapies for AIDS and immune dysfunction that can be used in addition to conventional medical care

$12.95 paper, 400 pages

☐ *Extended Health Care At Home* by Evelyn M. Baulch

Step-by-step advice on coping with the problems that arise during any extended home health care: finding a home nurse, dealing with physical and emotional issues, obtaining supplies and equipment. Includes a section on the special needs of people with AIDS.

$9.95 paper, 272 pages.

☐ ***Face to Face:*** A Guide to AIDS Counseling

by James W. Dilley, Cheri Pies, & Michael Helquist

A guide to dealing with emotional and psycho-neurological problems encountered with AIDS—suitable for patients or counseling professionals. Addresses the special needs of various affected populations—minorities, IV drug users, women, and gay men.
$14.95 paper, 350 pages

☐ ***AIDS Law for Mental Health Professionals***

by Gary James Wood, J.D., et al

The legal and ethical issues confronting therapists when they treat people infected with or concerned about HIV infection, with an emphasis on California law.
$19.95 paper, 272 pages

Gay fiction and literature

☐ ***...So Little Time*** by Mike Hippler

Over 50 essays on gay life, from an award-winning columnist, on topics ranging from politics, family, sports, and travel, to religion, sex, AIDS, and role models. Includes some of Hippler's most popular pieces, including *Dear Abby, Am I Too Gay?, How to Meet Lesbians*, and the wrenching *Visit to an AIDS Ward.*
$11.95 paper, 288 pages

☐ ***Kvetch*** by T.R. Witomski

A humorous collection of scalding, controversial essays from a master of searing wit, including *101 Things to Do with a Straight Man, How to Cruise the Met*, and *Zeitgeist or Poltergeist: Why Gay Books Are So Bad.*
$7.95 paper, 132 pages

☐ ***Longing*** by Paul Reed

Hailed by the *New York Times* for its style, this haunting novel of gay life in the San Francisco of the early 1980's also made the *Christopher Street* bestseller list.
$7.95 paper or $14.95 cloth, 192 pages

Available from your local bookstore, or order direct from the publisher. Please include $1.25 shipping & handling for the first book, and 50 cents for each additional book. California residents include local sales tax. Write for our free complete catalog of over 400 books and tapes.

Ship to:

Name _____

Address _____.

City _____ State ____ Zip _____

Phone _____

Celestial Arts

Box 7327

Berkeley, CA 94707

For VISA or Mastercard orders

call (510) 845-8414